Messa [barcode: D0440396]

"Taylor loves Whitman and Nasruddin, his students a̶n̶d̶ t̶h̶e̶ ̶a̶-̶ wakenings that come in conversation. This is living Sufism and wonderful sorbet. Sufis love to sit together and have this kind of mysterious free exchange, sometimes in silence, sometimes talking, as though around a fire late at night."

—Coleman Barks, author

"This is a most praiseworthy book. I couldn't put it down. Huxley did a good job in *Perennial Philosophy*, but I like the way this keeps at it. And the writing, with a background of Gurdjieff, has the immediacy and spontaneity of Rumi's poems."

—Julia Older, poet and writer

"Taylor Morris is tackling the biggest mystery of all, life and how we attempt to understand its design and purpose. Through student dialogues exploring Sufi stories, he allows us to find our own clues. In the hands of a talented writer like Taylor Morris, this very readable journey is a joy and a marvelous undertaking, My only regret is that he hadn't written sooner."

—Jake Eaton, author

"*Message From the Sparrows* is a good book for our generation because it gives us a different perspective, a different viewpoint—our own! It's easy to read and very insightful."

—June Sczymecki, college student

"This book was written for anybody who has ever had the feeling that there is 'something else' they've been missing. I can't think of one person who wouldn't benefit from reading *Message From the Sparrows*, although everyone who reads it will be forced to re-think and review, and maybe revise everything that they thought they knew."

—Aimee Miller, college senior

Message From the Sparrows

Engaging Consciousness

by Taylor Morris

HEARTSFIRE BOOKS

The author acknowledges the following for permission to reprint material:

Osho International Foundation: Excerpts from *The Tantra Experience* by Osho, © Osho International Foundation.

Yale University Press: Excerpts from *Women in Middle Eastern History*, by Nikki E. Keddie & Beth Baron, © 1991 Nikki E. Keddie & Beth Baron.

J.M. Dent: Excerpts from *Leaves of Grass* by Walt Whitman, published in 1993 by Charles Tuttle Co., Inc., Bantam.

Edwin Honig, trans.: Excerpts from *Poems of Fernando Pessoa.* © 1986 Edwin Honig.

Simon & Schuster: "Indian Camp," by Ernest Hemingway, from *The Conscious Reader*, © 1992 MacMillan Publishing Co.

Penguin U.S.A.: Stories from *Tales of the Dervishes* by Idries Shah, © 1967 Idries Shah. Excerpts from *The Way of the Sufi* by Idries Shah, © 1968 Idries Shah.

Random House: Excerpt from *Sex, Art, and American Culture* by Camille Paglia, © 1992 Camille Paglia.

Alfred A. Knopf, Inc.: Excerpts from *The Psychology of Man's Possible Evolution* by P.D. Ouspensky, © 1974 P.D. Ouspensky.

Rider: Excerpts from *The Book of Certainty* by Abu Kakr Siraj-ed Din.

Cover design by Marjoram Productions
Cover art by Louis Jones

For information write:
Heartsfire Books
500 N. Guadalupe St., Suite G-465, Santa Fe, NM 87501
Distributed by:
Hampton Roads Publishing Company, Inc.
134 Burgess Lane, Charlottesville, VA 22902
(804)296-2772
FAX: (804)296-5096
E-mail: hrpc@mail.hamptonroadspub.com
Internet: http://www.hamptonroadspub.com

If you are unable to order this book from your local bookseller, you may order directly from the distributor. Quantity discounts for organizations are available.

Call 1-800-766-8009, toll-free.

ISBN 1-889797-02-2

10 9 8 7 6 5 4 3 2 1
Printed on acid-free paper in Canada

To Jan and the kids—

Tita, T-Bone, Jackie, Lulie, Bevverlee, Miguel, Daveed,
Leela—and to Bill and the Walkers.

Two sparrows were sitting high on the roof of a building. The old one said to the younger: "Some time ago things were much better. There was the clip clop of the horse-drawn carriage and then, suddenly, a wonderful aroma and deposit in the streets. Our food and sustenance. Now? A terrible noise, noxious fumes, and after all that an inedible black spot of oil."

(G.I. Gurdjieff, All and Everything)

Introduction

Contrary to what we might think of ourselves we do not, ordinarily, welcome new ideas. Our idea framework is something that we have taken years to put together. Whether we have put it together consciously or unconsciously, whether with care or haphazardly, it is ours—our way of looking at the world—and we are comfortable with it. Anything new threatens that comfort.

Perhaps because he knew this, P.D. Ouspensky, one of the best-known students of G.I. Gurdjieff (mystic and enigmatic "Western-Sufi" master of the twenties, thirties, and forties), spends a good deal of time talking about the difficulty of making people realize they are going to hear something new (Ouspensky, *The Psychology of Man's Possible Evolution,* xii).

For example, he declares, Darwin's idea of mechanical evolution—the idea of massive, unconscious, or automatic evolution—simply cannot be accepted. It is probable, he adds, that we have been regressing instead of progressing, especially in the last fifty or so years. Certain works of architecture, he claims, cannot be reproduced by modern man so there is reason to believe that "ancient" man was superior to his modern counterpart (Ibid., 7).

Without arguing Ouspensky's views, I would emphasize his main point: individual evolution, which takes place through "work on oneself," is the only kind of evolution possible. The typical Sufi approach is similar without being argumentative. Sufism—more an approach to life, a way of living, than a religion—does not deny others' beliefs. Sufis are convinced that they have gathered the best from all religions and they practice these ways, from all religions, without being bound by any of them.

And it is very clear that the Sufis, through tales and in other ways, insist there is something to be done down here on earth and that it can not be accomplished by simply "believing" in something, or going through the motions—any motions. "He who tastes knows" is an oft-quoted Sufi dictum. In other words, experience—not books or credos—is the teacher. This is particularly interesting given the importance of stories and teaching tales, which play an essential part in the training and making-ready of a Sufi adept.

The Sufi way involves examining, studying, observing man's condition, and *experiencing* those phenomena for oneself. This cannot be done in a laboratory with immaculate white gown while looking through a microscope, but in the hurly burly of life itself—"in the world but not of it," by which is meant actively participating but not being "identified" with the subject of investigation. The Sufi tales are a rather special examination of man's condition.

A good deal of learning how to go about changing the nature of one's condition—asleep, unconscious, subjective— requires a teaching master and the attendant practices and exercises. For Westerners, accustomed as we are to "independence" and our "right" to question every step of the way, this can be a difficult proposition. However, the necessity for help outside of ourselves, and the difficulty of being objective, was unintentionally summed up by my son who, when he was four years old, made the following observation: "I can see behind your back. And you can see behind my back. But *I* can't see behind *my* back."

That we can learn from four-year-olds, from our most-hated enemy, from dogs or a picture or a knock on the head is part and parcel of the openness and willingness of the seeker on any level and, of course, is not confined to Sufism.

Teaching and Learning

1

The Last Degree of Esoteric Wisdom

The last degree of esoteric teaching is plain common sense.

—A.R. Orage, *On Love*

I introduced the idea, during one of the early days of the course, that there was something amiss with our educational system. Perhaps because, according to Mark Twain, common sense is the rarest commodity on earth. At any rate, by itself and without anything to support it, the statement would, I knew, win support. Everyone has his or her complaints about what is done in schools and classrooms, whatever the system, especially students who are in the middle of the "wash" cycle (i.e., sophomores and juniors).

However, shortly after that a student asked me what I had against academia.

"My main complaint is that there are courses about absolutely everything, everything in the world, but there are no courses about *you*. Not even philosophy courses, although one is free to make the connections—"

"How could there be a course about *me* or *you*?" she asked.

"I hope that by the end of the course you'll see that it's not only possible but that we've done it. Let me see how else I can answer you. Is there anyone in here who has taken a course in mythology?"

Three hands went up.

"Okay, tell me the story of Isis and Osiris."

Holly, who had objected to any criticism of academe, began, "Well, it's from, I think, from Egyptian mythology. Osiris, the king, is killed and his body's scattered into a thousand pieces."

"I think it was only fourteen," Sara offered.

"*Any*how," said Holly, "Isis, who was his daughter . . . and something else . . . his *wife?* Anyhow, his daughter/wife Isis had the task of gathering the pieces together and . . . reuniting them."

"Yes?"

"And that's it."

"Okay, now I'll add something, because right now it is not clear why it was scattered into fourteen or a thousand pieces. And why the pieces should be collected."

"Well, so many of the myths are like that," a couple of students answered. "That's just the way it is."

"For the proper burial of a loved one?"

"That's a good civilized answer, but let's look at it in a different way. Another way, the esoteric way. Osiris's body is a wish to understand. Okay? His body, symbolically, is a wish to understand. And his body was ripped into a number of pieces, and scattered . . . to the winds. And his daughter (flesh of his flesh) *and* wife, same person, have to collect the pieces and put them together so he will once again be one, one wish to understand. Okay? And that's what they don't teach you in Mythology 305. First, because they don't know it, and, second, because the myth, alone, is enough."

Someone jumped in with "Wish to understand? Understand *what?*"

"That's what I was going to ask. Understand *what?*" asked Holly.

Another student added, "Where did you get that explanation?"

"It was a message from the sparrows."

"No, really, where did that come from?"

"Your question should be: does it make sense? No matter who said it or where it came from. Does it make sense and how does it apply to *you*. These myths apply to you. If you understand them."

"Well, I don't see it making a lot of *sense* in either case," said the big tall guy in back, Mike.

"Think only about the wish to understand. Instead, one day we wish to learn French. Next day we wish to play the guitar. Next day we wish to get in shape. Then we wish to be married. Then for a while we wish to write a great novel. Our 'body' is scattered in fourteen different directions."

There were some nods, some puzzled expressions.

"What if all of those wishes could be unified under one heading: a tremendous wish to understand?"

"Yes, but understand *what?*"

"You answer that."

"Ourselves?"

"Maybe so."

"Life?"

"That's good enough. Instead, school gives us a little bit of history, a little literature, a little sociology, and so on. And a little bit of mythology: Isis, the one who cares, the one who *minds*, had to collect the pieces of her father/husband which were scattered all over.

"Let me put it in a more general way, about education and what's wrong." I told them about a good friend who had been through four years of undergraduate work, then graduated from a famous film school, then went through graduate courses in Social Guidance and Counseling. He was now 'fitted' to counsel others and guide them through life's reefs and shoals. But, after all of this schooling, at the age of forty-five, he had no idea what he wanted to do with his own life. And was still living with his mother, afraid for her or afraid of what would happen if he left.

"Many people, upon hearing a story like this, ask, 'What has education got to do with his personal life? Are you going to hold Princeton or Brown or Harvard responsible for the fact that he is helpless when confronted with life's problems?' My answer would be: yes, precisely.

"He was never, during his years of education, forced to make connections between his life and all of his courses. And the fact that someone might be astonished at the idea that schooling and life should be connected is more distressing than what we have. I look at you and wonder . . . can we do this? And my answer to myself is that *if* it is going to happen at all then *we* are going to have to get out of school. What does that mean to you? When I say that? Anyone?"

"It means to take it in a different way. This course in a different way," said Carole.

Mike interrupted. "You're asking us to 'get out of school,' but this is a classroom we've all had courses in. I had Biology and Western Civ in this room. This is a college classroom, so it's a little—"

There was a chorus of agreement.

"Well, in this room or some other, you've not only got to get out of school but have to realize that I'm not the enemy. I'm not the enemy. Maybe I browbeat you, I badger you to get answers, but I'm not the enemy. Ignorance is the enemy. Our common enemy.

"As for getting us physically out of school, I'm going to work on that. I will get us out, somewhere.

"This is not a graded course . . . and maybe," I spoke as it came to me, "maybe we should even drop the Pass-Fail."

"How would that work?" one asked.

"Alright, let's say you've all passed the course. You've all passed but you agree to come to every meeting. If you can make that commitment then I'll make the other."

"So, where will we have the classes . . . uh, meetings?"

"I'm working on it."

The college has a building on an "island" only half a mile away. It is rarely used and then only for small banquets or gatherings. It is a large log cabin with one huge room, two baths, a kitchen, and coatroom. In the large room there is a table big enough for any board of trustees to sit at. The area is called an island although it's surrounded on three sides by water, the lake, Pearly Pond, and on the fourth side is connected to land by a bridge which passes over a marshy area just off the main road to the college. It would be perfect for our use and completely "uncontaminated" by use as a classroom.

"Meantime, here is a story that pertains to you. The story came to me a few days ago while I was still in bed.

"When I was living in Mexico, teaching school for the Pan American Sulphur Company, some of us used to gather on certain evenings to play badminton; it was a mix of Americans and Mexicans, engineers and technicians. I was the teacher and principal of the little school which employed eight other teachers and which all of the higher-echelon employees' children attended.

"In the way these things happen, I became very friendly with a young Mexican engineer who had married his high school sweetheart. Within three years they had two children. That was as much as I knew about him until that night. It was a time in the evening when the badminton had stopped and people had turned to drinking and talking. It was also the awkward time marking the end of another evening. The heat of the day had lifted and it was getting on. Victor, my engineer friend, about ten years younger than I at the time, suddenly began telling me about life. Well, partly about life and partly about *his* life.

"'You're a little kid,' he said, from his deck chair to mine. 'You're going to school. Learning things. You have your eye on the girls but you're too young for that. Then, first dances and so on. Then suddenly you're in high school. Eventually, you get the car, and things are more serious. You fall in love. Maybe you go through a number of romances. Start college. Graduate. You get married. Your mother and father are suddenly older. Then you're working at a job. Your wife is pregnant. Then you're a parent, a father. Your parents are now grandparents. You . . . you take the children by the hand and see them through all of the steps. They're walking . . . first words. Then *they* start school . . .'

"Victor turned to me to see if I was following. In a way I was amazed. All of the steps were coming in this shorthand manner. But he wasn't finished, only checking me out. I was nodding for him to go on. But he had stopped. For that's where he was now, with his two children. One in school and one in kindergarten.

"'And then . . .' He was looking into the abyss, the future. 'So they go through school. *Your* parents are getting feeble. Even your wife is not as young . . . well,' Victor said, 'you see what I'm driving at? *Your* children get married, *your* parents die off, *your* children have kids . . . and you're suddenly a grandfather. And . . . and, you see?' By this time we were both laughing.

"'Yeah?' I said, still wondering how and why he had singled me out to talk about this. I couldn't believe that he was coming to the point.

"'So?' he said. 'Is that *it?*'

"I was laughing, but I was laughing because I was pleased. 'In a way, yeah, I guess so,' I said.

"'So? That's it? You grow up, marry, have children, work, they grow up, your parents die, your children marry and have children and then *you die? And that's it?*'

"Since that long-ago conversation in Mexico, there have even been bumper stickers about it: 'Life's a bitch then you die!' Six words for a conversation that took hours.

"Well . . . this course is about what *else* there is. If life is going along like this . . .' I drew a horizontal line on the board, with slight ups and downs but generally straight across. '. . . then our course is about *this!*' I drew a line going up from the horizontal.

"So that's what Victor and I talked about that night, the next day, and for weeks afterwards. Sufism is about this, this vertical line.

"Peggy Lee used to sing a song called 'Is That All There Is?' And it's about what Victor was talking about. After you've been to some mad parties and gotten drunk a good number of times, explored the sexual thing and are married and are living not just with a friend but with your wife or husband. And then along come the children . . . well, at some point you look up suddenly and ask, 'Is that all there is?'

"Maybe you say it quietly to yourself. Maybe you hardly dare breathe the question, even to yourself. So that's it? That's life? You wonder. So, this course is about *what else there is* . . ."

I repeated it, walked across with the chalk, marking the horizontal line again. "If that's the ordinary life-line . . . then this course is about . . ." I went up the perpendicular line again. ". . . about . . . *this!*

"Let's take a break. Be back in ten minutes."

* * *

"The first part of this . . . material is about teaching. It's also about *un*learning. Our ex-president used to talk about 'learning how to learn.' He thought it was a very clever thing to say. For you, now, you must realize that there is also a process of *un*learning some of the things you've learned.

"Here's a promotional blurb about a book by a man named Gatto. It's called *Dumbing Us Down*. See if it rings a bell.

Dumbing Us Down reveals the deadening heart of compulsory state schooling: assumptions and structures that stamp out the self-knowledge, curiosity, concentration and solitude essential to learning. Between school and television, our children have precious little time to learn for themselves about the community they live in, or the lives they might lead. Instead, they are schooled to merely obey orders and become smoothly functioning cogs in the industrial machine.

"It goes on to say that what is needed is 'large doses of solitude and a thousand different apprenticeships with adults from all walks of life . . . if we are to break the thrall of our conforming society.' Gatto urges us to 'get schools out of the way,' in order to regain control of our culture and our society.

"So, when I tell you we have to get *out of school* I am talking about your minds and, as well, unlearning what 'they' have done to you, under the pretext of education.

"One more quote, from a blurb advertising another book. The book is *Deschooling Our Lives*, by Matt Hearn.

> *Deschooling Our Lives* details the destructive effects of mass schooling on the lives of our children and communities. It examines how the day-to-day experience of school—of bells and whistles, narrow curricula, rote learning, violence, boredom, and constant discipline— teaches subservience and undercuts children's natural love of learning while undercutting their self-esteem.

"Okay, I can't teach you about this, our subject— Sufism— until I teach you about . . . life itself. But how can I do that? In the first place, you already know all about life. Haven't you been on the planet for nineteen years? Twenty-one years? So, whether you think you know all about life, or whether it is true, doesn't much matter because, either way, you are convinced. So, you know about life. And I'll admit this much—you probably know more than I did at nineteen. I wanted to go to war and come back a hero. And at nineteen I not only didn't care but, as a matter of fact, *ran* from anything that wasn't life itself. And don't try to tell me about it. Then, up comes my daughter—years and years later—sixteen years old and full of beans.

"'Charlotte,' I told her, having watched her heaving and pulling at the few restraints we put on her, 'you know, life . . .' I paused to let it sink in, since I was giving her the gift of the ages. 'Life . . . is *not* a rock concert!'

"'*Ohh, yes it is!*' said she, so quickly and with so much conviction that I began to doubt my wisdom.

"Now whether life is or is not a rock concert I was getting nowhere trying to convince her and, besides, maybe . . . maybe it is. But a different concert than she had in her mind."

I ended the class, now discussion group, with a reading and writing assignment. They were to think about the question "Who am I?" or "What am I?" and read the story "The Idiot in the Great City."

THE IDIOT IN THE GREAT CITY

This idiot came to a huge city, and he was confused by the number of people in the streets. Fearing that if he slept and woke again he would not be able to find himself among so many people, he tied a gourd to his ankle for identification.

A practical joker, knowing what he had done, waited until he was asleep, then removed the gourd and tied it around his own leg. He, too, lay down on the caravanserai floor to sleep. The fool woke first and saw the gourd. At first he thought that this other man must be him. Then he attacked the other, shouting: "If you are me: then who, for heaven's sake, who and where am I?"

(Shah, *Tales of the Dervishes*, 69)

2

. . . And There's a Gourd Tied to My Right Leg

I confess, the first time I read "The Idiot in the Great City," I found it to be irritatingly obvious. At the time, it was my least favorite story in the entire collection. But after reading students' answers to the question "Who am I?" I began to appreciate how the story pertains to their lives and who they are.

Although one student admitted, "I really don't know myself," most described certain traits which they felt they possessed: sympathetic, understanding, love-to-play-tennis, short-tempered, flirtatious, shy, easy to get along with, hard to get to know at first, etc. They might as well have added, ". . . and there's a gourd tied to my right leg."

We went over various traits and put down characteristics such as nationality, gender, age, weight, height, year in school, in love or not, body type, family life, parents divorced or not, sisters and brothers, how many, and so on.

"After you have answered all of these questions, do you feel satisfied that the answers really distinguish you? Or take the answers you gave when I asked the question in the last class. Do you feel that satisfies the question of Who am I?"

They felt it was incomplete, that it was only a partial answer, that it would be very difficult to properly describe themselves, and came away from the question feeling slightly dissatisfied.

"You have a certain relationship to your parents, to an intimate friend, male or female, to your roommate who sees you in a special way, to me, to relatives, to your friends back home. To various people you are friend, daughter, son, cousin, bully, nice guy, aunt or uncle. You are also, whether you like it or not, 'home' to millions of bacteria . . . but which one is *you?* Or are you all of them? And more? Or none?"

The question was irritating to some. Such a simple question yet so difficult.

In addition to the student who said, "I really don't know myself," another responded: "I don't know exactly how man came into existence, let alone myself."

We discussed what we "know," what we think we "know," and how these things are not so certain.

I told them about Copernicus. And how, before the seventeenth century, we—people—thought that the earth was the center of the universe and that the sun revolved around the earth. Then Copernicus came along and said, "Sorry about that! The earth is not the center. *We* revolve around the sun."

"Do you think people loved Copernicus for that? He completed his work in 1530, including his findings about the sun and the earth. It was not published until he was on his deathbed, in 1543. Do you think people welcomed this new truth? As a matter of fact, they wanted to disinter and kill him again. *What? Earth is not the center of the universe? That's nutty . . . It's heresy!!!*

"So, you see, we live with these notions. Then someone comes along and tries to change them. We do not welcome the changes. But if our search is for the truth then why *shouldn't* we welcome not changes for the sake of change but a more truthful view?

"The Sufis believe that we're *all* idiots. In fact, there's a Sufi book called *The Wisdom of the Idiots*. And, on those days when we slam our fingers in a car door, or drop something valuable, haven't we called ourselves 'idiots' and worse? If we can begin to accept that, the next step will be to find out what kind of an idiot each one of us is. For one thing, we're idiots who take others' opinions for things.

"You come to me brainwashed—but when I tell you that, you might go away with hurt feelings instead of examining it."

I didn't find out for two more sessions that that remark was like a slap in the face to some. Three of the group members later told me that they immediately stopped listening. Determined not to hear anything I had to say. I went on, after the slap in the face, to tell them:

". . . brainwashed by your parents, by society, by television, by your teachers and schools, priests and relatives. And I say that to you despite the fact that all of those people who have been in on the brainwashing have had only the best of intentions toward you. I might as well bite the bullet and say that you have been brain-*painted*.

"1. Killer Whales, we can now see with our own eyes, at Disney World, for example, are not killers at all. They are as harmless (to humans) as dolphins. 2. Wolves do not attack humans and are not the savage man-hunters we were terrified of at one time. 3. Sharks do not necessarily attack humans and recent films have shown that sometimes they have to be provoked into attacking a piece of meat held outside of a cage. Sharks, it appears, would rather attack a piece of garbage than anything alive, moving, and able to struggle.

"These three examples are all black and white areas of how we were brainwashed and then unbrainwashed. But, interestingly enough, we take others' opinions about whales, wolves, and sharks without ever having experienced either the one thing or the other. So we don't know, for ourselves, whether wolves were *ever* the carnivorous man-haters they were once heralded as, and/or whether they really are, as now depicted, quite friendly and sensitive animals. We don't *know* either one, first-hand. And we don't know whether killer whales were ever man-killers and only recently have become 'civilized' or whether they always were as friendly as puppy dogs. All we know is that for a long time we were told one thing and now we are told quite another.

"Am I brainwashed as well? Of course," I told them. "When I was nine I asked my beloved cook what would happen to me if I ate an ant. I'm not sure whether she was impatient that day, or angry at my mother, but she told me, 'You eat a' ant you die!'

"Since it was coming from someone I loved and trusted, my mind made a fist around that bit of 'information.' And twenty-five years later when a psychology student offered me some chocolate-covered ants, I could hear my cook's voice as if she had just spoken those words. I ate the ants, and it was as if I was crunching up a piece of idiocy from my childhood."

I don't know whether this helped them accept the possibility that they too may have been brainwashed, but they did remember the story.

"'To experience is to know,' the Sufis say. And 'He who tastes knows.'

"These statements are more than simply interesting. In fact, the reverse is true so we might well say, 'Not to experience is not to know.' And, as well: 'He who does not taste does not know.' Put in this manner, the two become much more provocative. We can surmise, and we can listen to others, and we can watch on television but if we haven't tasted for ourselves we cannot say we *know*. More enervating still is the fact that unless we are fairly conscious at the time of the experience, we can undergo an experience and *still* not know.

"We can further define the kind of idiots we are by asking why we haven't discovered that we were brainwashed before now. Or, if we have discovered it, why we haven't done something about it.

"Look, not one of these questions we raise can be looked on as done with—as ironed, folded, and put away. They'll come up again and again. And I might as well say that *all* of the tales we take up are about the human condition.

"Here's a Sufi tale about a shepherd and his sheep."

THE SHEPHERD AND HIS SHEEP

A shepherd is driving the flock to market to be slaughtered. On the way, one of the sheep declares: "I'm not a sheep, I'm a lion!"

And the shepherd says, "Yes, you are and please don't attack me." This satisfies the "lion" sheep and they continue on their way.

Another says, "I'm not a sheep, I'm an eagle, the highest flyer of all the birds!"

"Yes, I can see that," said the shepherd, "And I have been admiring your wings, your glossy coat and powerful talons and beak, for lo these many miles."

On they go to the slaughterhouse, some of them without a sound, some believing they are lions, some eagles, but all bound for the slaughterhouse.

"What is the slaughterhouse? Who are the sheep, and who is the shepherd? Are all of the sheep really the same?"

Rather than have one or two respond, I had them write their answers. The responses were fairly similar. Many students felt that the "lion" sheep and the "eagle" sheep were a cut above the others because "at least they are aspiring to something better . . . they *believe* in something."

They argued that belief in something "higher" could make them more than they were. Some thought that the shepherd was Jesus. And that the slaughterhouse was "paradise" or "heaven."

Almost all felt that "sheep" stood for something else. The sheep were mankind, or students or humanity, or a congregation, the flock, etc. And Jesus, some said, is the shepherd.

"Okay, sheep—symbolic. Shepherd—symbolic. But slaughterhouse? That's more difficult, or maybe easier. . . . Would you say that the slaughterhouse is a symbol for heaven? Or death? Could Jesus be the shepherd? Would he lead the flock to the slaughterhouse? Would he lie to the 'lion' sheep? And the 'eagle' sheep?

"Sheep—symbolic. Shepherd—symbolic. But slaughterhouse? A slaughterhouse is a slaughterhouse is a slaughterhouse. There is no way it can logically become something wonderful, like paradise or heaven. That has got to be the end. And there is no hint, in the story, that there is something better beyond it. And unless there is a hint, in the story, that there is something beyond a slaughterhouse then we cannot presume there is.

"As for belief—to think I'm the world's fastest human doesn't make me the fastest human, does it? To think I'm a lion doesn't make me one, right? And if I am a sheep who thinks he's a lion, does that make me one? The Sufis say that to know the definition of health doesn't make me healthy. To say the word 'wine' doesn't make me drunk.

"To experience is to know. To taste is to know. To *have* health is to know it. To experience drunkenness is to know it. To be a lion is to know it. Or understand it, a better term. Someone said the 'lion' sheep and the 'eagle' sheep are, perhaps, a cut above the others. They have belief. Are they? I would say that the 'lion' sheep and the 'eagle' sheep are more alike than any other sheep. They are sheep with delusions."

This did not go over well. I was shooting down something precious. I was "destroying belief" or even faith. I had to plow on.

"What about the sheep who says, 'He thinks he is a lion. Maybe he is. I, however, am a sheep.' Who has the healthier attitude? Of those two?"

Most did not want to answer the simpler question; they were back on belief and faith still.

"Try to understand 'story.' Within the story a sheep thinks he or she is something else. Okay? Even in an allegory, where one thing may stand for another thing, we're faced with a problem.

Even if we can say, well, probably, sheep stands for mankind, to follow the story we still have to deal with the fact that the sheep or the man *thinks* he or she is something else. Now, *in* an allegory or *out* of an allegory that is a *delusion*.

"Another one of you said, 'Every one of them is different even though they look the same.' Couldn't you just as easily have said, 'Every one of them is the same although some of them think they're different?'"

Some, without prompting, thought that the shepherd represented society or the government. And the slaughterhouse was death.

I told them, "The shepherd could also be 'conventional thinking' which tells us not to worry; technology and science will solve all of our problems, go back to sleep. Just contribute to the United Way and let us worry about the big issues. And yet, with all of our technology and labor-saving and time-saving devices we seem to have less and less free time."

It was more difficult than I had anticipated to convince them that "thinking oneself to be different" has no force, no weight. That the sheep who thought he or she was a lion or an eagle was actually worse off than the others who knew they were simply sheep. The thing of belief seemed to keep coming up.

"Do you think that if you believe you have wings, and if you believe that strongly enough that you will, eventually, grow wings? I mean . . ."

One student brought up the case of a friend, Dana, who had recently been in a terrible automobile accident and who otherwise would have been in this group. She had been told by two of her doctors that she would never walk again. The student spoke of the power of Dana's belief that she *would* walk again.

"We were *meant* to walk," I told them. "That is entirely different from a sheep thinking it is a lion. . . . Besides, the sheep is simply hallucinating, without a concerted plan or design on even *how* it might become a lion. It simply says, I *am* a lion. With Dana, she has *got* to believe that she will walk again. She has to see herself walking again. That is her only hope. And, in fact, if she *doesn't* believe she will walk again then there is no way in hell that she will . . . do you see the difference?"

I think I won that battle but not without some casualties. I believe I know what the problem is—mainly with young Americans, late twentieth century. I think it is rooted in the idea that anything that *anyone* believes, no matter how far-fetched, is okay, is good—is, somehow, a part of certain freedoms guaranteed us all. It came up later in a less disguised form.

I then added a wrinkle to the tale of the shepherd and the slaughterhouse: "What if one of the sheep (the black sheep) said: 'Look, you guys. We're a bunch of sheep. And this guy, this shepherd, is taking us to the slaughterhouse. As a matter of fact, that's how he makes his money. He gets *paid* for this. Now, here's my plan. If we all bolt in ten different directions he might catch one or two of us but the rest of us can escape. What do you say?' And what would they say?"

"They probably wouldn't go along," one volunteered.

"'Hey, you're nuts! He takes *care* of us. He *feeds* us every day. He brings us in at night so the wolves won't get us.'

"'No! No! Don't you see? Don't you get it? He feeds us and takes care of us until we're nice and fat then he marches us to the slaughterhouse where he'll sell us for meat. If the wolves get us first that's his loss! He can't sell us then!'

"'I'll take my chances with him . . . he's always taken care of us, before this.' And on they go, to the slaughterhouse."

"Do the Sufis say that this, the story of the sheep and the shepherd and the slaughterhouse, is about the human condition?" asked Carole.

"Good question. What do you think?"

"I think it is a pretty grim picture."

"Here's another picture, one from which I learned a great

deal: Two years ago my father-in-law died. . . . I looked down at him in the casket and thought, yes, that's Bill. And yet it's not Bill. It is but it isn't.

"It happened very suddenly. We got a call from my mother-in-law. Something was happening to Bill. Get over here right away. By eight o'clock that evening we knew he was gone. A brain tumor. He died around midnight of the same night. Two days later I was looking at him in the casket.

"For the first time in years I was faced with the notion that the body is not 'I.' Then what and where is the 'I' that has this body?

"And so the thing which sees and which hears and only sees and hears *out of* our eyes and ears—in short, not our *shells* but the *life* inside the shells, the spark, the fire . . . that spark has left. Because, when Bill died I was looking at the face I knew so well. Everything was there; the eyes to see with, the nose to smell with, the ears to hear with and yet . . . no more hearing, no more seeing, no more tasting and yet it was as if the eyes were waiting to see again. Waiting like a computer waits. There sits the cursor, on the last word we've written. It waits but it doesn't wait. It doesn't care.

"So . . . even *waiting* was gone. Waiting and impatience were gone. The 'clothes' inside of the clothes had been deserted. The consciousness was gone. The life was gone. And yet the shell was still there. 'Bill' was still there."

Bill is gone, I wrote on the board, *but "Bill" is still there.*

"So, the question is, are we our bodies, or do we *have* bodies?"

I asked two of the group and they both, without conviction, answered, "We . . . I . . . *have* a body."

"Then, if we *have* a body, if *I* have a body, what is the 'I' which *has* the body? We have bodies but we are *not* our bodies. And so, are we simply a bunch of characteristics? A bunch of habits and fears and desires? Is it the personality? Or something behind the personality?"

Time was up. I gave out copies of Hemingway's story "Indian Camp," told them we'd take it up next time, and read a favorite quote:

> God made the illusion look like the real, and He made the real look as if it does not exist. . . . This world is an old sorcerer who sells you the moonlight as silk; in return he gets from you the gold and silver of your life. When you come to yourself you see there are no silk clothes, but instead you have spent your gold and silver pieces. And your purse is empty. . . . From this magic market you can take refuge in nothing but Truth.
>
> (Farzan, 25)

INDIAN CAMP

At the lake shore there was another rowboat drawn up. The two Indians stood waiting.

Nick and his father got in the stern of the boat and the Indians shoved it off and one of them got in to row. Uncle George sat in the stern of the camp rowboat. The young Indian shoved the camp boat off and got in to row Uncle George.

The two boats started off in the dark. Nick heard the oarlocks of the other boat quite a way ahead of them in the mist. The Indians rowed with quick choppy strokes. Nick lay back with his father's arm around him. It was cold on the water. The Indian who was rowing them was working very hard, but the other boat moved further ahead in the mist all the time.

"Where are we going, Dad?" Nick asked.

"Over to the Indian camp. There is an Indian lady very sick."

"Oh," said Nick.

Across the bay they found the boat beached. Uncle George was smoking a cigar in the dark. The young Indian pulled the boat way up on the beach. Uncle George gave both the Indians cigars.

They walked up from the beach through a meadow that was soaking wet with dew, following the young Indian who carried a lantern. Then they went into the woods and followed a trail that led to the logging road that ran back into the hills. It was much lighter on the logging road as the timber was cut away on both sides. The young Indian stopped and blew out his lantern and they all walked on along the road.

They came around a bend and a dog came out barking. Ahead were the lights of the shanties where the Indian bark-peelers lived. More dogs rushed out at them. The two Indians sent them back to the shanties. In the shanty nearest the road there was a light in the window. An old woman stood in the doorway holding a lamp.

Inside on a wooden bunk lay a young Indian woman. She had been trying to have her baby for two days. All the old women in the camp had been helping her. The men had moved off up the road to sit in the dark and smoke out of range of the noise she made. She screamed just as Nick and the two Indians followed his father and Uncle George into the shanty. She lay in the lower bunk, very big under a quilt. Her head was turned to one side. In the upper bunk was her husband. He had cut his foot very badly with an ax three days before. He was smoking a pipe. The room smelled very bad.

Nick's father ordered some water to be put on the stove, and while it was heating he spoke to Nick.

"This lady is going to have a baby, Nick," he

said.

"I know," said Nick.

"You don't know," said his father. "Listen to me. What she is going through is called being in labor. The baby wants to be born and she wants it to be born. All her muscles are trying to get the baby born. That is what is happening when she screams."

"I see," Nick said.

Just then the woman cried out.

"Oh, Daddy, can't you give her something to make her stop screaming?" asked Nick.

"No, I haven't any anaesthetic," his father said. "But her screams are not important. I don't hear them because they are not important."

The husband in the upper bunk rolled over against the wall.

The woman in the kitchen motioned to the doctor that the water was hot. Nick's father went into the kitchen and poured about half of the water out of the kettle into a basin. Into the water left in the kettle he put several things he unwrapped from a handkerchief.

"Those must boil," he said, and began to scrub his hands in the basin of hot water with a cake of soap he had brought from the camp. Nick watched his father's hands scrubbing each other with the soap. While his father washed his hands very carefully and thoroughly, he talked.

"You see, Nick, babies are supposed to be born head first but sometimes they're not. When they're not they make a lot of trouble for everybody. Maybe I'll have to operate on this lady. We'll know in a little while."

When he was satisfied with his hands he went in and went to work.

"Pull back that quilt, will you, George?" he said. "I'd rather not touch it."

Later when he started to operate Uncle George and three Indian men held the woman still. She bit Uncle George on the arm and Uncle George said, "Damn squaw bitch!" and the young Indian who had rowed Uncle George over laughed at him. Nick held the basin for his father. It all took a long time. His father picked the baby up and slapped it to make it breathe and handed it to the old woman.

"See, it's a boy, Nick," he said. "How do you like being an interne?"

Nick said, "All right." He was looking away so as not to see what his father was doing.

"There. That gets it," said his father and put something into the basin.

Nick didn't look at it.

"Now," his father said, "there's some stitches to put in. You can watch this or not, Nick, just as you like. I'm going to sew up the incision I made."

Nick did not watch. His curiosity had been gone for a long time.

His father finished and stood up. Uncle George and the three Indian men stood up. Nick put the basin out in the kitchen.

Uncle George looked at his arm. The young Indian smiled reminiscently.

"I'll put some peroxide on that, George," the doctor said. He bent over the woman. She was quiet now and her eyes were closed. She looked very pale. She did not know what had become of the baby or anything.

"I'll be back in the morning," the doctor said, standing up. "The nurse should be here from St. Ignace by noon and she'll bring everything we need."

He was feeling exalted and talkative as football players are in the dressing room after a game.

"That's one for the medical journal, George," he said. "Doing a Caesarian with a jack-knife and sewing it up with nine-foot, tapered gut leaders."

Uncle George was standing against the wall, looking at his arm.

"Oh, you're a great man, all right," he said.

"Ought to have a look at the proud father. They're usually the worst sufferers in these little affairs," the doctor said. "I must say he took it all pretty quietly."

He pulled back the blanket from the Indian's head. His hand came away wet. He mounted on the edge of the lower bunk with the lamp in one hand and looked in. The Indian lay with his face toward the wall. His throat had been cut from ear to ear. The blood had flowed down into a pool where his body sagged the bunk. His head rested on his left arm. The open razor lay, edge up, in the blankets.

"Take Nick out of the shanty, George," the doctor said.

There was no need of that. Nick, standing in the door of the kitchen, had a good view of the upper bunk when his father, the lamp in one hand, tipped the Indian's head back.

It was just beginning to be daylight when they walked along the logging road back toward the lake.

"I'm terribly sorry I brought you along, Nickie," said his father, all his post-operative exhilaration gone. "It was an awful mess to put you through."

"Do ladies always have such a hard time having babies?" Nick asked.

"No, that was very, very exceptional."

"Why did he kill himself, Daddy?"

"I don't know, Nick. He couldn't stand things, I guess."

"Do many men kill themselves, Daddy?"

"Not very many, Nick."

"Do many women?"

"Hardly ever."

"Don't they ever?"

"Oh, yes. They do sometimes."

"Daddy?"

"Yes."

"Where did Uncle George go?"

"He'll turn up all right."

"Is dying hard, Daddy?"

"No, I think it's pretty easy, Nick. It all depends."

They were seated in the boat, Nick in the stern, his father rowing. The sun was coming up over the hills. A bass jumped, making a circle in the water. Nick trailed his hand in the water. It felt warm in the sharp chill of the morning.

In the early morning on the lake sitting in the stern of the boat with his father rowing, he felt quite sure that he would never die.

3
Getting Out and Letting Go

"The good news is that we've got the place. The cabin is ours! The cabin on the island, or what they call the island. Do all of you know how to get there?"

Most knew and were explaining it to the others.

"So, we will meet there for the next time, tomorrow. Okay. On to 'Indian Camp.' This is not a Sufi tale. But there are some connections. I'll paraphrase the story briefly—"

"Don't do that," said Jodie. "We've all read it."

"Okay, okay, so, the doctor—actually it's Hemingway's father—and his son 'Nick' . . . so, the woman has been in labor for how long?"

"Two days," said Bess, "so he does a Caesarian—"

"Yes, with a jack-knife and gut leader," someone interrupted. Dan it was.

"Okay, good. And is the operation successful?"

"Yep."

"The baby is 'brought to life,' as we say. And is living, right?"

"Yes . . . pretty good job."

"See? We have to stop here. Do you all agree with that rendition? The doctor was called on, he goes over, delivers the baby and that's it."

They were looking at me, sort of waiting. I was looking back and waiting.

"Well," I asked them, "then . . . that's not exactly a story, is it? That's just an account. Indian woman in labor. White doctor called in. Goes over. Delivers baby. And that's it. No questions.

You guys sit there. Any reaction? Nobody's angry. No one's upset."

"Well, that's all there is to it," said Jodie.

"Wait a second. Doesn't the husband—although he's 'just an Indian'—doesn't he kill himself? Isn't that part of the story?" I waited. At least among the feminists I expected some reaction.

"I'll get to my point. And my point is, *how do we know that the doctor is a brutal sonofabitch?*"

"What? . . . What do you mean? . . . What *should* he have done? . . . He did what he was supposed to do . . ."

"Does anyone think the doctor is a brutal sonofabitch? No, that's not it, I'll go directly at it. I repeat: how do we *know* that the doctor's a brutal sonofabitch? Write about it. Just put it down. What you think. Take a few minutes."

Inside I was boiling. Maybe boiling over. I did *not* want to radicalize them. I wanted nothing to do with politics. I wanted them thinking, with no bias, no curves, no bends in the road. Not politics, just thinking. Just humans.

He goes in, never checking the situation. Not taking a minute to calm the woman down. Doesn't check on the father. The woman is screaming and delirious. Doctor tells his son her screams are not important. He doesn't hear them. Indian father slits his throat with an open razor. Father/doctor is sorry his son has been there to witness this "mess." "It was an awful mess to put you through." To put *you* through. His *son*. Not the Indian family, *his* family.

"You know, in literature it's good form to *show*, not *tell*. A good writer is not going to tell you; he or she is going to show you. In the same way that it means more if you give me examples of your roommate's stinginess, instead of telling me that she's stingy. Okay?"

"What does the story have to do with Sufism?"

"Nothing . . . but your response to it has a lot to do with it. One definition of Sufism is 'heart-wakefulness,' and your response, so far, has been heart-sleepiness."

There were defenses of their reactions and demands to know what the doctor had done that was so awful. I wanted, instead, their silence and their sober questions. I got neither.

I tried to move on, to introduce another story, but they practically demanded that I explain something more about "Indian Camp."

"I'm *not* going to explain it. If you don't see something in it, why should I explain it? I *told* you that a good writer is not going to take a stick and point at a character and say, 'Hey! You see that character over there? Well, he's a real sonofabitch. Okay? I warned you.' Instead, he is going to show the person in action and *you* have to judge."

"So? I don't see it. He—"

"Well, if you don't see it you don't see it."

"So? Maybe it's not *there*. Maybe, in your opinion, the doctor is a brutal so and so, but, *really* . . ."

"All I will say to you is to put yourself in the place of the characters. While you're reading this be*come* Nick. Be*come* the doctor. Be*come* George. Now, for the other side; be*come* that Indian squaw. Be*come* her husband. Be*come* her mother. Read the story and put yourself in the places of all of those people. Don't give me your usual views. Doctor goes in, delivers baby. That's it."

"But you're forcing us to come to your conclusion."

"No, I'm forcing you to think about it."

"And *then* come to your conclusion!"

"No, I'll be happy if you only *think* about it. Now, I promise that we will take it up again. Right after we take up Walt Whitman."

They made me laugh and I couldn't help it but I was laughing with them, at their exasperation and because, for once, I was not pulled into going along with them. There was a feeling across the room of doubt, of having no idea what I was looking for. For the moment let it be.

I gave them a break. When we came back, we would discuss "The Blind Ones and the Matter of the Elephant."

* * *

THE BLIND ONES AND THE MATTER OF THE ELEPHANT

Beyond Ghor there was a city. All its inhabitants were blind. A king with his entourage arrived nearby; he brought his army and camped in the desert. He had a mighty elephant, which he used in attack and to increase the people's awe.

The populace became anxious to see the elephant, and some sightless from among this blind community ran like fools to find it.

As they did not even know the form or shape of the elephant they groped sightlessly, gathering information by touching some part of it.

Each thought that he knew something, because he could feel a part.

When they returned to their fellow citizens, eager groups clustered around them. Each of these was anxious, misguidedly, to learn the truth from those who were themselves astray.

They asked about the form, the shape of the elephant: and listened to all they were told.

The man whose hand had reached an ear was asked about the elephant's nature. He said: "It is a large rough thing, wide and broad like a rug."

And the one who had felt the trunk said: "I have the real facts about it. It is like a straight and hollow pipe, awful and destructive."

The one who had felt its feet and legs said: "It is mighty and firm, like a pillar."

Each had felt one part out of many. . . . No mind knew all: knowledge is not the companion of the blind.

The created is not informed about divinity. There is no Way in this science by means of the ordinary intellect.

(Shah, *Tales of the Dervishes*, 25)

Sara came up to me while the rest were still straggling in. "I have no idea what you're looking for," she said.

"All I'll say right now," I told her, "is that this doctor . . . well, he's not changing a set of spark plugs, is he?"

She smiled a doubtful, doubting smile and sat down.

I collected their papers and we began anew. "As I said before, there is a lot to tell you and I hope some of it is sticking. I want to read about 'sleeping mankind,' and then we'll do 'The Blind Ones and the Matter of the Elephant,' maybe the most famous Sufi tale and one of the world's most popular stories.

"But first, Ouspensky on the subject of sleep. It is a huge and important topic. Try to connect this with the condition of mankind, as well as the Hemingway story and the notion that mankind is asleep:

There is nothing new in the idea of sleep. People have been told almost since the creation of the world that they are asleep and that they must awaken. How many times is this said in the Gospels, for instance? 'Awake,' 'watch,' 'sleep not.' Christ's disciples even slept when he was praying in the Garden of Gethsemane for the last time. It is all there. But do men understand it? Men take it simply as a form of speech, as an expression, as a metaphor. They completely fail to understand that it must be taken literally. And again it is easy to understand why. In order to understand this literally it is necessary to awaken a little, or at least to try to awaken. I tell you seriously that I have been asked several times why nothing is said about sleep in the Gospels. Although it is there spoken of almost on every page. This simply shows that people read the Gospels in sleep—

(Ouspensky, *In Search of the Miraculous*, 144)

"Do you get this? Now listen carefully to the next section because, if you are there for it, it can explain a lot about us, our society and how things got that way:

> As I have already said, as he is organized, that is, being such as nature has created him, man can be a self-conscious being. Such he is created and such he is born. But he is born among sleeping people, and, of course, he falls asleep among them just at the very time when he should have begun to be conscious of himself. Everything has a hand in this: the involuntary imitation of older people on the part of the child, voluntary and involuntary suggestion, and what is called 'education.' Every attempt to awaken on the child's part is instantly stopped . . . and a great many efforts and a great deal of help are necessary in order to awaken later when thousands of sleepcompelling habits have been accumulated. . . . In most cases, a man when still a child already loses the possibility of awakening: he lives in sleep all his life and he dies in sleep.
>
> (Ouspensky, *In Search of the Miraculous*, 44)

"There is so much evidence to support this but, just for starters, it is reported that the average person uses only about 6 to 8 percent of his or her brain power. Even Einstein was said to have activated only about 8 percent of his brain—and couldn't find his way home from the drugstore.

"As for children, they're helpless. What else would they do but imitate their elders? Watch parents and children. From laughter, to expressions, to sitting, to smoking, to swinging their arms, children imitate parents, who were imitating someone else. It's hard to break the pattern.

"The quote I read to you is not, strictly, a Sufi source but it is close enough. The Sufis are more subtle, not nearly so direct. They point in a general direction. If you don't look carefully you'll miss it. And if you miss it you miss it. Can you guess why the elephant story has been told and reproduced over and over?"

"Not a clue."

"Yes, I can," said Holly. "Because each one only has part of the truth, about the elephant, and it's interesting how—"

Someone else interrupted, "Do the people who were told—"

"Good, Holly. Okay, go on, Sam."

"Do the people who were told what the elephant was like *believe* the ones who have touched the elephant?"

"Yes, they're wrong and so are the ones who told them."

"I say that's the problem and that's the whole story, taking someone else's word for something," Joanne said, quietly.

"Believing someone's word isn't the problem!" said Holly.

They were off and running.

"We trust people, we take their word, and it turns out that they're wrong."

"No, that they're *lying*. That's a different ball game."

"No," some said, "maybe they really didn't *know* and thought they did know."

"But why didn't they know? They went in and touched the elephant and went out and blabbed about it as if they really knew all about it."

"Wait a second. Slow down. I once had a great teacher who said, 'Proper use of the imagination is to discover the truth.' So, just back up a second and reconstruct the situation. This is a village of the blind. Okay—"

"That makes it hard to believe right there. A whole village of *blind* people?" That was Carlito. Seconded by Sam.

"Listen, the thing about 'story' that you have to realize if you're going to discover anything from it is that you must accept the miracle or the premise of the story, which should come at the beginning. So, this is a village of the blind. That in itself could be taken a couple of ways. But the ones who rush out to 'see' the elephant are described . . . how?"

Bess was reading from the story: "'Some sightless among the blind . . . ran like fools to find it.'"

"Good. Now, remember, these people are not only blind but he describes the ones who ran to 'see it' as 'sightless.' Why would he say that?"

"Because . . . maybe they're not only blind but they lack . . . they lack insight as well, maybe." Surprising contribution from Sara.

"Good. Maybe so. Anyhow, he certainly doesn't praise them. He doesn't tell us that the wisest among the blind were the ones who went. And he tells us that they ran 'like fools' to find it. So, among the blind, they are described as 'sightless' and as 'fools.'

"But I wanted to go back to something Holly said. You said it's not the problem that we take another's word for things?"

"Well, it's not the central problem."

"But my God, it *is* a central problem. We take others' word for elephant and we walk away saying: 'Now I've got to remember this; an elephant is like a column, an elephant is like a column . . .' We even take tests on it! We take *exams* on it, and flunk courses if we don't feed back to 'them' the *wrong* information!

"In the early seventeenth century, students had to know that the earth was the center of the universe and that everything revolves around the earth. Wrrrrrrooonggg! But now we see how the expert got his, or her, information. The one that everybody listens to. The 'expert' felt one piece of the elephant and, perhaps frightened to death, got out of there."

"Yes, but if no one had gone in to see the elephant they would have known even less than they did. . . . I mean, that was better than nothing, right?" said Holly.

Before I could say a word, Carole had turned to her. "Really? Is an elephant like a rug? Is it like a column—?"

"Sometimes," Dan added, "*no* information is better than the wrong information."

"Would you rather know something wrongly or still be open to what it might be? You know, during the war I was a pilot. A lot of us thought we would go into commercial aviation because, after all, we already knew how to fly. Just a little transition time and we'd have a good job with an airline. Come to find out they didn't want ex-military pilots at all. Even pilots who had flown twin engine and four-engined planes. Why not? They would rather train people from the beginning than try to *break* or overcome whatever habits we had picked up flying for the military. They would rather have their trainees begin from scratch! They found it easier. We were stunned.

"It's the same thing here. You have some information and it is wrong. And yet, before long, after living with that information for a while, it comes to be gospel truth. It's the same as with old habits. They die hard. It is twice as hard to drop that old belief as it is to have the right information from the beginning.

"I can only ask you to use your imagination and try to put yourself in the shoes of the people (almost everyone) who were convinced that the earth was the center of the universe. Then come to find out that they were wrong. Would that be difficult to overcome?"

"You know, really," Sam suggested, "I don't much care if the earth goes around the sun or the sun goes around the earth. What difference does it make to us?" His last words were almost drowned out by most of the others, but I knew he had something to say.

"I kind of agree," said Carlito, whose agreement was almost feared by everyone. "We're like ants on a football field . . . only smaller."

"No," I added. "Like ants on a football field in Kansas, worrying about the China question. Go on, Sam . . . finish."

"I just get tired of these huge questions that are supposed to mean . . . just *everything* to us. I mean, in one way, it doesn't matter. I have to have a skill—farming or computers or something—or else I'll starve. And that's true whichever goes around the other."

"Sam, I was in Spain after the brutal Spanish dictator Franco died, and democracy was restored to Spain. I had just landed and was in a cab going from the airport to Barcelona, exhilarated, happy to be in the new-born democracy of Spain. And I asked the driver, 'What is it like, now that Franco is gone?' I thought everyone would be celebrating. Democracy! Freedom!

"What was his answer? His answer was like Sam's: 'Well, señor, yes, Franco is gone . . . but still we have to get up in the morning and go to work.' With or without Franco. Or, whether the sun goes around the earth or the other way around."

"Or, *even*, if there's life on Mars," said Carole.

"Exactly! Exciting as that may be."

"Yes, but the problem is, how do we know when we have the right information?" Holly asked. "I mean, information that *can* make a big difference in our lives?"

"He who experiences knows," said big Mike from the end of the table.

"Did you hear that, Holly? Begin to trust your own taste of something. How do we know? How do we really know? That takes education. Real education. Meantime, you begin to question the authorities. Who says so? Why? Where did you get your information? Exactly who to believe?"

"Well, what's the answer?" she asked.

"Listen to the sparrows."

Pandemonium.

"Look, what I'm faced with, what we're all faced with, are these fixed notions that we carry around with us. Can we get just a little loose from them so we can at least consider new ideas? If we can't, then we're suckers for every fast-talking salesman out there. And there are lots of them. And they're very smart.

"If we can't, then we're stuck with these old wives' tales. We're convinced that an elephant is like a rug. See? We're stuck with what we grew up with. I'm stuck with my mother's notion that no real man ever does 'it' until he's married, which is what she told me, and undoubtedly with the best of intentions. I'm stuck with believing that if I eat an ant I will die. These notions we grew up with, and will carry to the grave, unless someone makes us question them. And yet, if I tell you you've been brainwashed you get angry and decide not to listen to *anything* I've said."

"You called us brain*painted*, not just brainwashed."

"But, you see, does it matter? What I called you? It's either true or it's not true, and if it's not then forget it.

"To return to the story, these blind people have run like fools to get to the elephant, this fearsome, huge animal. Are they going to stick around and feel every part of it? And maybe get stomped to death? Or would it be more like . . . what?"

"They might just touch it and run."

"Exactly. 'I touched it and now I'm outta here.' And do they know in their heart of hearts that they do not have the entire picture? And more important, later, start arguing with the other fools as to whether it was like a column or like a rug? 'My cousin felt it and he said it's like a rug and I believe him.' 'Oh yeah, well, my *brother* felt it and he never lies and *he* said it's like a hollow pipe, awful and destructive.'

"You know, sometimes, this story is told as if one of the blind who had felt the elephant was a Jew, one a Protestant, one a Muslim, and one a Buddhist so, of course it has religious overtones, but we'll get to that later."

"When are you going to define Sufism?"

"We're defining it as we go. The same teacher, incidentally, the one who talked about imagination and the truth, Mark Van Doren, taught a course called Comedy and Tragedy and after three days a student interrupted his lecture—and that was never done . . . ahem, a very different kind of course than this one—and asked him when he was going to define Tragedy and Comedy. She had been waiting for three days for a definition.

"He smiled from his lofty perch—he was about six feet three—and told her that he did not intend to define them. He only hoped that by the end of the course that she would be able to speak more intelligently about Comedy and Tragedy than she could now.

"And I have the same hopes for you.

"I really can't tell you, any more than telling you, how important this story is. Suppose we say that the elephant is the truth. *The* truth. The whole ball. The entire truth. The truth of why we're here on earth. The truth of what we're supposed to be doing with our lives. The truth about life itself. Incidentally, the geologists have just discovered that at the very core of the earth there is a kind of liquid core, jelly-like, and it seems to be a pulse of some kind. So that people who say the earth is alive have now got the geologists on their side. Anyhow, that the elephant is a symbol for the entire truth. The truth about the beginning and end. The truth about the earth and its aspirations, if that can be spoken of. And these 'fools' have rushed wherever the truth is kept, and they've had a glimpse of it, and have run right out again and, instead of sitting down and wondering or contemplating what it was they had seen, or touched, and sat and thought about it for a while and realized that they had had only a glimpse of something so tremendous that it was really indescribable, and admitting their doubts about it, instead, when others asked if they had seen or touched 'the elephant,' they said yes. Instant fame.

"There's a Nasrudin tale, about a man from a small town who had gone to Moscow. When he came back he told everyone that the Czar had spoken to him. People were wild with excitement and ran to tell others. Only one little child remained there and the child asked him: 'What did the Czar say to you?' And the man answered, 'He said, Get out of my way.'

"And, now, which person would get more attention? The one who honestly says, 'Well, I only touched a piece of it,' or the person who says, 'Yes, I know all about elephants'?"

"You mean if both of them had really only touched one part of the elephant?"

"Yes."

I watched them go through the painful process and hoped what I was hearing was icons breaking.

"Listen. When I was going to graduate school, a number of us got a job at a place called the Wall Street Club. We worked three and a half hours for $5.00, tips, and a lunch of leftovers. One day a family came in and they all asked for iced tea. It was November but there was a barrel of tea and lots of ice. Sure, I told them. Later, after they left, an old-time waiter came over and said to me, 'You should never do something like that. Look, if a bunch of people ask me for iced tea I look around and tell 'em, Okay, I'll *try* to get you some but don't say anything to anybody. See what I mean?'

"'Why should I do that?' I told him. 'There's tea back there, and ice and glasses; it's no problem.'

"'Because,' he said, 'I'm working for tips. And who do you think is going to get the best tip? *I'm* doin' 'em a big favor, see? An' you're just bringin 'em iced tea.'

"If the ones who felt a part of the elephant had said 'I really can't say what it's like because I felt only a part of the elephant,' would the others have flocked around them?"

Mike had a hand up and had not answered for a while. "The moral of the story is don't act—or make up your mind—till you know all the facts."

"Thank you, Mike. And thank God for this story! Thank God. Will you please tell me, will you please tell me *when* we know all the facts? All of the facts, about anything?"

"Never," said Carole.

"We make a decision about a boyfriend, about a trip, about a course in school, about marriage. Do we know all the facts? No, we sum up a situation and decide. How it will work out we have no idea. We take chances.

"We were on a walk in France, near Vence . . . twenty-six students, my wife, three of my children. My daughter was very excited. She had just met an American who was going to find us a place to put up our tent for the night. She brought him over, young guy in his twenties, speaking all of the drug language of the day and wearing a baseball cap with a logo on it: 'World's Number 1 Asshole.' I shook hands with him, excused us, and told her we're not going to stay at a place with someone who advertises himself as the Number One Asshole in the world . . . even if he's actually, in the eyes of God, only in twenty-fifth place.

"Did I make a mistake? Or avoid a drug bust? I don't know. Without all of the facts I made the decision. Did I make a mistake taking this discussion group on? This too is a calculated risk.

"That trip we ended up in Munich, Germany, in a Munich beer hall one night, after having walked a good bit of Spain, France, Italy, Austria, and Germany. There were some Americans there from Kansas. They'd been in Europe one hour. They had gone from the airport to the hotel and then to the beer hall, and were in a big argument with us. They were shouting, 'USA number one!' No one in our group was against the U.S.A., but these guys had only just landed . . . direct from Kansas. They'll go back home after what? After touching the elephant's . . . what? The elephant's footprint? . . . After stepping in the elephant's *stool*? And report to the home folks. So? Is travel broadening? Eh?"

"It depends, sometimes, on the person who is traveling," said Carole.

"Excellent. That's it. Can an idiot be broadened by a trip around the world? It's doubtful. It depends on *who* is traveling and what he or she brings to the place.

"But the main thing is, to taste is to know, to experience is to know. And that does not mean having someone else taste it for you. Or someone else experience it for you. So, you ask, how do we know if certain information is correct? By tasting for ourselves. Experiencing for ourselves. And learning, over time, to trust ourselves. And *how* to trust ourselves.

"Okay? I think our time is up. Tomorrow, we'll take on 'The Man Who Was Easily Angered.' See you then. And be on time. . . . Oh, one other thing, before you go."

They waited.

"A little task for now, tonight, and tomorrow. Here it is: I want you to think about your name. Your given name. As you know, as you must know, with even a moment's thought about it, you had no choice about your given name. So, your task is to think about your given name. Think about changing it. What would you change it to? And what are your feelings when thinking about this question?

"Okay, that's it. See you tomorrow."

THE MAN WHO WAS EASILY ANGERED

A man who was very easily angered realized after many years that all his life he had been in difficulties because of this tendency.

One day he heard of a dervish deep of knowledge, whom he went to see, asking for advice.

The dervish said: "Go to such-and-such a crossroads. There you will find a withered tree. Stand under it and offer water to every traveler who passes that place."

The man did as he was told. Many days passed, and he became well known as one who was following a certain discipline of charity and self-control, under the instructions of a man of real knowledge.

One day a man in a hurry turned his head away when he was offered the water, and went on walking along the road. The man who was easily angered called out to him several times: "Come, return my salutation! Have some of this water, which I provide for all travelers!"

But there was no reply.

Overcome by this behavior, the first man forgot his discipline completely. He reached for his gun, which was hooked in the withered tree, took aim at the heedless traveler, and fired. The man fell dead.

At the very moment that the bullet entered his body, the withered tree, as if by a miracle, burst joyfully into blossom.

The man who had been killed was a murderer, on his way to commit the worst crime of a long career.

There are, you see, two kinds of advisers. The first kind is the one who tells what should be done according to certain fixed principles, repeated mechanically. The other kind is the Man of Knowledge. Those who meet the Man of Knowledge will ask him for moralistic advice, and will treat him as a moralist. But what he serves is Truth, not pious hopes.

(Shah, Tales of the Dervishes, 79)

4

What's in a Name?

M y thoughts while driving to the log cabin made me anxious to get to them. I thought of Carlito, defending psychotherapy, against no one, in a conversation after class: "Well,
I think psychotherapy really helps . . . *some* people." Yes, Carlito, and chocolate helps *some people*; so does whiskey.

Of Dostoyevsky, defending idiocy: "I don't mind people's
idiocy. That's not it. I love people's idiocy, when it's their own.
The trouble is it's not their own idiocy, it's someone else's." Got
to tell Holly. Let her clasp that to her bosom.

As for our new location and what it can do for us, I guess it's
like going to Paris. Paris is great, if we can leave ourselves at
home.

When I was a kid and first heard about "the truth," I
thought, what's the big deal about truth? Do people just *make* it
difficult? Two and two equals four. Isn't that the truth? What's
the problem?

Across the rattling and flimsy bridge connecting the main-
land to the "island," another fifty yards, and I was parking the
car along with seven other cars. There they were, talking, lying
in the sun, playing hackysack. At home in the world. Well,
fine. I think we were all glad to see each other. And our new
private group room was a relief.

I fitted the key into the somewhat rusty door lock and opened
it. Everyone went for the windows and soon there was a breeze
blowing across from the lake. Jodie and Bess got rags and dish

towels from the kitchen and, without a word from anyone, wiped off the table and the chairs; soon we were sitting at the board of trustees table, with room for the eleven of us and more.

"Okay, I asked you to do the story, and the task of your given names. Let's do the story first: 'The Man Who Was Easily Angered.' First question: Is the man of knowledge interested in the easily angered man's temper?"

"Probably not."

"Amen. Probably not."

"Another question . . . anyone?"

"Maybe this doesn't make sense, but the man of knowledge doesn't say a word about 'temper.'"

"And why not?"

"I don't know." And no one seemed to hazard a guess.

"Well, for one thing, is the man's temper connected to everything else in the man? Or is it hanging out of his pocket like a dirty rag?"

"It's connected."

"Yes. John Muir says everything is connected to everything else. Only Muir says it about everything in the world. That it is *all* connected. Well, if that's true, then certainly it's true that our different traits are part of the whole, right?"

I could see in their faces that it was still a problem of reading carefully, or rather of not reading carefully. "These stories are complicated. Read it again, quickly, and keep in mind every reference to his temper."

* * *

"What did you discover?"

"He's had a bad temper for a long time, and he loses it often."

"He's had the problem all of his life."

"And he's been in difficulties because of it."

"Good. So, he's interested in getting rid of his temper because it gets in his way. Is he really interested in learning about himself? Or, even, is he interested in becoming a pupil of this wise man?"

"No, I don't think so," said Carole. "He just wants his clutch adjusted. Everything else is fine."

"Right! Now, in the same vein, does the man of knowledge give him any promises? I think Joanne already answered this."

"Not really."

"No, he just tells him, go out and give water at the crossroads."

"What do you mean 'promises'?" Jodie asked.

"He didn't tell the man, 'If you go out and give water to people for thirty days you will get rid of your temper.' He just said to go out and *offer* water. And does he do it? Pretty well?"

"Yeah, but—"

"Yes," said Joanne, "and he takes it very seriously."

"So, that's the situation at the beginning of the story. And then he becomes known as the person who does that. So, does the man of knowledge—we are told he is a man of deep knowledge—does he think that the man who is easily angered is *ever* going to get rid of his anger? His bad temper? What do you think?"

"There's no evidence for or against that," said Holly.

"Good, but what does he do? Does the man with the temper do the predictable thing?"

"Yes, he loses it . . . again."

"And how do we know that his terrible temper hasn't been improved in the least? You know, there are cases in New York where one kid kills another with a knife or with a zip gun because another kid didn't speak to him or was wearing a jacket he didn't like. Or because he 'had a sneer on his face.' These are actual cases.

"And what made the man in the story, the man who was easily angered, lose his temper?"

"The other man didn't take the water."

"Here, have some water. Oh, you won't take it, eh? Bang! He kills him. . . . Shades of New York. Now, when that happens, a lot of other things happen. Such as what?"

"The tree suddenly bursts into bloom."

"Yes, and the tree had been withered before. Now, just as the bullet enters the body of the murderer, on his way to commit the worst crime of a long career, the tree blossoms. It's as if nature has smiled on the deed."

"Nature sounds pretty bloody."

"You know," I told them, "one of the big questions about this story is whether the man of deep knowledge planned the whole thing and knew exactly what would happen."

"It's a question of what you believe . . ."

"You guys . . . you've got to stop that. It's *not* just a question of what you believe. Not just *belief*, but does it really happen? That someone can see ahead? That *someone* can know about an event before it happens and do something in the way of, let us say, 'world maintenance' to prevent it? That a person, or people, can know not only that something is going to take place but exactly how and where and *when*, and do something to prevent it?

"There's a story about a motorcycle gang who were going to blow up a huge mansion where the rock group The Grateful Dead were giving a concert. They were going to row across the lake to the mansion, plant the dynamite, and blow up the whole place. Well, the story goes that when they neared the middle of the lake something happened and the boat tipped over, spilling the dynamite, and so their plans never materialized. Is this just coincidence? Or did something or someone intercede?"

"What do you think?" Sara asked me.

"I think, really, that there are some forces at work which can't be explained in any easy way. I can think of a couple off-hand, when we were walking across Europe—the story of the knife and what happened the day of the chickens. We were walking through Yugoslavia, when Yugoslavia was a country. Two of the girls were walking through the woods; Jenna had a Swiss army knife and after walking on a tree which had fallen across a stream, she carved her initials in the tree. Beth said to her, 'I'd really like to have a knife—'

"'I'll lend you mine when I finish,' said Jenna.

"'No,' said Beth. 'I want a knife of my own.'

"About half an hour later, a young Yugoslav boy, about sixteen, walked out of his house, came up to the girls, started talking Serbo-Croatian, which neither one of them understood. He spoke no English but, suddenly, he handed a pocket knife to Beth.

"I was the first one to see the girls after this incident and, I swear, their hair was almost standing up while they told me about it."

"Maybe he had been in the woods and heard them talking about the knife," said Holly.

"He didn't speak English. It was a couple of miles away from the woods where they had been walking. They were alone in the woods and no one was around when Beth mentioned that she wanted a knife. His house was a couple of miles from where they had been. He didn't speak English and they didn't speak Serbo-Croatian."

"What do *you* think?"

"I say that there are things that happen that can't easily be explained."

"What about the chickens . . .?"

"Listen, there's a lot to do and we can't take up the whole time with stories."

"But that's also important. You called it 'the day of the chickens.'"

"Okay . . . on a long walk across Europe, in '89, we were a group of twenty-four. We were walking through Italy. We had just left Venice. Wayne, one of the walkers, was dying for some fried chicken or some barbecued chicken. He kept on 'dying' for fried chicken or barbecued chicken. Our food budget was much too modest for chicken in Italy. He kept talking about it. I told him to dream on, or something like that, because chicken was much too expensive, and we went to sleep. The next day I was about quarter to a half mile behind Wayne and two other walkers. Suddenly I came upon three of them sitting by the side of the road, chewing on something that looked like brown leather. It looked like they were eating their shoes. No, it was chicken! They had found a box of thirty-six barbecued chickens, still warm, each chicken carefully wrapped in white butcher paper. A box of thirty-six barbecued chickens had fallen off a truck, or out of the sky. Remember, this was the day after Wayne, on the previous night, had been wishing for chicken. I say it is more than coincidence and I don't know what it is.

"At any rate, those are like little miracles but what we're talking about in the story of the easily angered man is knowing something *ahead,* and if that is possible. Did the man of knowledge know that this temper could and maybe should be used in another way? The man who was easily angered was not a murderer and, in a strange way, may have, finally, killed his temper in killing someone. Remember, he was only supposed to *offer* water. Nothing more—"

"Did people have to take the water? I mean, were they supposed to take the water?" Carlito asked.

"No, his discipline was simply to offer it. But getting rid of his anger was not the interest of the man of deep knowledge. The anger was used, perhaps, to stop a greater wrong.

"Do two wrongs make a right? In the purest sense, no; however, a confirmed murderer was about to commit the worst crime of his career and was stopped by the man who was easily angered. Did the man of deep knowledge prevent the killing of ten or twenty people? In return for killing the 'confirmed murderer'? Remember, we're down here on earth, we're not in heaven. And these are life choices. Kill the murderer or keep your fingers lily-white and don't do anything, and let twenty or so people get killed. Like it or not, there is a sort of poetic justice to it. Did the man who was easily angered lose his temper in the killing? Lose it forever? We don't know."

"I have a lot of questions about this," said Sam.

And so did some others.

"Good! Let's hear them."

"How do we know for sure that this man is a confirmed murderer, and how do we *know* that he's on the way to commit this terrible crime?"

"Yes," said Carole, "and does he know that things will happen, the man will lose his temper and kill the other one, the 'confirmed murderer'?"

"These are good questions. But, again, we are in the world of story. He is a confirmed murderer because the story tells us he is. He is on the way to committing the worst crime of his career because the story tells us he is. *In* the story these things are 'true.' I used to tell my children a story at night and sometimes they would ask me, 'Dad, is that a true story?' I always felt they had been infected by the modern world. I couldn't but I wanted to say, what the hell does it matter? It's true *as a story*. It's a true *story*. As for *this* story, we are saying, what if? What if it's true? And given the story, exactly as it's told here, what can we learn from it . . . about truth. Do you see? Given, given, given the story as it is. So, for us, for this group, don't waste time with these *real* questions. Get into the story and use your imagination to discover the truth, about the big questions—"

"Such as?"

"Such as, can someone actually see the where, the how, the when? of events in the future? And use them for, let us say, the good of mankind? And how much would you have to know about the course of events before you would know exactly what the good of mankind is?"

Carole shook her head. "I don't remember anyone in here asking *that* question."

"Well, I got carried away—"

"But why would the wise man be responsible for not doing anything? I mean, he's not responsible for whatever the murderer does, is he?"

"Well, if he knows this is going to happen—that presumes he can look into the future—and if he *knows* a certain crime is going to take place, then doesn't he have *some* responsibility?"

"Just because he *knows?*"

"Yes, in the same way that if the train tracks have been switched, even if you didn't do it, but you know it and you know that the next train will be wrecked if it's not switched back, and you do nothing about it and the train is wrecked and people are killed . . ."

"Then the person who knows is partly responsible?"

"I think, in law, it's similar to being an accessory. But think about it. Think about it and tell me.

"I used to have a terrible temper and I asked my teacher about it, my real teacher, how I often lost my temper and ended up hating myself. He laughed and said, 'Wouldn't it be wonderful if you could lose it, once and for all.' And maybe that's what happened here."

"Well, maybe the man lost it once and for all in killing someone else," said Dan.

"Danny, he just said that."

"Well . . ." Mike raised his hand. "There's a lot about this story that I don't understand. I mean, suddenly the tree flowers . . . I don't get it."

"I don't either, Mike. All I can say is that whatever method he, the master, was using, was not direct. When the man came to him, the master didn't say, now, here's a pencil and paper, sit down over there and write, 500 times, 'I will not lose my temper, I will not lose my temper.'

"Once in grammar school I had to write 'I will not spit in Marilyn's hair' 500 times. And it kept me from spitting in her hair, at least until I finished writing it. I don't remember being remorseful or that it, in itself, made me change my ways. Incidentally, I was madly in love with Marilyn.

"As for the flowering tree, I do think there's a kind of consciousness in nature that may have said, for *once* he has lost his temper in a good cause. In any case it is a poetic touch. And one thing more. Let's not lose ourselves in what we can't understand. Work with it but don't let it stop you. Maybe come back to it later. But consider: the easily angered man wants to learn how to get rid of his anger. Maybe the man of knowledge knows it's not going to happen so he'll use the temper in a good cause.

"There is also the thing of levels. It could be taken as an entirely internal story. The exoteric or 'outside' man goes to his own wise man inside of himself and asks what's to be done about his temper. The internal, or wise man inside of him, says observe a certain discipline until you see that part of yourself which must be slain. He observes the discipline. Identifies that thing in himself which is his temper. Kills it. And the tree, which is his soul, and has been withering all of these years, suddenly flowers. These are simply possibilities. You could come up with your own. After all, these are teaching tales. They are all hundreds of years old and have been passed along from mouth to ear and mouth to ear. They don't teach facts. They teach a way of approaching problems.

"A couple more notes and we'll move on. This brief quote pertains to the story. In *The New Man*, Nicoll cites Matthew 10:42: 'And whosoever shall give to drink unto one of these little ones a cup of cold water only, in the name of a disciple, verily I say unto you, he shall in no wise lose his reward.' However, Nicoll is talking not about water, literally, but the handing on of truth, however poorly. Water as truth. And 'little ones' means 'of little understanding.'

"Finally, about the issue of whether or not certain people can see ahead . . . remember, he is described as a man of deep knowledge. At the end of the tale is the following statement about the dervish master, the man of deep knowledge, who figures in the tale:

Najmudin was one of the six hundred thousand people who died when Khwarizm in Central Asia was destroyed in 1221. . . . The great Mongol Genghis Khan, aware of his [Najmudin's] reputation, offered to spare him if he gave himself up, but Najmudin went out with the defenders [to defend Khwarizm] . . . and was later identified among the dead . . . [but] Having foreseen the catastrophe, Najmudin had sent all his disciples away to safety some time before the appearance of the Mongol hordes.

(Shah, *Tales of the Dervishes*, 80)

"Now, you have to decide whether this is possible or not. For someone to be able to see ahead, in time, and make plans for catastrophes and such. That part is not 'story' but is an account of what happened. According to Western science it is not possible. But, of course, Western science cannot explain many many things, such as a premonition of death for someone, or someone knowing about a death at the exact time of the accident of a loved one many many miles away, maybe even thousands of miles away. I just say that they have no explanation for it. But that, as they say, is only the tip of the iceberg of what they don't know and can't explain.

"There are stories in which the person who is being helped is not a good candidate for help, but is helped anyway. Just as in 'The Man Who Was Easily Angered,' perhaps a higher purpose is being served. There is one story where the man finds his food floating down to him in the river, at almost the same time every day. He is convinced that God is sending him this food. But he must make sure. It takes him through many hardships and brave deeds to finally enter the castle and find the princess of the castle. She tells him that because he has broken the spell which had left her captive she will answer any question he wants. *Any* question. So he asks where and how he was getting the food of paradise every day. It turns out that it is the remains of her daily toilet, which she threw down into the river every day after her bath. Only when he gets the answer

57

does he realize how trivial his question is. And how he's wasted his question.

"Last week I went to a meeting with a Buddhist monk. It cost $15.00 to get in. I had heard that his translator was sick and for some other reasons decided not to go, but went toward the end of the session to pick up my wife. It was the time for questions, so I listened at the edge of the crowd. The crowd was composed of professional people, graduates of all the best schools in the eastern U.S. I wondered what they would ask.

"'Sir, how long have you been teaching?'

"*What??* I couldn't believe my ears. We're in a small New England town and we have a chance to ask a question of a Buddhist monk from Japan. And the question is *How long have you been teaching?* I could have answered that question and satisfied any listener: 'Twenty-seven years.' Okay? 'Sixty-four years, three months and twenty-one days.' Okay? 'One week!' What does it matter?"

"Well, what *does* matter?" asked Sara. "What would *you* have asked him?"

"Sara, that is a better question than anyone asked all night. What matters? Well, how about: What books would you recommend for Westerners? What has gone wrong with our society and what would you recommend for it? Would it be difficult for a Westerner to get into your monastery? What is the history of some who have tried? And so on. And all the time there is no guarantee that this Buddhist monk is any more enlightened than the man next door but maybe, by his answers, he would give some indication. At least challenge him with the questions, whether he knows the answers or not. Don't ask him, 'How do you spell your middle name?' I mean, doesn't it make you want to strangle someone?"

"Ah ah ah, don't be easily angered."

"Check."

It was time for a break. We stopped for ten minutes.

I collected their papers on the 'names' task, to read while they were outside.

Sam passed where I was standing and told me, "I think you should have asked him some questions, whether you paid the admission or not!"

"I think you're right," I told him, and of course he was.

* * *

Their "name" responses were similar—almost identical. Not one wanted to change the given name. Jodie "would consider" changing to Joan or Joanie, which was her given name, but liked Jodie. Carole now liked her name but would consider Charia or Christina. Mike would change his given name Michael to Mike and thought the exercise "silly, mildly amusing but harmless." Holly was "not the least bit interested" in changing her name and said, "Just thinking about it fills me with a sense of loss." Sam hated his name "for a long time" but said, "Now I'd be nothing else."

"I've read your papers. No one, really, wants to change his or her name. I'm surprised that I didn't foresee that. But 'Who am I?' And 'What am I?' figure prominently in this. In addition to not being our bodies we are, equally, not our names. But we become identified with them. Just as we identify with our bodies or our professions. In the same way we identify with our names. A name is serious business. We answer to it, introduce ourselves by it, go to court and are fined; we sign books, paintings, tests, exams, applications, car loans, house mortgages with these names; we answer when someone calls—so do cats and dogs. We are limited all of our lives by names, labels, and definitions.

"You are not, repeat *not*, 'Mike'! And you are *not* 'Holly.' Or are you? Well, are you?"

"Well, at present, I am . . . I am *known* as Holly."

"That's better than *being* Holly but it still falls short. Your body-mind-sense complex answers to the name of Holly. The Spanish say, *Como se llama?* And it translates into, 'How do you call yourself?' We, in English, just say, 'What is your name?' But even we don't, in language, anyway, confuse the 'self' with the name. You are not your name."

"I'm *not?*" Dan chuckled.

"No," I said, without a smile, "you're not. But it might take a lifetime for you to discover that simple fact."

> Look for the moon in the sky, not in the water!
> If you desire to rise above mere names and letters,
> Make yourself free from self at one stroke.
> Become pure from all attributes of self,
> That you may see your own bright essence,
> Yea, see in your own heart the knowledge of the
>   Prophet,
> Without book, without tutor, without preceptor.
>   (Rumi poem, quoted by Nicholson in
>   *The Mystics of Islam*, 70)

"The poem is particularly apropos to 'The Idiot in the Great City.' He is not a-gourd-tied-around-his-ankle. And we are not our names. Our names are an exoteric cover. The markings on the box we come in.

"The reason angels can fly is that they take themselves so lightly. That's not original but I like it. And we will not fly as long as we're identified with names, labels, our habits, our characteristics. Do people want to move on? Do they want to learn?

"The man in the story just wants to get rid of his anger. He wants nothing to do with learning. Just take away my anger and I'm fine. The rock song goes, 'Girls just want to have fun.' But, as usual with these generalities, so do boys. As for actively seeking the truth? In the main we have had that knocked out of us early on: 'obey,' not 'discover,' has been the school answer.

"When I was in school, I mostly just sat through classes. I sat there mooning away and sometimes, *sometimes*, something really exciting would happen. Like the day a candy wrapper got stuck to the elbow of our history teacher. We followed the fate of that candy wrapper for maybe half an hour as this teacher— actually strong enough to pick up 'Chicken' Hodgkins by the belt and stand there with him through one entire recess—well, the candy wrapper was waving along with her arm like a little flag while she yelled about historical events. Great moment.

"Then, in college, we learn about different peoples and tribes: South American, African, and South Pacific tribes. How easy to assimilate information about tribes in some other part of the world. But we must begin to see ourselves as tribe members. You, Jodie, are a representative of the Lapiana family, Nation Americus, Springfield tribe, Massachusetts territory. Do we see ourselves like that? Or is it always looking out, *out there*, to the world of *others*?

"The Sufi tales don't try to convince you of anything. A wise man puts another man at a crossroads and that man ends up killing a notorious criminal on the way to commit a terrible crime. What do we do with the story? What can we get from it?

"Next time we'll take up 'The Ancient Coffer of Nuri Bey.'"

THE ANCIENT COFFER OF NURI BEY

Nuri Bey was a reflective and respected Albanian, who had married a wife much younger than himself.

One evening when he had returned home earlier than usual, a faithful servant came to him and said: "Your wife, our mistress, is acting suspiciously. She is in her apartments with a huge chest, large enough to hold a man, which belonged to your grandmother. It should contain only a few embroideries. I believe there may now be much more in it. She will not allow me, your oldest retainer, to look inside."

Nuri went to his wife's room and found her disconsolately sitting beside the massive wooden box.

"Will you show me what is in the chest?" he asked.

"Because of the suspicions of a servant, or because you do not trust me?"

"Would it not be easier just to open it, without thinking about the undertones?" asked Nuri.

"I do not think it possible."

"Is it locked?"

"Yes."

"Where is the key?"

She held it up. "Dismiss the servant and I

will give it to you."

The servant was dismissed. The woman handed over the key and herself withdrew, obviously troubled in mind.

Nuri Bey thought for a long time. Then he called four gardeners from his estate. Together they carried the chest by night unopened to a distant part of the grounds, and buried it.

The matter was never referred to again.

(Shah, *Tales of the Dervishes*, 31)

5

Four Hundred and Ninety? Or Stop Counting?

I gave out paper and asked three questions: 1. What's in the chest? 2. Is that important? and 3. Was Nuri Bey right? Explain.

I wanted them simply to react to the story. There were so many things to be noted and in such a condensed story it is easy to overlook them.

They decided that the story was about the idea of "trust." The agreement on this aspect—either "trust" or "love"—was almost unanimous. Those who differed but then listened to others grudgingly admitted that "trust" was a good enough theme. Still, almost all of them admitted that they either wanted to know what was in the coffer or *they* would have opened it, "not out of distrust, you know, but . . . just to see." In any case, the discussion hardly strayed from the idea of "love" or "trust."

To the question, "Does it really matter what is in the coffer?"

"Hell yes, it matters," said Carlito. "Of course it matters!" Despite that, despite Carlito, the consensus was no, in the final analysis, the contents of the box were not central to the story, although Mike thought that Nuri Bey's grandmother's bones were in the box. I never found out how or why some bones would be left in the coffer and/or what the bones had to do with the story, but every time I took up this story at least one person would tell me that Nuri's grandmother's bones were in the coffer.

"I find the story a little irritating. He *never* opens the box?"

"It's irritating to you, Carlito, because *you* want to find out what's in it."

"Damn right I do."

They began to agree that it didn't matter. But that came only after some consideration. This seemed to change some other opinions, and threw more weight behind the idea of trust. At the beginning even those who felt that trust and the relationship were the themes of the story felt that the chances were good that the wife was hiding a lover in the box. What was their evidence, I asked.

"Because the servant *said* the box was big enough to hold a man," a couple answered. Others jumped in.

"*That's* not evidence!" said Holly, the budding young lawyer.

The ones who felt that the wife had a lover were slow to give up the idea. "She left the room . . . dis . . . disconsolately."

"No," said Bess, "she left . . . here it is, obviously—"

She didn't get to finish before others were seconding her finding that she had left "obviously troubled in mind."

"That doesn't prove anything, anyway. Maybe she's sad because she knows he doesn't trust her," Carole said, furiously. "There could be a hundred reasons why she's sad."

A comforting moment in the life of a teacher.

"But," Carole added, "my roommate gave me a note about this story. May I read it?"

"Sure."

He wanted her to think he trusted her and she *knew* it was a no-win situation. He thought so too, so he did the oh-so-wise move of burying the chest. He accomplished all sorts of things at once—avoided the confrontation which would have destroyed the marriage, got rid of the lover who was probably inside, punished the wrong-doers, and put the whole matter to rest forever. And indeed, forgave her and never mentioned it again. He had the last laugh, so to speak. Yes, he understood that to open the chest would be to destroy the trust. So—great solution—he said "Okay, I trust you; I won't open it." And then he buried the lover! The wife's distress? She knew it was a no-winner. And yes, she did save the relationship by sacrificing the lover within the chest!

"So," said Carole, "what do you think? Kathy, my roommate, wants to know."

Perhaps it matched what many had been thinking but didn't put down. Or speak. In any case, they were all looking to see what I'd say.

"Tell your roommate to turn off the TV."

"And *that's* your answer?" said Carole, ready to throw something at me.

"Well, we could go on for hours about her note, but I think it's lurid, and the indications are that both the marriage and the participants, the husband and the wife, are more worthy than she sees them."

I asked about the idea of forgiveness; and whether forgiveness had anything to do with the story.

"Forgiveness for what?" asked Holly. "What has she done?"

"I agree," said Joanne. "I see it as a battle for power. The young wife, his servants in the big . . . castle, I'd guess, and the master. I think she has come to live with *him*, in his castle and estate. And the servants are jealous."

"Whatever . . . under all of these circumstances . . . did he do the right thing? Not only is he going to drop the matter, he is going to bury it forever. And it will never be mentioned again."

"Well," said Sam, "he can bury it. And forget or forgive, or whatever, but he doesn't need to close his eyes . . . in case something is going on."

"If he gets suspicious and keeps a close eye on her, doesn't that mean that he distrusts her? As for forgiveness—and I agree with Holly; she has really done nothing to be forgiven anyhow, as far as we know—to bury it and never mention it again means that he drops it. Forever. Which is like forgiveness," I told them. "Any other way of forgiving is not really forgiveness. Jesus' answer to the question 'How many times should we forgive?' was not seven but seventy times seven. Does that mean four hundred and ninety? Or does it mean, stop counting?"

"Stop counting," said Joanne, who always sat across from me but spoke quietly.

"Good. On the same subject Gandhi once said, 'Forgive another until he or she becomes worthy of your trust.' The same answer."

"You seem to think he's accusing her of something. Is he?"

"Find it!" said Carole. "*Find it!*"

"Right. He doesn't. He just buries it. So, let's leave that for a moment and discuss his wife. How do we know that she is not just after his money? And desirous of living in this big castle? What did she do before giving the key to her husband? What does the key signify? I mean, what the hell is going on here?"

"The key is really the key to their relationship," said Holly, the English major.

"Okay, good. And how did she let him know that it was serious and important?"

"She gives him a *long* look. 'You better pay attention to this.'"

"That's interesting, Holly. Let's see your long look—"

"You know what I mean. When you want to tell someone, a boyfriend, let's say, to look out, and you don't use any words, just the look?"

"Ohhh, the *long* look."

"Yes, you know?"

"Good. So she gives him the *loooong* look. And does it work? Does he wake up and begin to take it all seriously?"

"Why did they dismiss the servant?" asked Mike.

"Does that mean they fired the servant?"

"Noooo, Carlito, they just told him to leave."

"Go cook supper, or something."

"Was that the right thing to do?"

"It was none of the servant's affair," said Sara.

"Right. It's really between the husband and the wife. And would Nuri have broken the bond of trust if he had opened the coffer and looked inside? Is that why he didn't? In other words, did he do the right thing? Did he handle it well?"

"I'd have looked inside the box."

"Carlito, don't you understand?"

"I don't care, I'd have looked inside."

"Of *course* he did the right thing," said Jodie. "The second he opens the box the relationship is destroyed. Just like *that*." She snapped her fingers at Carlito.

For a while the discussion was fierce, mainly between the men and the women.

Then came a different view. "Well, they did things differently in those days. . . . And we can't judge, from the twentieth century, a story written in the—uhh—thirteenth century, or whenever it was first written." That was Dan's contribution.

I think most people, at whatever age, are fond of seeing themselves on top of a heap of brainless neanderthals (e.g. all those who were born before them). They, the new generation, are the shining examples of at least 2,000 years of straight-ahead progress. To have them admit that our emotional lives and relationships with one another are identical to what they were in Shakespeare's day is to fight an uphill battle.

"I still have one big question about this story," said Dan.

"We'll get to it, Dan. Just a second. It might take most of our time to convince you otherwise but, for right now, please give the people in the story credit or discredit for acting as stupidly or as wisely as we would ourselves—people in the last years of the twentieth century. Without belaboring the point, I would say that in our relationships and in the eternal battle between the sexes that we have made no progress since Jesus' time, and before. Might as well continue and say, except for automobiles and gadgets to destroy entire populations, we have made no progress. And when you begin to confuse those technological advances with progress, we are in trouble. Gurdjieff put it very succinctly: 'People, people, why are you people?'"

"But, that goes against—"

"Can we just let it go, for the moment? There's a wonderful quote, I think it comes down to us from 8,000 years before Christ, the words of an Egyptian mother. It goes something like: 'Kids nowadays are disrespectful and care about nothing but their own pleasure!' *Nowadays*—did you get that? An Egyptian mother, not 8,000 years ago, 8,000 years before Christ."

"Can I ask my question?" said Dan.

"Go ahead."

"There's another way of looking at it. I think Nuri Bey's a pretty slick customer. I don't think he really trusted her and I think he buried her lover, so he got rid of her lover and still kept her trust. It was the best thing he could do for one person. That one person was he himself."

"Dan!" said Jodie. "That's almost exactly what Carole's roommate said."

"Well, then, I agree."

Hands were up, Dan was the subject of spitting female fury from at least two of the women. Others were laughing, talking, arguing.

"Look. Hold it down. This is great. And Dan is certainly free to make that interpretation and that's what makes it a great story. But what is the evidence that there's a lover in the box?"

The argument went on and on. Some seemed to be stuck in whatever position they had first taken. So it seemed they were defending themselves, not even a position.

"Okay, okay. This could go on forever. But remember a couple of things. Number one: these are teaching tales. Two: we are talking about the *right* thing to do, under *all* the circumstances.

And even Dan will admit that, under all the circumstances, he did the wise thing. You cynics can continue to believe that he has murdered his wife's lover but, remember, she gave him the key and indicated, even with the *long* look, Holly, that she was leaving the situation and the decision up to him. Finally, in the very beginning of the story, we are told that Nuri Bey is a 'reflective and respected Albanian.' This is a very short story. Every word must be taken seriously. Now think—would a reflective man, one in his position, take on some floozie for his wife?

"To go a little deeper, and take it from a different level, we're talking about the three sides of man-woman. In each of us there is the physical, the emotional, and the intellectual. In this particular story the servant represents the physical body, Nuri's wife represents the emotional side, and Nuri represents the intellectual side. Ideally, the body should be a good servant. The body should never command. The head, guided partly by the heart, the emotions, should be in command."

"Taylor, do you believe in progress?"

"General progress? I'll believe in progress when it can be pointed out to me. Until then, no. In individual progress. Individual evolution. That's what we have to worry about. You know the Lord's Prayer: Give us this day our daily bread . . .? Bread, in exoteric terms, is the stuff we eat, at breakfast and for sandwiches. In esoteric terms bread means understanding. That's how we grow, increasing our understanding day by day, bit by bit."

"And we've made *no* progress since Jesus' time?"

Before I could answer, Carole, who was on fire with what she had to say, turned the conversation: "I feel like something else needs to be said about 'The Coffer of Nuri Bey.' For Nuri Bey to react like that, as he did, is extraordinary. But what about her? She *makes* him see! She not only got rid of the servant but she made him realize this was no ordinary argument. That he can't take this in the ordinary way. She leads him to see it. And the fact that he does is the measure of their love. Real love. They are, like, God and Goddess to each other!"

"Wow! Carole, that is really . . . beautiful!" said Sara.

"Yes, Carole, he bows to her, her clearer understanding of the situation and how she forces him to make a conscious decision about it; only then does she give him the key, and then she bows to him, and what he'll do about it.

"And Carole, to your roommate, thank her for the offering. As for the soap opera reference, I was only partly serious. But she really *has* painted the picture of a marriage made in hell. Both of them, according to her, are deceitful and hypocritical. One is a murderer and the other an accomplice to the crime. But I think also, especially in a marriage, and even more especially when there are issues that simply will not go away and simply cannot be resolved easily, or at all, that the way we should approach these issues is . . . to bury them. To *drop* them.

"This one single story could be discussed for much longer. But let me give another insight to it. I once taught at a prep school. The custodian of the school building was a Mrs. Murphy. And, in a very real way, Mrs. Murphy *ran* that school. No one crossed Mrs. Murphy. In the same way sergeants run the army. Even the generals think twice before they cross the top sergeants. In Nuri's case there is his 'oldest retainer,' a person who probably brought him up as a boy, and had been working for Nuri's father, working there before Nuri Bey was born. Now, what is the dilemma about? This chest? This coffer? I'm stuck with this coffer? That's what the argument is about? Then I'll bury it. I'll get it out of the way entirely. Forever."

"So, you're saying that's the answer and the correct way to interpret it?" said Holly.

"Look! There *is* no . . . *correct?* I'm not, I can't do it that way. It's whatever you bring to the story. How far along are you? How do *you* see it? I'm not giving you answers. I want you to think about these things. Then it's important as to what you do with them. If something occurs to you a week from now, that's fine."

Carole wouldn't let it go. "But, these are not ordinary people, and *she* saved the relationship, by making him understand."

"Yes, yes! Did the rest of you see that? He's *capable* of understanding but *she* forced him to stop and really consider."

To teach is to learn. Each time I go over the stories someone brings a new angle to them. And more light.

"We talked earlier, briefly, about esoteric—the inner—and exoteric—the outer. Has it become clear about inner and outer? About esoteric and exoteric knowledge? Let's take a fairly difficult topic. Take 'cancer.' No one likes cancer and people are working day and night to find a cure for it. But it has become a business, if not an industry: the cancer-cure industry. People work and work and get nowhere. No one is shocked at the lack of progress and the whole process goes on and on.

"The esoteric view looks a little different. Fifty years and a few trillion dollars and, still, no cure for cancer? Well, since there's no cure doesn't it seem that we should, or could, begin working on *preventing* cancer before we get it? Are we polluting the air we breathe, the water aquifers under the ground, the oceans and lakes and rivers, which in turn pollute the water and the fish who swim in it? Are we injecting the cattle, hogs, sheep, chickens, the very earth, with chemicals that are, in turn, affecting the fish-eaters, the meat-eaters, the plant-eaters?

"The esoteric way of treating disease is preventive; fresh air, pure water, and organic foods. If we can't find a cure let's avoid it. But the medical establishment and the cancer institutes want a pill cure, a vaccine cure to stop it once it has begun. So, the exoteric approach is to cure cancer. Don't worry till then. The esoteric approach is to avoid it.

"There is not a great deal of research money for creating the conditions which would eliminate the disease. That is not the direction that 'medicine' takes. There is nothing dramatic about cleaning up the environment, the water, air, and the food we eat.

"In the East, generally speaking, doctors are paid for keeping one well. So it pays them for you to be healthy. This encourages preventive medicine. In the West, doctors are paid after you have become sick. The investment is in disease, not in wellness. I realize, that is only the general picture, but . . ."

Quite a few hands were asking for attention, but Bess, whose father is a doctor, blurted out, "Are you saying that doctors in the West are only interested in money—?"

"No—"

"—my father would kill you."

"He *would*? For speaking my mind? Tell me, is he an easily angered man?"

They enjoyed that. And so I added, "Let's just say that money is not the last thing on an American doctor's mind. Can we take a break? Ten minutes? I feel like saying, 'Can we? For God's sake?'"

* * *

ESOTERIC (inner)	EXOTERIC (outer)
Hidden	Obvious
Unorthodox	Orthodox
Conforms to belief	Conforms to society
What is real	What appears to be real
Jesus as teacher	Jesus as God
Mankind is asleep	Man sleeps eight hours a day
We don't know ourselves	I'm John J. Parkerson
Water = truth	Water = H_2O
Repent = re-think	Repent = be sorry for
Atonement = at-one-ment; state of being at one w/oneself	Atonement = do something to make up for wrongdoing
Final aim: truth/ freedom	Final aim: heaven

Spirit of the law	Letter of the law
Bible: written by man	Bible: written by God
Problems: Inside	Problems: Outside
Figurative	Literal
Bread = understanding	Bread = white, wheat or rye
Sin = miss the mark	Sin = to do 'bad.'
Sinner = one who missed mark	Sinner = bad person
Heaven: within	Heaven: up there
God = consciousness. Real 'I'	God = Higher being, up there
Hell: Internal state, ignorance	Hell: place down there

When they came back I gave out copies of the list and asked them to look it over.

"Although I want you to take these with you and study them, let's go over some of them now. Inner and outer—the shell of the walnut would be exoteric and the meat, the inner, is esoteric.

"Conforms to society—exoteric, and means only that the person follows whatever it is that's being done. In school a few years ago the proper 'uniform' for college students included ankle-high sneakers with the shoelaces untied. The shoelaces *had* to be untied. This was not out of preference but because that was 'kuool.' You also couldn't say 'cool' you had to say 'kewull.' The esoteric would be to follow one's own beliefs or desires, no matter what the herd is doing.

"Another item, quite important to the Sufis, is the apparent and the real. What appears to be so as opposed to what is really so. For example, on a cloudy day it *appears* that the sun is 'out' or gone. But, really, the sun is doing what it always does only we can't see it. It's not visible from our spot on the earth.

"The rest are fairly obvious; however, the esoteric meaning of 'repent,' for example, is to 're-think' one's position. The word comes from the Latin *pentare*, which means to think. So, 'repent' means to think again or re-think one's position. The exoteric meaning is 'to be sorry for or about something.' In the South, where I grew up, in the thirties and forties, we used to see signs on pine trees—REPENT YE SINNERS. Either that or signs saying REPENT NOW! JESUS IS COMING! We saw them all the time; we also heard about war, that war, war, war was coming—newspaper headlines and our parents talked about it. And, on the pine trees, those signs told us that Jesus was coming. Once a cousin of mine asked my uncle, while we were driving to the lake to go swimming, 'Dad, will Jesus get here *before* the war?' It caused a sensation among the grownups.

"At any rate, the esoteric view of Jesus is that he was a perfected human being, Man Number Seven in Gurdjieff terms, but definitely a human being, born and bred. The exoteric view is that Jesus is God (I'm thinking in terms of Christianity, of course). The esoteric view is that Heaven and Hell are states of *being* and not places outside of us. The exoteric view would be that they are places where, depending upon your behavior, you will go.

"'Repent, Ye sinners!' meant you were to throw yourself down and pray for forgiveness. And had nothing to do with change by way of re-thinking or re-examining your ways. The real meaning of 'sin'—according to the Sufis, and certain Greek and biblical scholars—is to 'miss the mark.' That is it. No more, no less. So a sinner in the esoteric view would be a person who simply missed the mark. The exoteric view of sin is to have done 'bad' according to some canon or some view or other. And so a sinner would be someone who has done 'bad.'"

"What's the *mark?*"

"Good, good question. the mark would be the truth. So, missing the mark would be missing the truth."

"The truth in whose eyes?"

"Okayyy! In this case, if what you 'hit' is the truth, the objective truth, then you didn't miss the mark. Although someone else can think you did."

"This is complicated."

"Yes. Let's say that a universal truth might be expressed as 'Don't hurt others.' Or some variation of the Golden Rule. To practice that would be to hit the mark . . . physically and psychologically not to hurt others.

"To continue with exoteric and esoteric—in Provincetown last summer I saw a T-shirt that said: JESUS IS COMING (SO LOOK BUSY)."

"One I saw said JESUS IS COMING," Sam announced, "AND IS HE *PISSED!*"

"*SHE,*" said Jodie.

"In either case," I told them, "the exoteric, or superficial, view would say, 'Not funny.' Esoteric viewers would see it as amusing because they don't see Jesus as part of the God-police."

"What about problems? The esoteric says 'Problems inside' and the exoteric says 'Problems outside.' What do you mean?"

"In general, the esoteric view is that we create problems; the exoteric view would be that someone else, or the world, created our problems. For example, if we get a flat out on the highway, is that a problem?"

"You better believe it!"

"Carlito, I can always depend on you. No! It's a fact. It's a fact that we have to acknowledge. Do you see?"

"No, I don't see. Especially if you don't have a spare."

"If you don't have a spare tire that is simply another fact . . . you have a flat and you don't have a spare; two facts."

"What if you have to get somewhere? You're late for a dinner, or a date?"

"Three facts."

"It still seems to me that the flat came from outside, a nail or something."

"Yes, of course. The nail is outside, the tire is outside, and the car is too. And also the *fact* that you are late. Four facts."

"So?" he said.

"So?" I said.

"Well, where *is* the problem?"

"That's what I'm trying to get you to see. There is no problem, until . . .? Do you see?"

"No! I don't see. Until what?"

"Until you make it into one. Ohhh, my God . . . I've got a flat! Then suddenly it's a problem. And where did that come from? From outside or inside?"

From the noises with which they greeted this "knowledge" they didn't seem happier. In fact, it was a sobering transaction but I was glad they were thinking about it.

They took another break, mainly for the smokers who had suddenly become very itchy. I thought it was good for them to have these breaks. They were being asked to swallow a lot and if, as I had every reason to suspect, almost all of it was new, they needed time to reflect, even if the reflection took place while they spoke of other things. I'm convinced that our minds continue to work on problems while we do other things and even think other things. Even in sleep, ideas and notions are being sorted out.

* * *

When they came back I read an article to them about schools, education, and discipline. They loved it. They even clapped when I finished.

"Okay, so, we have been doing this section of the course, of the discussion, which I have labeled *teaching*. But it is impossible to separate the differences and the connections between teaching/learning from superstition/religion/authority/fixed notions/change/human nature/fears. So, we are using the scatter approach. And the hope is that as you hear more and more of this it will begin to make sense."

"It does, already," said Carole.

"Not to me it doesn't . . . well, at times," said Sara.

"Good, Sara. Hang in there; you're not alone."

"Alright, the article I just read—'The Student as Nigger.' You liked it so well that you clapped. You agree. Students are niggers. Clap. Clap. You're out there on the old plantation and when you appear before the boss it is with cap in hand and shuffling feet, and 'yes sir,' to this and 'no, sir' to that. But do you make the jump? The leap? To the point where you can conclude that the article is about *you*? That *you* are the one they're talking about? And *you* are on that plantation? That *you* are *niggers*? You see the parallels, but that crucially important leap, that critical last step is the hard one.

"Yes, we are niggers. Now, how to get off the plantation? How to stop thinking with someone else in mind . . . do what he says, set the margins just right. Never mind anything, *Get the Grade*. And after twelve years of chasing grades they've got you:

> . . . Students don't ask that orders make sense. They give up expecting things to make sense long before they leave elementary school. Things are true because the teacher says they're true. At a very early age we all learn to accept 'two truths' as did certain medieval churchmen. Outside of class things are true to your tongue, your fingers, your stomach, your heart. Inside class, things are true by reason of authority. And that's just fine because you don't care anyway. Miss Weidemeyer tells you a noun is a person, place or thing. So, let it be. You don't give a rat's ass; she doesn't give a rat's ass.
>
> (Farber, "The Student as Nigger," 416)

"I think it's why you objected so much when I told you you were brainwashed. You made it an ego issue. But it's a *truth* issue. 'He called me brainwashed and I don't like that.' So, whatever I called you it wasn't out of an urge to insult you. I called you to try and get your attention. And, for a while, I lost it."

6

What If We Only Think We're Awake?

"The Spanish playwright Calderon de la Barca wrote a play called *Life is a Dream*. Shakespeare and others have used the same conceit. But it is more than a conceit. When Ouspensky talks about the demise of psychology he asks, in effect, what good is the practice of therapy on sleeping, unconscious, subjective human beings?

"What if we think we're awake but we're really asleep? We operate from the standpoint of *thinking* we're awake, but we're really not? Or put it in a more verifiable way: What if we think we're healthy and the x-ray shows lung cancer? What good did our *thinking* do? It was not even thinking; it was supposing. Health was our conception, not our condition. Our conception was that we were healthy but that was not our condition. Our conception is that we are awake. Our condition is that we're asleep. Does this affect us? We think we're lions but we're really sheep. Our conception is 'lion'; our condition is 'sheep.' Before too long I am going to prove to you that you are asleep, or at least unconscious. I will prove it to you. The question is what will you do with that knowledge?

"Take a different example. What if we think that a piece of rope in the road directly ahead of us is a snake. Do we become as frightened as if it really is a snake? Bess?"

"I have trouble with that kind of question. But I guess I might, if I was convinced it was a snake. I guess the fright might be exactly the same. Yes, I think so."

"It's *really* only a piece of rope, perfectly harmless. But we think it's a snake. It's not, but we're convinced it's a snake. What's the difference between the real thing and our thoughts about it? Are you just as frightened? Does the same chill close over your heart as when it *is* a snake? And yet what is the situation here? You reacted to 'snake' and yet it is only a piece of rope. Same reaction, different reality. What do you think, Sara?" Earlier, Sara had admitted a fear of snakes.

"Yes, I would be just as afraid, as soon as I decided it was a snake."

"Have you ever been scared as a kid? In a few seconds you realized it was only your big brother but for a second or two you couldn't have been more frightened by a real murderer. Isn't it amazing? We can fool ourselves into believing something and we have the *real* reaction to something that is not real at all. You guys, we have to pause over this because this is the human condition. And so many of the stories are exactly that, part of the human condition. We believe one thing and it is totally untrue. Totally."

All this time they were quiet. But listening.

"Once an excellent teacher in graduate school told us that the proper function of the imagination is to discover the truth . . . to discover the fact, the truth, the condition. So, according to him you could sit right here and discover the truth, or some truths at any rate. The Sufis say, 'He who tastes knows,' and that is even more true. But by listening carefully and applying imagination we can also learn. So, now, here is the test of whether you've been listening. The other day we talked about death and what is 'I.' We agreed that we are not our bodies. We *have* our bodies but we are not our bodies. And let's say, for the example I just gave you, that *rope* is the *condition* and *snake* is our *conception*. Got it? Rope is real and snake is what we conceive it to be. So, snake is our conception of the real. Okay, here it is: IS DEATH OUR CONCEPTION OR OUR CONDITION? Write on that!"

This brought a storm of questions. Explain it again. What do you mean by conception and so forth. I wouldn't answer the questions directly. "In some situations it is going to be worth your *lives* to listen. You have *got* to get it, the first time."

"Will you repeat the question, please?"

I wrote it out in big letters and held it up for them to see.

After about seven minutes I collected their papers on death and put two half-filled bottles on the table, one large and round, the other smaller and rectangular. The smaller, slim bottle had a skull and crossbones label from the pharmacy with the word "Poison" under the skull and crossbones. The other said "Blackstrap Molasses."

I held up a bottle. "What does this say?"

They dutifully said, "Poison."

"And what about this one?"

"Blackstrap . . . molasses . . ."

I breathed on the label that said "Molasses" and took it off. Breathed on the other one and my hot air loosened it and I took it off.

"Now, which is which?"

"The one on your right is molasses and on your left is the poison."

I reversed the labels. The Molasses label was now on what had been labeled Poison, and the Poison label was on the bottle previously labeled Molasses. I unscrewed the cap and held it up to my mouth and drank a bit of the dark bitter sweetness labeled Poison.

"Hey," I said. "It tastes fine. The label says Poison and it tastes fine. How come?"

"It *says* Poison but it's really blackstrap molasses."

"Well, what if I drink from the other bottle?"

"Screwed!" Mike said in a low voice, and giggled.

"Really? But it *says*, Blackstrap Molasses."

"Yeah, but it's *really* poison."

"Unless you've just stuck labels on them," said Joanne. But so quietly that no one else heard her.

"You mean I can't drink this stuff even though the label says Blackstrap Molasses?"

There were some grins and muffled remarks.

"So, somebody who didn't know what I'd done would walk up here and take a swig out of *this* bottle, marked Molasses, and could die, right?"

"Egg-zackly," said Carlito.

I unscrewed the cap, held it up, shook it back and forth, letting them see the difference in texture. I started to drink and stopped myself. They were watching. Not quite trusting what I would do or had done. I took a healthy swig of the milky molasses mixture and started choking, gagging.

Some were amused, others were alarmed.

"Hey, you guys said that was poison," I said to them.

"No, *you* said it was poison."

"No, I didn't. I just held up the bottle with the label on it. How did you know what was really in the bottle?"

"Because of the label."

"Suppose the label is a lie? After all, words on the outside of a bottle don't necessarily tell you what's inside. Your conception comes from the label. The condition, or reality, is that this bottle, now marked Molasses, previously marked Poison, is molasses with milk added to it. The other, previously marked Molasses and now marked Poison, is full-strength molasses. So, then, your conception was that this was poison but it is really molasses. The *conception* is poison but the *condition* is molasses. It is really molasses but because of the label you thought it was poison. Did it harm me? No, because the reality, the condition is, the *truth* is—molasses. Now, what has that got to do with the conception of death and the condition of death?"

"Wait—!" Bess yelled out. "There's something wrong with your experiment."

"Really?"

"Yes, we took your word for it that the labels were accurate—"

"Yes, and all of those people waiting to hear about the elephant took the word of those who had felt only a part of the animal. Isn't that the same thing? Isn't that what we do? Isn't that how we form our picture of the world? Not through direct experience but because someone *told* us what to believe? Or we drew a conclusion from only part of the evidence? And isn't that risky? Can we take people's word for things? Especially—"

"Sometimes we've *got* to! There isn't anything else—"

The group broke up into talking, twos and threes. I called them back.

"The objection is a sound one. We look, see a label, and we trust. Much of civilization is based on that. Also, much of our misconceptions are also based on that. Not too long ago there was a big crisis of confidence. Someone got a batch of Tylenol and put poison in the bottles and sealed the bottles up again. People were getting sick. The sickness was eventually traced to the poisoned Tylenol bottles. Their slogan at the time was: 'You can trust Tylenol.' Tylenol sales dropped off tremendously for a few months. New seals were put on the bottles and people were warned, 'Don't buy it if the seal is broken.'

"Our interest, for the moment, concerns labeling and what's really in the bottles. We see a label and our conception is that it contains what it says it contains. And 99 percent of the time our trust is justified; the conception and the condition are the same."

We were running out of time and had covered a fair amount, so I'd hold off any more till the next class.

"We'll stop here but we're not finished with the whole question of 'Who am I' and death and our bodies and what dies when, as we say, someone dies."

"When are you going to define Sufism?" Bess asked, almost insisted.

"Okay, okay, have patience."

"What about our papers on death?"

"I'll get them back tomorrow."

Sara stuck around after class and I was happy because she had seemed a little out of it.

"I don't know if I'm getting this. I feel like I'm missing something," Sara said.

"You have to have patience. We're just barely beginning. How did you do on your paper?"

"That's what I'm worried about. I'm confused about . . . the body and 'I.'"

How nice, how great that she was worried. I told her, "It's a big question. And we've lived most of our lives believing that we are our bodies. That we really are, and that's all there is."

"Well, it still seems to me that I *am* my body."

"I don't blame you. But are you your eyes? I mean, if your eyes were put out you'd still be living, right? There's a Chinese poem, attributed to Han-Shan, part of which goes: 'If someone would poke out the eyes of the hawks, we sparrows could dance wherever we please' (Han-Shan, 48). Does that mean the hawks are gone? Are dead? No, they just can't see the sparrows any longer, to torment them, to kill them. And think of Dana, who *might* not walk again. Yet she's still living. Is she her legs? Or even her back?"

"But what about my mind? And if my neck were cut off I'd die, of course."

"Of course. There are certain conditions that must remain for the life in us to be retained. Still it is not . . . look, see if you can think of it this way . . . you're given the gift of life, you're born into a certain family. You're cared for and loved as well as your parents and relatives and sisters and brothers can love and care for you. Okay, these are influences on you. And they're so strong and come at you so early that you forget about the time when you were just a pure and perfect being. Before the influences. You are something behind and above all of that. Even above and beyond your mind. But the mind takes on, takes on these influences and they are so strong, so powerful that we confuse them with the consciousness which is behind everything . . . even the mind.

"Look, Sara—this is very important. This should be to the whole class. Not just now, for one person. Let me begin with this tomorrow, okay?"

Good. She was happy or more relieved and off we both went.

I would have to face it head on.

7

The Soul and Walnut People

The question followed me home, into bed, into my dreams and was still with me when I woke up the following morning. At moments of exasperation I wanted to shout at them: "You're taking yourselves wrongly! There's so much more. Of *course* I'm trying to brainwash you."

* * *

"Yesterday, there was a discussion after our session. And I'm sure that the person who was puzzled was speaking for a number of others in the group. So I want to begin by discussing your papers on death and everything that connects with it. In addition to that I want to take up at least one more story today.

"First I want to mention something that probably disappeared with the beginning of your generation; plastic and toys with batteries took their place. When I was a kid we could buy a little kit: a rubber band and two halves of walnut shells with some tiny holes drilled in it for four matchsticks. The idea was to catch a fly, put it inside of the walnut shell, tie the rubber band around the two halves, and stick the matchsticks in the four holes. The fly, in trying to get out, banged into the matchsticks and made them move and so it looked like the walnut shell was alive and the little person's arms and legs were moving of themselves. Or, in other words, it looked like the walnut had a life of its own. Some fancier walnuts even had heads that could also move. The fly would buzz around inside till it collapsed and it looked like the walnut person had died. Of course, for a while you could shake the walnut and the fly would be motivated, or infuriated, to start flying around some more trying to get out but, finally, it would die. Now don't—"

"That's cruel," said Jodie.

"I was going to say, now don't start crying about those little flies inside . . . don't form a committee and elect a chairman to STOP MISTREATING FLIES!"

"I was thinking about it," she said, with a little smile.

"Anyhow, of course it was the fly who had died and the walnut had never been alive from the beginning. Some people would liken the soul to the fly, and the walnut to our bodies, and this is not so far-fetched as it might seem; since we can read fanciful tales about how the soul has been lured into our bodies and would like nothing better than to escape and return to the heavens. But here the analogy of the fly in the walnut ends because if you open up the body—the shell of the walnut, I mean—you will, sure enough, find the fly's body. Whereas if one opens the body of a 'dead' person, one finds all of the organs but no sign of life. Where has the life gone? Where is the fly that animates all of these veins and muscles?"

"Well, where *has* it gone?" asked Danny. "I mean, what do *you* think?" He sometimes said things for effect. And looked around to see if anyone thought well of his question.

"Danny, it is one of those things that is totally unverifiable. And anything I said would be pure guessing. The question is, do souls die? Or, if you wish, does the consciousness in us die? Or does it simply leave? I am using *soul* and *consciousness* and *fly* interchangeably. If you can see that, then it is the consciousness which sees through the eye and thinks through the mind and propels the legs and arms, through the muscles, into walking, eating, dancing, and all of the other activities in which we indulge ourselves. Even thinking, if you can call it that.

"So, when I ask you if death is our condition or our conception, that is what I meant, nothing more."

Relief was visible on at least five faces.

"Well . . ." Laughter from Holly. "Why didn't you *say* that?"

"I thought I had, in other words. But, also, maybe it's just as well to let you think about it in another way before explaining it away. In fact, I gave you a quote, which is worth repeating. It is from one of the first classes, from the Sufi book *The Tale of the Reed Pipe*:

> God made the illusion look like the real, and He made the real look as if it does not exist. . . . This world is an old sorcerer who sells you the moonlight as silk; in return he gets from you the gold and silver of your life. When you come to yourself you see there are no silk clothes, but instead you have spent your gold and silver pieces. And your purse is empty. . . . From this magic market you can take refuge in nothing but Truth.
>
> (Farzan, 25)

"What does 'illusion' mean here? What does he mean by 'real'? What does the deception 'moonlight for silk' signify? What does it mean to say the 'gold' and 'silver' of your life? What does it mean to 'come to yourself'? What do the following expressions mean: 'your purse is empty'? And the 'magic market'? And taking 'refuge in nothing but truth'? I made copies of that little quote for you to look at from time to time.

"Your papers were not bad, your 'death' papers. But I did want to comment on one. One of you said that death depends on your belief. You must stop thinking that things depend on your belief. The phenomenon death does not have anything to do with what you believe. Believe what you want, but we have to deal with the fact that two and two equals four. Now you can believe it equals three or five or even seven. But at the craps table when you get two twos you don't win unless you come up with another four.

"The question was: Is death our conception or our condition? But exactly *what* dies is what we're talking about. Bodies die. That is a condition of bodies. It is not just a conception. Bodies die. Now, if you identify with your body then your answer to the question would be 'death is my conception and my condition.' But if you say 'I *have* a body' then death is the condition of the body but not necessarily of 'I.' If you believe that 'I' is, really, consciousness then for our consciousness death is not a condition.

"One of our problems lies in the fact that while we can *say* 'I have a body,' in the way we live and take things it is the reverse—our bodies have *us*. We are slaves to our bodies.

"Okay, Holly, what did you say?"

"I said that it . . . depends on your belief."

"You mean that it is neither a conception nor a condition but depends on your belief?"

"Yes, basically."

"Look, I can't tell you how important this is. Holly, again—death does *not* depend on your belief. Let's take the color spectrum—in a rainbow, or when reflected from a crystal. The way the colors occur is a truth. A truth outside of us, an objective truth. Have you ever seen the reflection of a crystal on a wall behind a source of light? The colors line up in exactly the same way, regardless of what you may believe. The colors go from one to another and it never varies. As I said, this is a truth. And it, like the phenomenon death, does not depend on your belief. Believe what you want, but the color spectrum goes from orange, yellow, green, blue, red, and—unless you're nuts or colorblind—that is what will come up every time, because of the order of their wavelengths. In that same way, the body dies. The body dies. The only question is whether that life-spark in us, or our consciousness, or if you would rather use the word 'soul' . . . whether that too dies. Or whether it leaves the body at what we call death. And if it simply leaves the body, then the body continues its process of decay and 'life' leaves. Where it goes is not, right now, the question. So, death is not a way of looking at things; it's a fact."

"Well, I thought you said that *we* don't die, just our bodies die."

"I *did* say that. And, looked at from what is *real*, 'I,' our consciousness, the life in us does not die—"

"Well, I am totally confused. You—"

"But—"

"So, then, what I *believe* affects whether death is our conception or our condition."

"Okay, I see what you're saying. Okay. Look, it is a condition of the body that it dies. Alright? And if we have the *conception* that the body does not die then we are wrong. The body will die no matter what we believe. Slowly or quickly it will die. So then *death* is a condition of the body."

"I think I was putting it a different way. Let me think about that," she said.

"What if I don't agree with the whole notion?" asked Sam.

"Well, are you thinking about it? Is it still up in the air? Are you turning it over?"

"Yes . . . yes, I've been thinking about it a lot. I just don't know if I go along with it. Especially about the word 'soul.'"

"Perfect. That's all I ask. You don't have to agree. You know, Buddha is supposed to have said, 'Don't believe anything that doesn't make sense to *you*. Not even if *I* say it.'

"And another thing—please . . . don't walk out of this, this discussion group, and tell people about Sufism. You really know little or nothing about it. This is simply an introduction to some of the ideas. If you have to say anything tell them it is a discussion group about ideas. That is all.

"After the break we will take up 'The Story of Fire.'"

Some of them, led by Carlito, went for a quick swim in the lake, only a few yards from the cabin.

* * *

THE STORY OF FIRE

Once upon a time a man was contemplating the ways in which Nature operates, and he discovered, because of his concentration and application, how fire could be made. This man was called Nour. He decided to travel from one community to another, showing people his discovery.

Nour passed the secret to many groups of people. Some took advantage of the knowledge. Others drove him away, thinking that he must be dangerous, before they had time to understand how valuable this discovery could be to them. Finally, a tribe before which he demonstrated became so panic-stricken that they set about him and killed him, being convinced that he was a demon.

Centuries passed. The first tribe that had learned about fire reserved the secret for their priests, who remained in affluence and power while the people froze. The second tribe forgot the art and worshipped instead the instruments. The third worshipped a likeness of Nour himself, because it was he who had taught them. The fourth retained the story of the making of fire in their legends; some believed them, some did not. The fifth community really did use fire, and this enabled them to be warmed, to cook their food, and to manufacture all kinds of useful articles.

After many, many years, a wise man and a small band of his disciples were traveling through the lands of these tribes. The disciples were amazed at the variety of rituals which they encountered; and one and all said to their teacher: "But all these procedures are in fact related to the making of fire, nothing else. We should reform these people!"

The teacher said: "Very well, then. We shall restart our journey. By the end of it those who survive will know the real problems and how to approach them."

When they reached the first tribe, the band was hospitably received. The priests invited the travelers to attend their religious ceremony, the making of fire. When it was over, and the tribe was in a state of excitement at the event which they had witnessed, the master said, "Does anyone wish to speak?"

The first disciple said: "In the cause of Truth I feel myself constrained to say something to these people."

"If you will do so at your own risk, you may do so," said the master.

Now the disciple stepped forward in the presence of the tribal chief and his priests and said: "I can perform the miracle which you take to be a special manifestation of deity. If I do so, will you accept that you have been in error for so many years?"

But the priests cried: "Seize him!" And the man was taken away, never to be seen again.

The travelers went to the next territory, where the second tribe were worshiping the instruments of fire-making. Again a disciple volunteered to try to bring reason to the community.

With the permission of the master, he said: "I beg permission to speak to you as reasonable people. You are worshiping the means whereby something may be done, not even the thing itself. Thus you are suspending the advent of its usefulness. I know the reality that lies at the basis of this ceremony."

This tribe was composed of more reasonable people. But they said to the disciple: "You are welcome as a traveler and stranger in our midst. But, as a stranger, foreign to our history and customs, you cannot understand what we are doing. You make a mistake. Perhaps, even, you are trying to take away or alter our religion. We therefore decline to listen to you."

The travelers moved on.

When they arrived in the land of the third tribe, they found before every dwelling an idol representing Nour, the original fire-maker. The third disciple addressed the chiefs of the tribe: "This idol represents a man, who represents a capacity, which can be used."

"This may be so," answered the Nour-wor-shipers, "but the penetration of the real secret is only for the few."

"It is only for the few who will understand, not for those who refuse to face certain facts," said the third disciple.

"This is rank heresy, and from a man who does not even speak our language correctly, and is not a priest ordained in our faith," muttered the priests. And he could make no headway.

The band continued their journey, and arrived in the land of the fourth tribe. Now a fourth disciple stepped forward in the assembly of the people. "The story of making fire is true, and I know how it may be done," he said.

Confusion broke out within the tribe, which split into various factions. Some said: "This may be true, and if it is, we want to find out how to make fire." When these people were examined by the master and his followers, however, it was found that most of them were anxious to use fire-making for personal advantage, and did not realize that it was something for human progress. So deep had the distorted legends penetrated into the minds of most people that those who thought that they might in fact represent truth were often unbalanced ones, who could not have made fire even if they had been shown how.

There was another faction, who said: "Of course the legends are not true. This man is just trying to fool us, to make a place for himself here."

And a further faction said: "We prefer the legends as they are, for they are the very mortar of our cohesion. If we abandon them, and we find that this new interpretation is useless, what will become of our community then?"

And there were other points of view, as well.

So the party traveled on, until they reached the lands of the fifth community, where firemaking was a commonplace, and where other preoccupations faced them.

The master said to his disciples: "You have to learn how to teach, for man does not want to be taught. First of all, you will have to teach people how to learn. And before that you have to teach them that there is still something to be learned. They imagine that they are ready to learn. But they want to learn what they *imagine* is to be learned, not what they have first to learn. When you have learned all this, then you can devise the way to teach. Knowledge without special capacity to teach is not the same as knowledge and capacity."

(Shah, *Tales of the Dervishes*, 39-41)

"The difficulty with Sufism," I began, "is that there is no way to separate all of the different aspects. Learning goes into teaching and back to learning; how to learn goes into listening or paying attention, goes into fixed notions and religion, which goes into superstition, to fear and authority, freedom, family, sex and punishment, age and tradition, to rose windows and churches, priests, incense and sin, cathedrals and hymns and choirs and tremendous organs and relics and mighty stone monuments and history and tradition, back to teaching and learning again.

"That is, for now, my own introduction to 'The Story of Fire.' What is the story about? In ten words or less. Write."

"How much time do we have?"

"Entries must be received before midnight . . . well, let's say five minutes."

The answers began coming in by twos and threes, slid across the big board of trustees table: It's about fire . . . It's about teaching . . . Superstition (The whole thing comes down to superstition. Seven words. Danny) . . . It's about locked-in ignorance . . . This story is about the administration of this school . . . It's about my roommate . . . The Story of Fire is about Carlito.

I collected the rest and we began.

"What is the moral of this story? That teaching can be dangerous? Just a joke. But can you see, by the device of 'story,' that when it is a matter of making fire, which we're all familiar with—fire, not making it—it is not something that *we* happen to be touchy about. If it involved a religion we were brought up with we might be equally stubborn about changing our view of it. But, here again, is the function of story. Because fire is not an area about which we're touchy we can laugh at the different tribes. The trick is to apply it to ourselves and areas in which our thoughts and attitudes are locked in."

"Couldn't we say that there is one religion, in the story, and the religion is Fire? Does that seem ridiculous?" It was Sara, and somewhat rare for her to offer it like that.

"Great! Go on . . ."

"I can't. That's it. Well . . . each tribe has a different attitude about it . . . about the same thing, fire."

"I agree," said Carole. "Different attitudes but all toward the same thing. As Sara said, about Fire. Like all of the different Christian sects are about Jesus. But they are hardly on speaking terms with each other."

"Okay, good. Let's stick, for the moment, to Fire or teaching of any kind, because it is about teaching, communicating. About overcoming language and emotional mind-sets. It's also about fixed notions. And we'll do something about fixed notions today."

"Not 'Later on'?"

"No, today." I know they were kidding me about all of the things I had promised to take up "Later on."

"Speaking of tribes, we in the U.S. are like a bunch of tribes under one governing body and all, or most of us, speak English. It is the language of our tribes. And when I was a kid at the movies, hardly suspecting that I was a member of a very powerful tribe, not even dreaming that I was brimming over with all of the prejudices of my tribe, there was a news program before the feature film, called The March of Time, and we often heard leaders from other countries, French or German or Arabian, speaking English. I was very critical. 'They can't even speak English,' I said to myself. It didn't once cross my little mind that I couldn't speak one word of their languages, whatever they were. I gave no credit to the fact that they were not completely fluent in 'my' language, and so dismissed what they were saying.

"Anyhow, does the master of the little traveling group know that Nour was killed? Passing on this knowledge? I mean, how do we know that he knows this is a risky business?"

"He has to know that Nour was killed."

"He says it. He says, somewhere . . . that—"

Holly read off the quote, "We'll go back and 'by the end of the trip, those who survive will know the real problems.' Who *survive*, he says."

"Good. What else?"

"Doesn't he *warn* the guy who wants to speak? Doesn't he warn him?"

"Yes he does, Carlito."

"Wow, the brain comes through." Carlito was beaming.

"Carlito," said Jodie, "you'd probably be the first one to speak up."

"And be knocked off," said Mike.

"Yes, he says: speak at your own risk. And he's killed."

"Or 'disappeared' to use the South American term," said Carole.

"There are many parallels to this. I was in the South when people from the North came down to help the civil rights movement in Mississippi, and I tell you, truly, I could feel the surge of anger around me and was even influenced myself: Who the hell are those yankees to come down here and tell us how to run things?

"It's very difficult to *teach* anyone. People can learn. But they can't be taught. I once picked up a little book called *Nobody Can Teach Anybody Anything*. I bought it for the title and don't think I ever read it but I loved the title.

"Do you see the connections? Between the different tribes in the story? And us? Americans? The way we are?"

"Just because we're number one in the world," said Jodie, although she was only half joking.

"Let's try and clear that up now. It does have to do with fixed notions and the story. I think we can all agree that we had nothing to do with being born here in the U.S. So, our nationality can be called 'accidents of birth.' The same for our religion. Did you grow up Jewish because your mother and father were Jews, and Protestant because your mother and father were Protestant? And Catholics?

"You were all born in America. What would you be like if you were born in China? Wouldn't you then be partial to China? As you are now partial to America? You'd be studying Confucius instead of Washington and Lincoln. Maybe you would never hear the name Jesus Christ and if you did it would be as part of the evil barbarian Western world which, in your terms, is not even civilized yet. Christianity, an upstart religion only two thousand years old.

"You would get goose bumps when the national anthem was played and would thrill at the sight of the Chinese flag passing by. And you would know, in your heart of hearts, that no country matches China. *Chiii-na, number one! Chiii-na, number one!* And you would say to others: I'm proud to be Chinese!

"Proud? Proud of a fact of birth? Do you see what I'm saying?"

"No; I don't see anything wrong with being proud to be an American," said Jodie.

"Do you see anything wrong with being proud to be Chinese?"

"No, not if they really *feel* like that."

This was greeted by shouts and whoops.

"And nothing I said about the *accident* of birth, the *accident* of birth, would make any difference to you?"

"I just said I don't see anything wrong with being proud to be an American . . . that's all."

"Nothing wrong with it, only it's like saying, 'I'm proud to be a chocolate ice-cream lover.'"

"I don't see the connection. I had nothing to do with inventing the flavor, or making chocolate ice cream."

"Did you have something to do with making America?" Carlito asked Jodie.

Jodie turned a murderous look on Carlito, who grew red-faced and grinned sheepishly.

"Jodie, I was born in Rayville, Louisiana. Should I run around declaring I'm proud to be a Louisianian? Or a Rayvillian?"

Jodie was annoyed.

"Look, the Sufis say we—in our present condition . . . of

sleep—are neither praiseworthy nor blameworthy . . . about *anything*. Now what does that mean? It simply means that in our present state, our present unconscious state, we cannot be blamed for mistakes we make (since we're sound asleep) and, equally, we can't be praised for things we do (since we're sound asleep). In other words, if I do something stupid, without thinking about the risks involved, because I am stupid and unthinking, but as a result of my action someone's life was saved and I become, in the eyes of the public, a 'hero,' the Sufis would say that since it was unconscious, in other words not having totted up the risks involved . . . look, haven't you ever heard someone described as a guy who 'has more guts than brains'? That's what they're saying. A person did it without knowing what he or she was doing. 'The Man Who Was Easily Angered' loses his temper and kills this murderer on the way to committing the most horrible crime of his career. Is it courage or just anger? Did the man who was easily angered kill the criminal because he knew he was on the way to commit a horrible crime? No, he killed him because he, this man whom he knew nothing about, refused a glass of water.

"So, we have our nationality, our customs and our pride, our way of doing things. Remember the Americans from Kansas? One hour in Europe, one hour spent in Europe, from airport to hotel to beer hall, and they were putting Europe down and defending America . . . from what? No one was attacking America."

"I think all of this is kind of depressing. We're not responsible for anything we do? It's all meaningless?" said Holly.

Before I could answer, Mike interjected, "What do you think of those guys? Those guys from Kansas?"

"Just a second, of course I have to explain that. Just one at a time. The guys from Kansas? I think it was kind of sweet. But also stupid. And we see a lot of that wherever and whenever people are very patriotic or nationalistic . . . and unthinking.

"Okay, Holly, I agree, at first glance it's depressing to be told that you're not, really, to be blamed or praised for anything. I see your point, that as we are we don't merit praise or blame—incidentally, there's a Sufi sect who call themselves the 'blameworthy.' And that's a little daunting. But the aim should be to 'wake up,' to become conscious and, thus, to become praiseworthy and blameworthy for the things we do."

"Then . . . nothing we do, now, according to the Sufis, counts for anything? Good or bad? It doesn't matter?" Dan was ready to dismiss it all.

"Not till we become conscious. Look, the important thing is to *wake up* to all of this. And it doesn't take place in a big explosion with a cloud of smoke, but little by little. That is of paramount importance. Meanwhile, of course, there are degrees of unconsciousness and consciousness. Some people are relatively aware. Other people don't seem to have a clue as to the effect of their actions. In simplified terms: in our present state of sleep we are neither praiseworthy nor blameworthy. Let me try to muddy the waters a little more—"

"Don't! My mind can't handle it."

"Sara, hold on. It doesn't mean that at whatever level you're operating from you should stop trying to do 'the right thing' as Spike Lee put it. It doesn't mean that you can think it's okay to begin taking things that aren't yours. Or that you can lash out and hurt someone just because some teacher said you are neither praiseworthy nor blameworthy. In fact, at every step of the way, as this unfolds for you, you should be objecting or accepting, as it makes sense or doesn't. Some of the questions will clear up; and some you should be asking about . . . *now*—"

"Well, *are* we praiseworthy or aren't we?"

"Well, was the man who was easily angered praiseworthy?"

"You mean, for killing the murderer? Not really."

"And, so, is he *blameworthy?*"

They decided he kind of was and he kind of wasn't. Carole brought up the twelve step program and how he was helpless in controlling his temper, almost as a diseased or sick person.

"Yes," I told them, "but he was aware enough to know that he had actually killed a person. And that the person had not done any harm to *him*. And when he calmed down again he must have realized that once again his anger had made things difficult for him. And that his task had been to *offer* water to the passersby. It had nothing to do with forcing them to take it, let alone killing them for refusing. *That* he can understand. And, as we discussed, this might have been the turning point in his life, to realize that his temper or his anger can result in the death of others. But the story leaves it there, with the death of the murderer and the flowering of the tree. And the point of it—"

"Yes, what *is* the point of it, exactly?"

"It says, as part of the story, that the Sufis serve Truth, 'not pious hopes.' In this case, 'pious hopes' would be to get rid of the man's temper without affecting anything else."

"So? What should he have asked the Sufi for? Guidance?"

"No, Sam; realizing his helplessness in curbing his temper, and realizing how it has always resulted in difficulties, all of his life, and realizing how his anger is tied to everything else about him and is not an isolated trait which, like a little growth can be cut out with a laser beam, he would have to ask if the Sufi can take him as a student. Without qualifications. Teach me. Or better, will you take me as a student. And that is a big big step. Because the teacher is not going to do what *you* think he should do. He will take the whole person and do what he *knows* should be done. And if he chooses to teach swimming, the student is not allowed to say, 'Okay, but remember, no water up my nose.' No! You sign on. And unless your attitude is correct, you will not last more than a few days before you are out, or are told to leave.

"That's enough. I don't care what time it is. This covered a lot of territory. It's time for a break, a *long* break. So, think about these things. See you tomorrow."

"Are you going to prove to us that we're asleep?"

"Yes."

"When?"

"How about beginning today?"

They were ready.

"Okay, here is your task: For the next five days, beginning today, I want you to pause just before you open the door, any door: the car door, bathroom door, house door, room door, screen door. Pause, come to yourself, whatever that means to you. Pause. Come to yourself. Realize who you are, where you are, just pause and take those two or three seconds before you open the door, then go through the door. I want you to keep a count of the times you succeed at this exercise. Now, listen— there is no way that you can fail at this. Except not to try it. If you determine that you will try it for the next door you pass through, and then you forget it, that is fine. Just remember the times you forgot. Redouble your efforts and try for the next time."

I had to repeat it. I did, slowly. Then I called out each name, pausing at each one: "Do you promise to do this, faithfully, for the next five days? Beginning now?" I waited till I got a serious yes from each one.

"Okay, that's it. I'm not going to mention this for five days beginning now."

8

The Pause that Reminds Us

As usual, I was making speeches to the car. Maybe my best remarks: "I am asking you to think about things, all sorts of things. Did any of your other brainwashers try to do that? Did they ask you what do you think? Or did they say, 'Now, I am not trying to influence you, but . . .'"

The clock goes around, the days go by, and the opportunity is slipping out of my grasp. I have until August 15, or the 14th if they have their way. I had told them that we have *got* to have some Saturday and Sunday meetings. I got them to agree about the weekend after this one. Both days of it. They agreed rather easily. After all, it was eight days away.

* * *

"Soon we'll take up some definitions of Sufism and the questions surrounding the topic of religion. You should be getting more from the stories now—"

"I *love* the stories," said Joanne.

"Aaamen. I love the stories!"

Even Bess favored the stories even though, until then, she had hardly added a word to the discussions.

"Okay, I want to read a short quote from Ouspensky. The kind of thing that has to be heard over and over, till it dawns on you that he is talking about *us*, warning us:

We must begin with man's general knowledge about himself. And here we come to a very important fact. *Man does not know himself.* He does not know his own limitations and his own possibilities. He does not even know to how great an extent he does not know himself.

(Ouspensky, *The Psychology of Man's Possible Evolution,* 11)

"The next thing I want to mention is the idea of fixed notions. Think of your own 'fix.' The things about which you cannot be budged. I don't care what they are. Can you let them go? Or at least loosen your hold, on those fixed notions, if you can't let them go?

"You are convinced that you are a very generous person. Can you take the opposite tack and decide, at least for a trial run, that you are actually very possessive and ungenerous? You think you are ugly? Try thinking you are, really, quite beautiful. You hate swimming? Try the opposite: 'I love swimming, and I love the water.' You dislike a person? Decide for this experiment that you are going to let that go. You *love* that person. You think you are just a little better than other people? Meditate on being exactly the same, or even inferior. You *hate* history? For this meditation you *love* it.

"Pick out what it is, what you are going to work on, and meditate on it for five minutes. Prepare yourselves beforehand. Don't talk. Prepare what it is you're going to work on and then we'll do a five-minute meditation on it. Do your five minutes at the same time, outside or in here, but don't talk. I'll keep track of the time. I'll signal when to begin. One minute to decide on a topic."

We began the five-minute session and, again, a time of watching them in silence, most with eyes closed or head in hands. And I suddenly felt a great hope. That we were actually doing things. I felt love for them and respected their bravery for putting up with this mind tussle day after day.

When the five minutes was up I asked them to write about their fixed notion and the result of their meditation upon it. I collected their papers and, as anxious as I was to see them, withheld that wish till I could get home and comment on each one. I do think there was a different reaction on their part as they let go of this effort and gave me their papers.

"There is a Nasrudin story—Nasrudin is the primitive, the fool and, also, in a peculiar way, dumb-smart or cunning— well, Nasrudin is the judge. He has to decide between two sides. Nasrudin hears the first person and after the man's story he says, 'You are right!' Then he hears the next person's story. The other side, the opposite side. When that person finishes, Nasrudin says to him, 'You're right!'

"His wife says, 'Nasrudin, they can't *both* be right!'

"'You are right, too!' says Nasrudin.

"Got it? Very funny. Very very funny. But what else? Nasrudin says 'Right!' to both sides of the argument. He even says 'Right!' to his wife who points out to him that both sides can't be right. What do you make of it?"

For once they were quiet. And did not want to be called upon.

"Could both be right? And, more insane, could all three be right? What about it, Sara?"

"I *knew* it, I knew you'd call on me."

"Well?"

"It sounds impossible. But . . ."

"What do you think? Carole?"

"I don't know. I agree with his wife."

"Does it depend on a point of view? Is that it?"

"I don't follow this," said Holly, who seemed impatient with the whole thing.

"How about this. I had a new two-wheeled red bike. I had just had it for one month. I was going away with a friend for the day. My little sister wanted to borrow the bike while I was gone. I didn't want to worry about my bike while I was away, even though I was teaching her how to ride it and she was doing pretty well. Then my mother got into it. What was the harm in letting her have it while I was gone?

"There are the three points of view. 1. My sister wanted to use the bike. Nothing wrong with that. 2. I didn't want her to, she might wreck it. After all, was it my bike or not? Nothing wrong with that. 3. My mother wanted me to let her use it. That's okay, too, only it was not my mother's bike. But who was really right and who was wrong?

"I was being selfish, said my mother. No, just afraid for my bike. Can both be right? Can all three be right?" I asked. "What does it depend on?"

Silence. I could feel the wheels grinding.

"It depends," said Sam. "On . . ."

"Yes? On what?"

"There could be a situation like that, in which . . . well, all three are right."

"I think all three *were* right; although I didn't at the time. And so, what does it depend on?"

"*Who's* looking at it. On who's looking at it. And . . . how they're looking at it," said Bess.

"My God, Bess, yes! Bess . . . yes! . . . Great! That's it."

"I agree—*how* they're looking at it. *How! How! How!*" said Holly.

"*How!*" said Dan and made the Indian sign of greeting.

"Point of view," said Jodie.

"Exactly. You're all right," I said. "Although that's not the best way of saying it. 'Right' and 'wrong' are relative. Who's judging things? From what viewpoint? Nasrudin says they're *all* right. His wife too."

"He's right, too. That makes four," said Dan.

"Okay, okay."

"No, I'm serious. He's more right than the other three because he sees all three viewpoints."

"And you're right, too."

They were clapping hands together.

After the time was up, I stalled, pretending to do some papers. The group was talking and taking off in their cars. We had made this place ours. Our lake house. Now it was mine.

Strange, the place so alive, all the words, gestures, and now silence. The words are still hanging there. On the walls, in the air between us. All the words, and the force behind them. "And you're right, too!" Gestures and the ghosts of gestures, antics, movement, action. Their youth, smiles, so full of life and so life full, so much listening, so little. Life cruising through us, time. And what is happening. Little steps? Nothing? "He sees all *three* . . ."

The feeling began as I walked out of the door. My life had recently been: home to car to cabin to car to home to car to cabin. I stopped, and walked behind the cabin to a large stone at the edge of the lake and sat down.

I sat on the stone out of sight of cars and people and something dropped away from me. I was alone for the first time in what seemed to be days. I looked down. Closed my eyes and decided that when I looked up again I would not impose on the scene . . . not beautiful, not relief that the class was over, not tiredness, not happiness; for once just look and see . . . I would just see.

I closed my eyes, waited, took a breath, let it out. One more breath then I opened and looked.

For one long moment, something breathed in, in, in, and, in a great exhalation of the whole area, breathed out again. More than air. More than breath. I held it. Not even perfect. Something beyond that. The lake, the hills, shoreline, trees and the school but as if I had never seen these things before. There it all was. And as soon as I began to try and analyze it, in that instant it was gone.

Desireless for one instant. And until then I had never understood it. An instant of not wanting. Of having it all.

Once in college, after a class in Abnormal Psychology, I had asked the teacher about nirvana, and she had told me,

"The state of desirelessness? But what fun would that be? To be totally without desire? Would you really want that?"

At the time I walked off half-satisfied.

For one long second I had had a glimpse of it, I had been in that glimpse. Then it was gone and I was left describing the memory of the moment. A sniff, a glimpse of the world as it really is? If we only allow it?

The psychology teacher had never known it. You wouldn't want that? What fun would that be?

Desireless is to have it all; if only for a moment.

Desireless be*cause* I had it all. Nothing left to want.

We have it all and don't know it. Whitman says it, over and over. Only ignorance stands in our way.

Ninety thousand conferences with God, and when he got back the water from the glass, knocked over when he leaped out of bed, was still running out.

And my small cup of water to them: please drink, please please drink, won't you? For "whosoever shall give to drink—"

Then a voice was breaking through the dream. How long had I been there? My voice was cracking, as if I had not used it all night.

Was I okay?

I was fine, I told the voice.

As I got up from the rock I was stiff and sore; I might have been sitting there for years. I crossed back to the path to the cabin. Joanne was standing there, worried.

"I went for a short walk," she said, "came back and your car was still here. I wrote a note which I want to give to you . . . I looked in the cabin. I'm sorry, I—"

"It's okay."

"Hope I didn't disturb you." But the look on her face was that she had.

"It's okay."

"Here's the note, but don't read it right now." And she was off.

"Wait! How long were you . . . I mean how long has it been since the group?"

She laughed. "About ten minutes."

"Do you need a ride?"

"No thanks."

I put the note in my pocket to read later, got in the car, and drove home. The whole ride I was thinking about what happened. Only the urge to sit down and be still. Just to sit for a while. Just sit. I sit and look at the water. Look down. Close my eyes. I was sitting with their papers. I opened new eyes on the world. And I had it all for whole seconds at a time.

9

Fixed Notions and Taking Chances

Before class I read their papers:

"I tried loving my father . . ."

"My whole family are Catholics. Priests and nuns. I tried to not be Catholic."

"I don't want to say, but I really tried something. To see something I do as if it's good. That it's okay."

"My brother is a macho bully to his wife, me, our mother, and his children. I tried to take it *off*. To take that view *off* and, gulp, to love him. Inside I was a battlefield."

"I hate my period and PMS and I, instead, tried to welcome it and realize it is connected to being able to have children, which I want very much, one day. It made me cry."

"I tried to like the way my roommate eats. And laughs. And blows his nose. It made me realize how much I hate it, and, maybe, hate him too."

"I tried hating my little brother. It didn't work. I love him so much. I want to try something else. Maybe loving instead of hating."

"Please, if you read these out, don't say whose this was. I tried . . . this is difficult to even write down . . . I meditated on the idea that I am beautiful. And I think what I first have to have is more confidence. It wasn't very successful."

"This is a topic I think of all the time. I tried to stop hating the divorce. And my father. That the divorce was a good thing. And that I love my father. And that I understand him. It was very upsetting, although I try not to show it. It made me realize how much time I spend thinking about it and yet when I was forced to think about it my mind kept wandering away."

"I always feel that I never have enough. I got rid of that notion and imagined that I have plenty of money. It worked . . . in snatches. Do you know what I mean?"

* * *

"First, I'm very impressed by the things you tried to do. You're taking chances and there's something courageous about that. I'll give back your papers with comments, but I wanted to make some comments in general. I so often think about what would happen if teachers took their thumbs off your minds. That was the idea of the long-distance walks. Just get out of school and allow you to think your own thoughts with no assignments. What I didn't realize is that you, *you*, have also got to take your thumbs off your own minds.

"The reason it is difficult for some of you to take in new ideas, to have you answer not from a set of preconceived notions but from a new mind-set—not what society has forced down your throats—is that you're operating from your old perspective. And how in the hell can you *hear* anything new if it's being blocked by what's in your heads already? In a little while—today, not later—we'll take up a story that deals with that. As you are now, you plant the new on top of things you have picked up before, as Ouspensky said, so when you hear something that doesn't jibe with what is already in your minds then you automatically reject the new, not because the new idea doesn't have merit but simply because you are comfortable with the old. You've worn it around for years.

"Well, these fixed notions . . . it's good to confront them. To confront them is to take a look at how fixed they are. Also, we can see how much time we waste while these things churn around inside of us keeping us from getting clear. And yet, as one of you said, you think and think about it but never face it and put it away, once and for all. This is the beginning of the way we fall in love with our suffering. But I won't go into that right now."

"Are you adding that to the pile of things to be discussed later on?"

"Well . . . no. I'll tell you a short story about that right now. Once a prospective student came to Gurdjieff and asked him if he could become his student. He told Gurdjieff he would give up anything and everything in return for his acceptance. He would give up smoking. He would give up alcohol and liquor. He would even give up women. Gurdjieff asked him, 'Can you give up your suffering?' And the man went away completely puzzled."

"I don't get it."

"Neither do I. In *love* with *suffering?*"

"Well, hang in there. Meantime, for starters, what you are suffering with now are your various fixed notions. 'I hate my father and I can never forgive him.' 'I hate my mother *and* my father for getting a divorce.' 'My brother is a bully.' 'Everybody in my family is a nun or priest; how do I get out of it?' Eventually it becomes your story. You have run it by your mind so many times that it has become very very familiar to you. Soon enough you are looking for someone new to tell it to. To get sympathy from, about how terrible it is. And gradually you can't do without it. It is like a shot in the arm, a fix, yes, a *fix*. Mothers-in-law about their sons-in-law or daughters-in-law. It is a favorite topic. And then, pretty soon, it is like another leg. By that time you love it. That is a shorthand version of loving your suffering.

"These are the things we must get loose from. Yes, even that we are *Americans*, that we are male or female, to the point where we can say about ourselves: I am a seeking, searching human being. I am on a search for the truth, and I will put aside everything that doesn't help me find it. I'm not a Catholic, I'm not an American, I'm not a feminist, I'm not even male or female, I'm not a Democrat, I'm not a socialist, I'm not a Republican, I'm not young or old; I'm looking.

"You're not a Catholic, you're a human being. And you're not a bully, your brother is. Give thanks, and go on your way. It's his burden, not yours. Understand these things but don't identify with them. And when someone says 'What are you?' you can say 'I'm a seeker!'

"And speaking of that, there's much to be done. For tomorrow I want you to read Walt Whitman's *Song of the Open Road* and *Song of Myself*. Now remember, I'm not trying to say that Walt Whitman is a Sufi, okay? I'm not trying to say that he *is* but there are some things that he says that are very close, very reminiscent.

"One last word about your struggle with fixed notions. To struggle against Hate is not only healthier than to struggle against Love but maybe to go against Love is the wrong struggle. To try and understand both is one thing. And it would be a very Sufic thing to realize that Love is real and Hate is not. Hatred is simply a lack of understanding, or it is ignorance. In yourself or about someone else."

There was a restlessness, a casting-about that seemed to permeate the entire room of us. Attention shooting off in a hundred different directions.

"Let's try a meditation," I asked and told them. "This should take about fifteen or twenty minutes. I've been wanting to do this for a while but, after yesterday, I think the timing is right. Remember, there are two kinds of meditation; one where you meditate on a topic and another where you try and follow, as in this, which will be a guided meditation."

"I don't know anything about meditating," said Mike.

"We did it for five minutes yesterday, Mike. And so . . ." A few other hands went up.

I told them, "A great Indian teacher said once, no, he said it twice or three times: Meditation is recalling the mind. When it wanders, to recall it. It is as simple as that. But we will do a guided meditation. I'll be asking you to consider certain things and think certain things. Simple requests but it will require your attention, naturally. When you find your mind is wandering, don't waste time cursing about it—that's what minds do, they wander; just call your attention back."

We left the windows open but darkened the room as well as possible. I told them to sit comfortably, backs straight but not to worry about Lotus positions or any position that they were not used to. And began after a silence of a minute:

"Can you let the sun . . . and the moon and the stars . . . be as they are . . . exactly as they are?" I paused and let the words sink in.

"Can you let the mountains and the lakes and the rivers . . . be, exactly as they are?" I paused and forced myself to slow down even more. Waited a minute.

"Can you allow the trees, and the streams, and the houses, to be exactly as they are now? Let them be? Visualize these things . . . let them *be* as they are." I paused a long time . . .

"Can you let the people of the world . . . can you allow them to be as they are . . . without trying to change them? Accept them as they are? Asleep, awake, eating, drinking, just sitting?

"And now, can you let your friends and relatives be . . . let them be exactly as they are? Let them be . . . as they are. Exactly as they are? Think about them . . . and allow them to exist, just as they are? The things you judge, things you dislike, or like? Let them be.

"Now, can you let your mother and your father and your sisters and your brothers, can you let them be . . . exactly as they are now . . . without wishing to change them? Let them be exactly as they are?" I waited for a long thirty seconds.

"And can you let your closest, dearest friend, or lover, wife or husband, be exactly as he or she is? Without wishing to change that person in any way, can you accept that person . . . exactly as he or she is? Only let that person be . . .

exactly as he or she is? Without trying to change even one hair of that person?" I let them think about it for another minute. Then . . .

"Finally, can you let your*self* be, exactly as you are . . . with no wishes to change anything, at all. Let yourself be exactly as you are. Exactly as *you* are.

"The color of your hair, exactly . . . ears . . . head . . . neck . . . exactly as they are?

"And your shoulders and arms, and your hands . . . exactly as they are? And each finger, exactly as it is? Without wishing for one thing to be different?

"Your chest, your stomach, your lower body, your legs and knees, and calves . . . ankles . . . and feet . . . and toes . . . exactly as they are? Without wishing to change anything? Not even so much as one hair? Your weight . . . your skin color . . . everything, exactly as it is? Exactly as you are. Let it be. Accepting yourself as you are."

We sat in silence for five more minutes, then Jodie had to run to the dining hall and would be right back. We paused for a minute.

Two strange things took place after the meditation. I do not attribute either one of them to the meditation and yet it is hard not to. One with Jodie and one later that afternoon, with Carole, after class.

I took out Joanne's note from yesterday:

> I was raised a Catholic. As I got older, later teens early twenties, I found that when I did attend church I would always cry at a certain point in the ceremony and feel an overwhelming sadness. This used to bother me a great deal. When I shared this with my mom she figured it for an excuse not to go anymore. I always figured I'd have to wait until I died to get the answer. Well, yesterday it occurred to me that I cried because it wasn't the *truth*. What you read yesterday touched

me as the real truth. A small part of what I've been searching for.

Joanne.

Jodie came back, gushing with her good news. During the meditation she had had a very clear notion that the Housing Director, whom she had been trying to track down for more than a week, who was always in a meeting or unavailable, would, right then, be in the dining hall. She borrowed a car, raced over there and, sure enough, caught him as he was leaving. She straightened out the problem and would be able to move off campus in the fall. "It *came* to me. Clear as a bell. Almost like a message, while we were meditating," she said.

"Great. Okay, we'll take a break and then we'll take up 'The Horseman and the Snake.'"

* * *

THE HORSEMAN AND THE SNAKE

There is a proverb that "the opposition" of the man of knowledge is better than the "support" of the fool.

I, Salim Abdali, bear witness that this is true in the greater ranges of existence, as it is true in the lower levels.

This is made manifest in the tradition of the Wise, who have handed down the tale of the Horseman and the Snake.

A horseman from his point of vantage saw a poisonous snake slip down the throat of the sleeping man. The horseman realized that if the man were allowed to sleep the venom would surely kill him.

Accordingly he lashed the sleeper until he was awake. Having no time to lose, he forced this man to a place where there were a number of rotten apples lying upon the ground and made him eat them. Then he made him drink large gulps of water from a stream.

All the while the other man was trying to get away, crying: "What have I done, you enemy of humanity, that you should abuse me in this manner?"

Finally, when he was near to exhaustion, and dusk was falling, the man fell to the ground and vomited out the apples, the water, and the snake. When he saw what had come out of him, he realized what had happened, and begged the forgiveness of the horseman.

This is our condition. In reading this, do not take history for allegory, nor allegory for history. Those who are endowed with knowledge have responsibility. Those who are not, have none beyond what they can conjecture.

The man who was saved said: "If you had told me, I would have accepted your treatment with a good grace."

The horseman answered: "If I had told you, you would not have believed. Or you would have been paralyzed with fright. Or run away. Or gone to sleep again, seeking forgetfulness. And there would not have been time."

Spurring his horse, the mysterious rider rode away.

(Shah, *Tales of the Dervishes*, 140)

"I think there are things about the story that are a little strange. Can you pick out anything? Yes, Sam."

"I cannot picture a poisonous snake crawling down a person's throat. I don't care how deep a sleep it was, or what he was drinking or what drugs he had the night before. I have a problem with that."

"Anybody else?"

"I agree. It makes me take the story less seriously."

"Okay, I have the same problem but remember, in a story, the cardinal rule is, if there is to be a miracle put it at the very beginning. Don't bring it in at the last minute. And the story begins that way. From his point of vantage, the horseman saw a snake go down the man's throat. The sleeping man's throat. Yes, Carole?"

"There's an old saying, you can lead a horse to water but you can't make him drink. The horseman not only forces the sleeping man to drink but also forces him to eat rotten apples. That's pretty unbelievable . . . and it doesn't come at the beginning."

"Yes," said Sara, "and wouldn't all of that struggling make the snake bite him?"

"It seems to me," said Bess, "that the whole struggle takes hours. The struggle went on and on. Because it says, around dusk, the man fell to the ground exhausted and *then* he threw up everything. I guess I'm saying the same thing as Sara. If the snake was going to bite him wouldn't he have done it during the struggle?"

"Should we dump the story and go on?" I asked them. There was laughter and pleasure at the suggestion.

"Let me say this about it. I think it is a rather clumsy effort to say something allegorically, despite the warning not to take it allegorically. However, the venomous snake is supposed to represent poisons that we imbibe, and have to throw up, like racism, like hatred, like superstitions, like old wives' tales; we have to get those things completely out of our systems before anything new can be put in their place. It has to do with the saying that you can't put new wine in old bottles.

"Just one question. Did he learn anything from the experience?"

There was a pause. Joanne hesitantly offered, "I don't think he is a good bet. Even after he sees what came out of him he's not in shock. He just says, 'Well, if you'd only *told* me, I would have happily done what you asked me.'"

"Sure," said Carlito, "I would have *happily* eaten all those rotten apples and that other stuff."

"*What* other stuff, Carlito?" asked Jodie. "It was only rotten apples and water."

"*Only?*"

"You don't believe the man—"

"I *know*—"

"I was asking Carlito. I just wanted to follow it up."

"No, I think the guy's still full of it . . . even though he just threw up."

"Well," I told them, "it's a story. And all of them can teach us something. We have to get rid of the poisons within us. And that is not easy. And the man could be any one of us. After we begin to know even a little about ourselves we look back and laugh at our former selves, without remembering it wasn't *our* doing but that of someone else who came along and helped us see something about ourselves. There's a story from *The Book of the Secrets* that pertains to this:

"The man in question has never gone outside. The teacher has to get this person out. But the 'inside' person has seen only his four walls and so that is all he knows. What is the good of talking about the flowers? The person-in-the-room has never seen flowers so he'll think you're crazy. What is the good of talking about the sun and the sky and the clouds to this person who has never seen anything but walls? But he does know about fire. That spells danger. And so the teacher approaches the subject from what the person knows. In order to proceed from the known to the unknown. So the teacher begins screaming, 'Fire! Fire!' This the person understands and, finally, he runs out of the house.

"Once outside, the person begins to understand that yelling 'Fire' was just a device to get him out of the house, but forgives the teacher because there is the sky and the sun and the flowers. And then begins to realize that without the device he would never have left the room. So, in the story we have just rejected, the rotten apples were a device to get the man to throw up his poisons. Even if the story is clumsy it has value.

"Nicoll says:

> Just as we are today finding out about . . . penicillin and streptomycin, so do we have to advance to the study of the poisons of the mind and the emotions . . .
> (Nicoll, *The New Man*, preface)

"But the story itself is only that, only a device to get you to see something. No matter how clumsy or weird, if it makes you see something it is worth it. Even if the story is a lie. Or if I lie to get you to see something. So the apples were a device, and yelling 'Fire!' was a device. And these stories, in themselves, are devices, to prompt you to see something about the human condition. Even this group is a device to have you see something different, something new.

"Anyhow, the story is about the horseman and the snake. The man in the story is merely a prop. The horseman not only *knows*, he knows poison—prejudice, our dear opinions (of ourselves and others) which have a death-hold on us; our poisoned relationships which keep us from growing—hatred of a father, of a situation you find yourself in—of religions which we have outgrown but are fearful to let go of on the chance, on the merest chance, that these things might be true, that God might be shaking His Finger at us even now.

"Rumi tells us, apropos of the horseman and his cure:

Till he (the physician) cleanse your corrupt humours with medicine, how will the indisposition be removed, how will a cure be effected?

(Nicholson, *The Mathnawi*, Book IV, 402)

"Water in Sufi terms is truth. So, with the aid of his method, a mixture of rotten brain food (the apples) and truth (water) he makes the man—forcibly—'eat.' The man regurgitates . . . everything; all the poisons in his system. He is now empty. He is ready to learn. But is he?

"It would appear that one poison still remains, his good opinion of himself. He doesn't thank the horseman (man operating from a higher vantage point) and mildly criticizes him for not really understanding what a fine truth-loving gentleman he really is. He talks about what he would have done if he had only been reasoned with. Since he has thrown up everything—truth, the Sufi's devices, *and* poison—he seems ready to take in more poisons (i.e. is still blind to himself). The horseman rides away. But, again, the story is not about the man who has taken in poisons; it is about method, or device, and those who can see and those who can't.

The people who pretend that you will know the most suitable method for *yourself* are the ones who pretend that what you like is what you need. Man probably does not know the way for himself. He needs someone to arrange the circumstances . . .

(Shah, *Thinkers of the East*, 11)

"What I need right now is a drink.

"That comes from *Thinkers of the East* by Shah. Not the part about needing a drink, the rest of it.

"My wife was brought up Catholic. She used to feel sorry for her friends who were not Catholic because they were all going to hell. Someone has never had a chance to hear about

Catholicism—in darkest Africa, or some Australian Bushman—that person is doomed. Straight to hell, because he or she is not Catholic. Would that view keep a person from hearing something new? Her attitude about hell and how candidates are selected?

"My son grew up hating little birds. Why? Because his mother, God bless her, said she knew he'd eaten those cookies because a little birdie had told her. Those damned little birds again."

"Sparrows? Were they sparrows?" Sam asked me.

"Of course! So, whatever you think of the story of the Horseman, it is very definite with the Sufis, and most other systems or ways, that we do not see ourselves as we are. Outside help is needed."

And we *needed* one more class before we could begin the section I have called Religion.

I told them that we'd begin with Walt Whitman next time but, instead, something else came up, and we approached Whitman from a different angle.

10

Introducing Dr. Walt Whitman

Carole told us the strange story: "After class yesterday, and the meditation, I went to the library and some girl, whom I've never seen before, came up to me and told me, 'You have *got* to see this tape; it's wonderful.' And she gave me this video tape. It's called *Beautiful Dreamer* and it's a film about Walt Whitman."

"Our hands are tied," I told her. "We've got to see the film."

Danny and Sam went back to the library, got a VCR and screen, signed for them, and were back in about fifteen minutes.

We saw the film and, although it is far from an action film, everyone watched with complete attention. They had already read a good deal of Whitman and, although some didn't understand it, Sam, Joanne, Sara, and a number of others thought Whitman was wonderful.

"Sam," according to his adviser's report, "hasn't a clue as to what he's doing, what he wants, or where he's going. Other than he *thinks* he wants to write." It was as if Sam had been waiting all of his life for a particular door to open, a door marked Walt Whitman.

A sentimental film-maker might have called the film *Love Conquers All*. It's about early mental institution procedures—which doesn't, to this observer, seem terribly different from what goes on today except for the surface niceties—and how Walt Whitman helped the progressive doctor treat patients as human beings not as caged animals. That is not even a hasty summary and does not include Whitman's influence on the doctors around him, the absolute conviction of his rightness, his exuberance for life, his love for all things, his joy, and views of absolute equality between men and women.

When we'd finished watching the movie I couldn't wait to ask them: "Okay, here is one of the first of all of the Later questions. All of those things I have been telling you that we'd get to Later. So, you saw the movie, you've read at least some of Walt Whitman's poetry. You've discovered that he identifies with women and men. He's gentle, he's kind, he's loving. He's open to the whole world—the skies and flowers, cities and streets, white men, red men, black men *and* women. That he's in love with the world and all it contains. And that he puts himself above no one. Okay, now think back to 'Indian Camp'—"

"I *knew* you were going to ask about that," said Sara, who usually groaned, "I *knew* you were going to call on me," just when she hadn't a clue about the answer.

"Yesss, and the doctor. And the Indian woman. And the operation. And I want to know, in writing, how Walt Whitman, as the doctor, would have handled that operation. How would he have done things differently from the doctor in 'Indian Camp' who, actually, was Hemingway's father who . . . well, no matter."

"What?"

"Who killed himself. Just as Hemingway did. But that doesn't distinguish the brutes from the others. Anyhow, that's your assignment. Using your imagination, of course, re-create that scene in the little Indian hut, Doctor Whitman doing the operation."

"Oh, that's impossible!"

"Can you make up a story?" I asked them. "A true story? And use your imagination to re-create the truth? Ask yourself these questions: Would he have taken his son with him? Would he have—"

"Okay, okay. I've got it."

"Yeah, well, I don't," said Mike.

"How do you *re*-create the truth when the *truth* is . . . it never happened?" said Bess.

"Listen, all of you. Maybe this is your *chance* . . . to really *prove* that instead of having to experience *everything* that maybe you can actually discover the truth . . . of some things, right *here*. You know, Einstein said, 'We must think in a new way if we are to survive.' He also said, 'Imagination is more valuable than intelligence.'" I looked at them. I wanted to get down on my knees; instead I said it: "I feel like begging you to *throw* yourselves into this. The proper use of the imagination . . . got it? To discover the truth! Alright? To dis*cover* it. Do it! Discover the truth of this situation even if it never happened. You can do it! *Make* it happen. *Make* it true. *Make* Walt Whitman do the operation, as Walt Whitman would have done it. Don't you *see?!?*"

I was one second away from pounding the table, running outside and diving in the lake, banging my head against the nearest tree. I felt a scream rising inside of me that I stopped only because I might have lost the whole game.

Some were already writing furiously. Others were turning to it. Then, the inevitable question.

"How long do we have?"

Carole, Joanne and Sam glared at the culprit, who happened to be Carlito, but there were two or three others who would have asked it if he hadn't.

I too had to get out of time and assignments.

"You have *forever*," I said. "Got that? *Forever* . . . and if you're finished by tomorrow, we'll take up Religion! If not, we'll keep on writing about 'Indian Camp II.' I'm taking a break. You guys write."

I went outside, looked at the rock, the lake, looked back at the cabin and, suddenly, I was feeling gleeful. They were doing it. They were putting things together and coming up with the story of what could have happened but never did.

I went back in and announced, "Listen, I'm going to be gone for about ten minutes. If you finish, leave it on the table and take a break. I'll be back shortly. We're not done with this session."

I went and had coffee, and even read the newspaper for a few minutes at The Greek's out on the highway, and all the time I was tickled at the thought of what was going on back at the little cabin.

I drove back and, oddly enough, only Joanne, Mike, Carole and Sara were still working on their stories.

"Mike, you might have talents in you that you never dreamed of."

He grinned and considered that. "Yeahhhhh," he said.

* * *

Indian Camp II

Chief Whitman put on his headdress and went to answer the call . . .

Well, I'd have to expect some of that.

* * *

The rain was coming down in sheets and made streams down his cheeks. But he knew the area well and went right to the teepee where Morning Sun was trying to have her baby. He walked in, drew a deep breath and looked around him. Morning Sun's mother was there and greeted him as if he were one of the tribe. He gripped her hand and went to the rough matting on the floor. Morning Sun was delirious but she still recognized him. She knew he was not like the other white men who looked upon Indians as dogs or lower animals. He understood Indians and their ways. He asked for hot water and clean chamois cloths. He soaked the chamois cloths in the hot water, rinsed one, squeezed the excess water from it and bathed her forehead calmly and slowly. While he did it he sang a white man's song about the river, and how the river goes on forever and forever, and little by little she put herself in his hands. Her limbs stopped their involuntary shaking and she was able to relax. When her delirium had passed a little, he asked for her husband, Blue Heron, and discovered that he was in the upper bunk and had an injured leg from an axe wound. The doctor turned to Morning Sun's mother and spoke with her briefly. She left the hut and when she came back she had three braves with her. They explained to Blue Heron that it might be better for him to leave while the doctor helped Morning Sun with the baby. After some discussion Blue Heron let them carry him out of the hut to a place near the river. Before he left he spoke with the doctor and asked him to take care of Morning Sun and if the baby was brought safely into the world Blue Heron told the doctor that he would name his son after him.

The man worked skillfully and very gently and, with his hands on her stomach, while he talked gently to Morning Sun, he helped shift the baby's body around so that the head was, at last, in the right position. Morning Sun's mother was there, helping her daughter, telling her how *soon* the pains would be gone and in place of the pains there would be a new child in the world.

One hour later, in a burst of waters, the baby's head poked out into the world and when they told Morning Sun she smiled her first smile for a long time. The next tremendous push and there, caught by the doctor and Morning Sun's mother, was a baby girl. Morning Sun collapsed with a smile and with her baby daughter in her arms went to sleep. And that's how Morning Sun's daughter came to be called Walt."

* * *

The doctor was roused from a sound sleep by a banging on his cabin door. When he opened it he saw three Indians almost as dumbfounded as he was. The spokesman pleaded with the doctor to come quick to the Indian settlement on the other side of the river. Indian Squaw cannot have child, in big trouble. The doctor explained to his son, ten years old, where he was going, not to worry. He'd be back as soon as he could.

He had to turn back when he realized he'd forgotten his instruments. But he was cursing himself for not having brought his favorite surgical knife with him. As they rowed across the quiet river they explained more. For three days she had been in great pain but the baby would not come.

His mind was racing ahead to what he would need, how he would go about this. Too bad he did not speak the tongue of the Ojibway tribe. "Does the mother speak English?"

"She work for white family. She speak little."

That was all, as they continued across the river and beached the canoe, then hurried through the dripping trees to the teepee.

"Here," said the tall one, delivering the teepee to the doctor. Then he left, as if his duty had been done.

Mustering all of his courage, and his strength and common sense, because he knew that in the final analysis that great wisdom was only common sense (did you like that?) he entered the smelly airless teepee.

The would-be mother screamed at the sight of the giant bearded white man and huddled against her son who, although he was only twelve was ready to protect his mother against anyone, and drew his hatchet against the doctor.

"I am here to help you," said the doctor. But he had to repeat it ten or more times before the woman decided that he might be okay. She had words with her son who finally decided that the big white man would not hurt his mother. The son went over to the upper bunk and roused his father who was suffering with a very bad leg wound from an axe. Since the mother couldn't be approached, the doctor took a look at the father's leg wound.

It was in very bad shape and was badly infected. Very carefully he began to wash it and, in a short time, the Indian was convinced that the man was there to help him. Meantime from the area of the mother's bed was silence. An apprehensive silence. He sprinkled some medicinal powder on the cut leg and slowly and carefully bandaged the leg after making sure it was cleaned properly.

While this was going on the Indian began talking to his wife in a soothing voice and soon she was talking back to him. Her voice now sounded normal and, finally, the husband said to the doctor, "She will now listen to you. She is prepared to let you help her."

As if the Indian husband could read the doctor's mind, he held up a straight razor and gave it to the doctor, after demonstrating that it could cut a single hair with one swipe.

Good. That was all he needed. That would do as well as his surgical knife.

Even though he did have to do a Caesarian, he convinced the squaw that he would hurt her as little as possible. And sure enough, inside of two hours were born the first twins in that village for many years. One they named Doctor and the other they named Walt.

* * *

When I said the doctor did his job (Indian Camp #1), I meant technically that he did. What this exercise made me realize is that when you're frightened, and don't know what's happening it exaggerates everything. So, I'm no story writer but I know what you mean. Walt Whitman, I mean Dr. Whitman, would not have frightened her. The Indian woman. He would have calmed her down so it would make his work easier. I mean "her" work also. *Their* work. I had to go and read the story over again and I saw things I didn't see before. For the doctor to say that her screams weren't important and to say that they weren't important because *he* didn't hear them, is so gross that it's enough to make you throw up . . . the doctor (Indian Camp I) was only interested in *his* work, not in . . . the total situation, which involved the mother, the baby, *and* the husband. He didn't talk to the mother before the operation, during, or after. It seems inhuman. The manner of the doctor was typical of the statement: Operation a success; the patient died.

* * *

Because Dr. Whitman didn't know what he was doing, and could not improvise and *use his imagination*, the baby died, the mother was sick for months afterwards and the father went on a rampage and killed three white men from the nearby town before killing himself.

P.S.: But there was a happy ending after all. Dr. Whitman, who was singing songs to the mother and holding her hand while her baby was dying, fell in love; they were married Indian-style, and eventually went on to have five children, all healthy, all brought into the world by that famed baby doctor, Dr. Clinton Holbrook, of Amherst, MA.

* * *

Win some, lose some. Perhaps Bess was still angry about Western medicine. I considered various comments, rejected them all, and, after giving back their papers, asked if Dr. Holbrook was any relation.

"My father," she said, embarrassed, pleased and abashed all at once.

"I would never have guessed."

"The question was: How would Walt Whitman have done the operation on the Indian woman as opposed to Hemingway's father?

"Would Whitman have gone in there and 'done the job'? Or would he have said, I'm dealing with a human being. And every single part is connected to the whole. And our fears, sometimes, are worse than whatever is going to be done to us. And so I first better spend a little time trying to get to know the person and trying to calm the person down. After all this is not an oil change that I'm doing. This is not changing the spark plugs or doing a front end alignment. This is not a car. It's more complicated than that. Wouldn't it be worth a lot to sit with her for a while? To hold her hand? To smile at her? Instead of ignoring her screams? Not even 'hearing' them?

"Let me tell you a story. One time when we were living in Mexico my four-year-old daughter stepped on a nail. I told her we would have to go see the doctor. 'Is he going to stick me with a needle?'

"'Yes,' I told her.

"'I'm going to cry,' she warned me.

"'I tell you what. Don't cry till it hurts. Okay? Then, if you want to cry, it's okay.' We got in the car. 'Does it hurt yet?'

"'No,' she said. And she got into the game.

"We drove to the corner. 'Does it hurt yet?'

"'No.'

"We got in sight of the hospital. 'There's the hospital! Does it hurt yet?'

"'No,' she said, but now her smile was a little apprehensive. I parked the car, we got out and walked hand in hand to the office.

"While we walked to the office I asked her, 'Does it hurt yet?'

"'No.'

"We got to the emergency doctor's office, and walked in. 'Does it hurt yet?' No. She was still smiling, sneaking glances at me. We sat down and he sat down next to her. The doctor took her arm and swabbed it with alcohol.

"'Charlotte, did that hurt?'

"'No,' she whispered to me in a loud voice.

"He took out the needle, put the vaccine in. I leaned over and whispered in her ear, 'Does it hurt yet?'

"'No,' she said.

"He took hold of her arm, stuck the needle in and out, and swabbed and rubbed her arm vigorously.

"'There! It's all over. Finished.'

"'It's finished?'

"'Yep!'

"'*I didn't even cry!*' she said."

I admitted that a Caesarian and a tetanus booster were hardly comparable, but it was Hemingway's father's attitude that needed focusing.

Naturally, I wanted more and better from them. But I was

reminded of the words of a Sanskrit scholar and teacher of Vedanta: In any situation we either get exactly what we expect, more than we expect, less than what we expect, or something totally different. If we're waiting to cross the street in order to catch a bus we either get across safely and catch the bus (what we expect), or a friend comes along, sees us, and takes us to the very door of where we're going (more than we expect), or we cross the street too late and miss the bus (less than we expect) or we get something totally unexpected, like ending up in the emergency ward, after being hit by an automobile while trying to cross the street.

Again I promised that tomorrow we would take up Religion. And, another Later, some definitions of Sufism.

11

The Devil: Man's Terrible Power

"I've told you too often that there are no marked distinctions between any of the aspects of Sufism. I have refrained from a discussion of definitions or religion simply because, well, because . . ."

I noticed at these junctures—wherever, whenever—they suddenly became very interested as if they, the group, knew I was in doubt, and wondered how I would get out.

". . . Because you needed the background and it would, well, mean more to you after more general information. I still don't know if your background is sufficient. Are there any questions? Pertaining to what we've covered?"

"Only a few hundred," said Holly.

"Well, Holly. I hope you never lose that curiosity and always have a few thousand more questions than answers. Thomas Edison, inventor of the light bulb, telephone, movies, and at least a hundred other items, is supposed to have said: 'We don't know one millionth of one percent about *anything*.' Maybe he was exaggerating a little; maybe we know one-thousandth of one percent about a couple of things. In any case, he was known as The Man who Invented the Twentieth Century, and if this genius claims we're ignorant, and includes himself, modesty demands that we join him in confessing our own."

"I have a question," said Sara, "about esoteric and exoteric. About the devil, for example, and other things."

"Okay, the term 'devil.' In Sufi terms, the devil is not some evil character with horns, who runs around creating havoc, the one who made you get drunk and start smoking again; the devil is man's terrible power of misunderstanding everything . . . the power of wrongly connecting everything. So the 'devil' is right at home in us, not some creature who haunts your footsteps—although it's more fun to think of the devil out there, lurking around dark corners; he, or she, is much closer than that. The devil—our amazing power of misunderstanding things—is built into us, and comes with mother's milk."

"Is that what is meant by 'esoteric,' by the esoteric view, of seeing problems *inside* of us and 'exoteric' as viewing problems *outside* of us?"

"Yes, exactly. It is also on the way to becoming responsible. If something is *your* fault then, at least for that particular thing, admitting it is to take responsibility for it."

"What about things like . . . well, like rape?"

"What do you mean?"

"If you're raped, is that a problem that you, somehow, are you saying, *you* brought on yourself? Or is that a problem outside of you?"

"Is this a trap?"

"No . . . but . . ."

"That's a really tough question. So much is involved. I'm not avoiding this but I don't think it's for us, now, this discussion group."

There were all sorts of questions about my response. Weren't we, the group, able to discuss anything? Wasn't "Sufism" able to handle this? Was there nothing that could be said about it?

"Well, I could say that this thinking involves the thinking that 'your being attracts your life.'"

"Would you translate that?" asked Carole, who seemed to be bristling for a fight.

"Yes, but, actually, that whole concept demands a good deal more in the way of background than we've had. But, put more simply, the way we are attracts the things that happen to us."

"You mean, basically, that whatever we do—?" said Holly.

"That it's our fault? Whatever happens?" said Jodie.

"Look, I'm really sorry we're into this. The background for my being able to say anything worth hearing is just not there . . . yet. It involves a lot of self-observation . . . *working* with these ideas, not just talking about them. Even if I tell you, for starters, not to get drunk in some bikers' bar it sounds—"

I couldn't even finish for the screams and howls from the women. Finally, Carole and Joanne could be distinguished and the one followed the other, although I'm not sure which one came out with it: "You mean just because you got drunk that gives people the right to rape you?"

"That has nothing to do with what I said. I'm not talking to a bunch of rapists—I'm talking to rapees and potential rapees. Of *course* rape is despicable. But despicable things happen—"

"We're not free to—"

"Look, Carole—and all of you—I've already told you that for the purposes of this . . . discussion, there are certain things we need more background before being able to discuss. Until then, you are 'free' to do whatever you want . . . well, put it like this. You come to a corner. You have the right of way. The guy coming from the other direction has a STOP sign. You go through and the other guy plows into you. You were right but your leg is broken, and maybe your neck. You're *right*. And in the hospital.

"Do you see? You are free to do whatever you want. And so are the bikers. And your freedom and theirs run into each other. And since it would be easier to rape this drunken girl who is in 'our' bar, let's take *her* . . . now to answer your question, as you gain more knowledge of the world, you see and understand certain things about it. And as you grow you become aware of just how free and just how *not* free you are. And if you do certain things simply to prove that you are free there will be others around who will exercise what they think is *their* freedom. And if they're stronger than you are, your 'freedoms' are liable to suffer. This has nothing to do with what is *right*. Only with what *is*. If you want to be out on the front lines you'll probably be looked on as very brave. You are also liable to be shot.

"This is so tough. Problem inside or outside? Did your 'being' attract the event? But where did your 'being' come from? Is it karma? Fate? Accident? Your 'choice'? And what is *that*?

"On the '85 walk across Europe—we were in Yugoslavia, in a town not far from Trieste, a tough little town—one of the girls, dressed in shorts and halter, stayed back at a restaurant and wrote in her journal for a long time. There were three locals there at this bar and they kept eyeing her. All of the walkers had left a long time before. When she got up to begin walking they followed her. Then one was walking with her. She was trying to be polite. He tried to hold her hand and she politely refused. Suddenly he picked her up, jumped over the wall with her, and tried to rape her. She got away and ran to the highway and flagged down a car. The car took her to where some other walkers were and she was okay there.

"The question is *not*, I said *not*, that she brought this on herself but, think, if she had been a little more savvy . . . she was in a strange country, didn't know the language or the customs. Should she have remained back there for so long? Do you see what I'm saying?"

"No!"

"Wasn't it a little naive?"

"You haven't said one word about the *guys*," said Holly.

"So?" said Jodie. "Are you saying she brought it on herself? That she wanted to be *raped?*"

"Are you guys listening to me? The discussion is about a situation in Yugoslavia, although it could have been in any one of our big cities as well."

The discussion went on and on, and even two hours would not have cleared it up. At a certain point nothing is being heard.

"Look, this course is not exhaustive. We're only scratching the surface of some very complicated ideas. But, as I said, the course is not exhaustive. Carlito, do you know what 'exhaustive' means here?"

"Yes," said he, bravely, "it means that we shouldn't exhaust ourselves over it."

"Carlito, I love you. Let's take a short break."

I *knew* this time I would be roasted. I was chauvinistic, and whatever else. Had we made any headway, since the beginning?

* * *

When they got back, I asked for a cease-fire. That the discussion was not finished, that we would take it up again and I'd continue with them and give them equal time to get their points over and to hear mine. Further along, maybe we can clear up some points.

"Later, later," said Jodie, but she managed a smile.

I wondered if they really felt like that. I felt that I was parceling out information and some of it just couldn't go before other things.

"Meantime, let me bring up one of those old points that I deferred till later. Remember the story of Nuri Bey and the coffer? Well, we pretty much agreed that the story was about trust and the relationship. And, in the end, that Nuri Bey, in burying the coffer, did the right thing. I know, Carlito, you never quite went along with that. But now I want to add something more. Here is what Osho has to say about it:

> Your possibility of transformation is in your future. The past is dead and gone and finished. Bury it! It has no meaning any more . . . it is unnecessary luggage.
>
> (Osho, *The Tantra Experience*, 42)

"So, is it the coffer that causes the disagreement?"

"No, not really."

"Then what?"

"Maybe their attitude toward it."

"Exactly. What'll we do about the coffer? Bury it! Why?"

"Because," said Bess, "it is now history. It is in the past."

"Hallelujah. Thanks, Bess. Yes, as Osho says, our chance for transformation is in the future."

"Listen. One time in Mexico, when we had only two children, I took my son in to the market in our little VW bug. When I got back my daughter, the oldest, four years old, was furious. Why hadn't I taken her? Because she was playing with her friend three houses away. 'But I wanted to go *with* you!'

"'Look, I promise I'll take you next time I go.'

"'*But I wanted to go THIS time!*' she said. I could not get it over to her that I could not turn back the time. Next time would not do. She wanted to go *last* time.

"Some of our wishes are just that impossible. We have *got* to bury the past and work with what's possible, the 'now' coming up.

"One last note on the 'The Horseman and the Snake.'"

"I hate that story."

"Well, this is it. Last mention of it and then we'll bury the story. The Sufis see humanity as sound asleep. And so the sleeping man, remember how it's worded, 'he sees *the* sleeping man.' It doesn't say *a* sleeping man. He sees humanity in general. And men and women, in general, are convinced that, as they are now, they are fine. And are determined not to wake up.

"The story helps us realize that as we are now we will not accept anything new because we are satisfied with our old truths, just as the sleeping man has no idea about the poisons until he *sees* them come out of him, in the form of a snake. And he can see it only *after* the poison has been forced out of him. Until then he is happy with himself as he is. But the horseman knows that before the sleeping man can learn anything new, he must get rid of his old ways of thinking, his old poisons. He knows that we cannot put new wine into old bottles. And wine in Sufi terminology means spiritual truth.

"A different way of approaching the same topic is Nicoll's plea that 'We have to slay the mind dragon.' This has been said in a dozen different ways. Osho says, 'We are never doubtful of the mind, and the mind has brought us to the mess we're in . . . You can doubt any teacher, any master, but you never doubt your mind . . . And your mind has brought you to the mess, to the misery that you are in.'

"*Think* about it! One last thing. I want a brief report on the task I gave you five days ago . . ." There were groans and exclamations even as I spoke to them, and they remembered about the doors. ". . . to pause before opening every door. It was a five-day experiment. So?"

I went around the room. Most had totally forgotten it. Didn't even think of it once. Others had thought of it, remembered once or twice then had determined to try. Forgot again. Dropped it. Others had "always thought of it just after I went through a door . . . well, not *always* but I never once thought of it before getting to the door." Sara had actually done it three times, on the second day. And not again.

"Okay, remember. I told you there was no way for you to fail at this. How's that possible? Mike?"

"You fail only if you don't try!" said he.

"Excellent," I said, unable to believe my ears. "But if you fail to do the task? Or fail to pause before opening the doors?"

"Well, that's failing in another way."

"Yes, but, as you pointed out, the only real failure is not to try. Because if you really try and don't do it, then you should have discovered something."

"That you didn't try hard enough?" said Bess.

"That we're unconscious," said Joanne.

"Yes! Both! The two are connected because we think we're conscious, as we are. Okay? I told you I'd prove to you that

144

you're asleep. This is a chance to discover that fact."

"Alright," said Sam, "let's try it again. I *know* I can do that."

Others joined in. *This* time would be different. I was pleased. At least this time they'd give it a better shot.

"Let's vary it, just a little. Instead of pausing before opening doors, try pausing twice a day at certain times which I will assign to you. Come to yourself, take three or four seconds—"

"Please explain what you mean by 'come to yourself'?"

"However or whatever that term means to you. Stop whatever it is you're doing. Examine yourself: 'I am Tom. I am standing here in the hallway at 5:00 P.M. I'm in New Hampshire. My attention is on myself. I am simply pausing and collecting myself.' That's enough. In a way it's like shaking hands with yourself. Like a meeting with yourself."

I gave different times to each one. They wrote them down. I talked about preparation beforehand: "If your times are 8:30 in the morning and 4:30 in the afternoon, write the times down and think of them. Think of where you might be, or where you usually are at those times. Determine, as you think about this task, that you are going to get ready and stop, at those times. You might start checking your watch at 3:00 or 3:30, determining not to forget. Check again. Wait for it. Four-twenty, and you're getting ready."

"What if you don't have a watch?" said Dan.

I didn't have to say anything. A dozen suggestions were hurled at him, to the effect that it wasn't a huge stumbling block.

"Alright, Dan. For you, and maybe one or two others, I want you to pause before breakfast, lunch, and supper. Even if your breakfast is only a cup of coffee, before you pick up the spoon to stir the coffee, pause, come to yourself, three seconds, then stir your coffee. If for lunch, you have a sandwich, pause before the first bite, three seconds. Then eat. For supper, before picking up the fork, before eating, pause. That's *three* times a day, before each meal."

Three others wanted to try the pause at meals. I let them. Noted it down. It would be a three-day task and they'd report at the end of that time.

"See you tomorrow. Wear your Sunday best. It's time for Religion."

Religion

12

Love, Crime, and Ignorance

God is where a man's blood is not shed.
                    —G. I. Gurdjieff, *All and Everything*

"It's difficult to say that Sufis believe this or that because no one person speaks for Sufis. It is not an organization. But Hazrat Inayat Khan, who wrote a multi-volume series called *The Sufi Message*, said something that seems central to much of Sufi thought: 'All ignorance comes from a lack of love, all crime from a lack of love' (Khan, *The Sufi Message*, I:19).

"Maybe the most daring statement on love that was ever made. All ignorance . . . only a lack of love! All crime only a lack of love. Only a lack of love! Think of it. Turn it over for a few minutes. What if it's true?"

I paused for a few seconds.

"What do you think of the woman in the news recently who drowned her two children?"

"Wait—sometimes, we really have to stop and consider the things that have been said. I don't mind talking about these issues of the day, because, after all, if we don't deal with them, the life problems, then what good is our discussion? But sometimes things are said and no sooner are they out of my mouth than you have a question, instead of allowing time for the idea to be considered. I tell you a *new* thing and you take it as any *old* thing. Tell me, have you ever heard that before? That all ignorance is due to a lack of love? *Ignorance!* And that all *crime* comes from a lack of love?

"We live in a country with the highest prison population in the world. And what is our answer to the high crime rate? *More* prisons, *more* police, and longer sentences. Are any alternatives being offered?

"Maybe it's a lack of love. Maybe a lack of *time* for love. You want your child to be intelligent? Don't push encyclopedias at him or her; just love the child."

"Do you believe that?"

"I think it's an astounding statement. About crime and ignorance. It's the kind of statement one should walk out in a field and think over. Sit down a whole day with. By oneself. Should meditate twenty-four hours over. In any case it's not something one should accept or reject in a minute. Or an hour.

"About the woman you brought up—I saw a tabloid headline that declared in giant letters: *Child Killer Has Evil Heart!* When hearts were being doled out, was the 'child-killer' given an 'evil' heart? Or were certain things done to her, certain things not done *for* her? Was she a child who was loved in some sensible way? By even semi-conscious people?"

There was heated discussion and I felt somewhat saddened to have been taken from "love" to tabloids. I called them back.

"There are so many things to be said about the Sufis and religion, but a comment on love is a good way to begin. Let me begin again, with the view of a person who was being brought up in a strict religious atmosphere and why he moved away from it. This is Maurice Nicoll:

> I was brought up, in regard to religious ideas, with the sense that only the conviction of sin was important. Everything was sin, briefly speaking. In consequence, religion was a very gloomy business and personally I loathed it. Morality was only sexual morality. Virtue was only continence, and so on, and, in general, sin

and the feeling of being a sinner was the main idea of religion.

(Nicoll, *Psychological Commentaries*, I:8)

"In the same passage he admits that he could not understand the parables. No one else seemed to care. One Sunday he dared to ask the headmaster about the meaning of one of the parables.

> The answer was so confused that I actually experienced my first moment of self consciousness—that is, I suddenly realized that *no one knew anything*. . . . As you know, all moments of real self-remembering stand out for ever in one's inner life, and one's real life is not outer events but inner states.

"Nicoll, the stuttering little kid who dared to ask the question about the parables, grew up, learned Greek, and came to be a biblical and Greek scholar . . . a very different psychotherapist, and wrote at least six volumes of commentaries on Gurdjieff's method and two books on the esoteric meaning of the bible.

"This is not, this discussion, is not meant to be exhaustive; I'm simply introducing these ideas and a lot of them need more time and more information, and practice, before they can mean something to you. Meantime, I want you to turn your attention to the basics. To how things work. To how you work. To how you don't work but wish you did. To why we believe this and not the other. Even to use the word 'religion' is a turnoff. Filled with what you must do, or not do. No joy. No happiness, and lots of rules.

"I'm not talking about that. Or anything that doesn't make sense to you. But I *am* talking about sense. About making sense. About pursuing the truth. Not to keep you from doing anything you like. Even to make us happier. And you're not going to be happier if you keep on insisting that two and two equals three, or six. And you have to find out if that's what you're doing."

"You keep using that expression," said Sam, "and maybe it sounds stupid but I really don't know what you mean by it. Two and two equals four . . . I don't get it."

No one laughed at Sam's question and I realized that we had come to know each other and listen to each other. He was speaking from himself, from his own doubts and, because he was, it touched the doubts in a lot of the others.

"The question is simple and profound. But, aside from the arithmetical truth, when I say two and two equals four, I mean that we have to tell the truth, because if you don't the truth will come up and knock you in the head. You'll also die a physical death if you think your car can beat a train to the crossing and you've overestimated what your car can do ($2 + 2 = 6$). Or underestimated the train's speed ($2 + 2 = 3$).

"Let me begin, off-target, with a card that someone sent me. A man is holding up his checkbook and saying, 'I *can't* be overdrawn, I still have some checks.' That is a simple example of not adding two and two because . . . well, you're a book-keeping idiot, or you are hoping against hope that it will not add up to four. But the bankers keep track of your account even if you don't. I think all of us have written checks and wondered and hoped, and even prayed, that it will clear. That is a modified way of praying that two and two will not equal four. But the banker is not interested in your prayers.

"It has been said that 95 percent of our prayers are 'Please God, don't let two and two equal four . . . just this once.' And I have to stop and ask one of you, please explain that prayer to me."

"Well, I don't know if I'm exactly clear about it, or which question," said Jodie, "but it's like wishing against . . . against the truth. Everything tells you it's not going to work and so not to do it but you go against . . . what you *know* . . . I can't explain it—"

"Well, 'wishing against the truth' is really it," I told her. Jodie would not have taken that chance, even ten days ago.

"To run a red light at a blind corner and pray that no one is coming from the other direction," said Carlito.

"You sleep with someone who has AIDS and pray you won't get it," said Holly.

"Well, both of those have to do with chance. Sometimes you can get away with it; you can beat the odds. But there's really nothing chancy about $2 + 2 = 4$. You wake up on Monday morning and start wishing it was Sunday. So, does that help?"

Sam nodded and seemed satisfied.

"Of course, if two people marry and they have eight children, then one and one equals ten, but that's biology and not arithmetic. However, most of our prayers ask that two and two not equal four because we desperately want it to be otherwise."

"Okay, I've got it," said Sam.

"Just a second, you've got me started and I've got to go on a little more. Look, it's the way you take yourselves and your own abilities, what you *can* do and what you *can't* do. And knowing yourselves. For example I'm sure most of you felt that you could easily remember to pause before a door and, only then, go through it . . ." I think, for the first time, this thought was coming home to roost.

"For example, you face a challenge, or there's a chance to do something that you might think is out of your reach, because for years you have been saying two and two equals three, so you think, 'I can't do that!' Because you think it only equals three you decide not to try it. Do you see? It *is* within your reach, within your abilities, but because you don't know what you're capable of or because you're lazy you add two and two and come up with three. It is your excuse not to do anything, or your fear of failure which says no to the effort, not lack of ability.

"On the other hand, you might credit yourself with more than you're capable of doing. Oh, two and two? Two and two equals six. You mean I just have to pause a couple of seconds before opening a door? Every time I go through one? No problem! And then you forget all about it. That is a case of not knowing yourselves. What you *can* do and what you can't do.

"In a Senior Life-Saving course we were told that if a person who is drowning is bigger and stronger than you are then you should not try saving that person, because you will end up being drowned. Similarly, when you size up a situation you've got to decide whether *it* is too big or too powerful for you. William Blake the great mystic poet said: 'You never know what is enough until you know what is too much.' Drink eight beers and you're fine, drink ten beers and you throw up. Somewhere in that area is 'too much' . . . for you . . ." Of course that brought the usual remarks.

"Listen, I'm not advocating anything; it's only an example of not knowing oneself, and only through experimenting and being honest about the results can we know ourselves.

"To begin anew, let's define, or try to define Sufism. Here is the *Columbia Encyclopedia*'s attempt:

> Sufism: An umbrella term for the ascetic and mystical movements within Islam. While Sufism is said to have incorporated elements of Christian monasticism, gnosticism, and Indian mysticism, its origins are traced to forms of devotion and groups of penitents in the formative period of Islam.

"An 'umbrella term'? That means it is a catchall term. The 'ascetic and mystical movements'? That also covers a great deal and, unless you were a specialist in ascetic and mystical movements you would still be in the dark as to what they're talking about. And if you *were* a specialist you might object to the linkage between them and a definition of Sufism.

"And 'elements of Christian monasticism' and 'gnosticism'? But *what* elements of Christian monasticism? And which elements of gnosticism? As for 'Indian mysticism'? Just a dash of

'Indian mysticism'—is this a recipe for stew?—Ha! the country of India is a boiling sea of mystics and mysticism and anyone who knows India would laugh himself sick at such an ungraspable definition.

"And 'within Islam'? There are a good number of authorities on the subject who believe that Sufism was, really, alive and flourishing well before Islam. That there was never a time when it didn't exist—under different names, perhaps.

"And 'groups of penitents in the formative period of Islam' were the originators of the movement? That meets with the same objection as above. Some will give a date as to when Sufism began, and others don't try, while others say it has always been.

"Does that help us? I'll answer that . . . no. Although Sufis say that Sufism is not *a* religion, that it *is* religion, the word 'religion,' from *Webster's Ninth New Collegiate Dictionary* uses the word 'religious' three times in its brief definition: 'religious faith . . . religious beliefs . . .' or 'the state of a religious' (as, for example, a nun). The use of a different form of the word being defined is known as the dictionary fallacy. In looking up word A you are sent to B and at B are sent back to A.

"*Webster's New World Dictionary* is a little better: 'Religion: Any specific system of belief and worship, often involving a code of ethics and a philosophy, e.g. the Christian religion, the Buddhist religion.'

"The problem with Sufism, and these definitions, is that there is no 'specific system,' no holy book, no bible, no single view. It is, rather, a *way*. In *The Mystics of Islam*, R.A. Nicholson, a renowned Sufi scholar, simply states:

> Although the numerous definitions of Sufism which occur in Arabic and Persian books on the subject are historically interesting, their chief importance lies in showing that Sufism is indefinable . . . (p. 25)

"He goes on to illustrate by referring to the story of the Blind and the Elephant: 'So it is with Sufism: they can only attempt to express what they themselves have felt . . .' He also says, 'For creeds and catechisms count for nothing in the Sufi's estimation.'

"So, you see, it's not the ritual or the person; it is the truth expressed, regardless of the form or ritual."

There were hands calling for attention but I fended them off. "I know you want to be heard, but for some time you've been asking about definitions and I'm giving them to you, or at least some of the difficulties of defining Sufism. But you, those of you who have left some formal religion because you were made to believe certain things that you object to, or because you can't do this or that, listen up:

"Rumi taught, 'All religions are in substance one and the same' (Whinfield, 139).

"'All religions are one,' says Abu Bakr (Abu Bakr, 9).

"Hazrat Inayat Khan says, 'There is one religion, the unswerving progress in the right direction towards the ideal, which fulfills the life's purpose of every soul' (Khan, *The Sufi Message*, I:16).

"So, taking it from his words, is the *name* of the religion important to Khan? And is there one set of rules and regulations, one book to adhere to? No, it is going in the 'right direction' toward the ideal. Almost parallel to that is Orage's statement—Orage was a Gurdjieff student. 'There is only one art,' he says, 'the art of making a complete human being of oneself.' Substitute 'religion' for 'art' and the two statements are almost identical.

"There's an old story about the Greek philosopher who went about with a lighted lantern in the daytime. People asked, 'What are you looking for?' He said, 'I'm looking for a human being.'

"So, between 'love' and becoming a human being, and seeking the truth, and tasting and experiencing, you have a good handle on what Sufism is.

"As for bibles and holy books, perhaps the thing with Sufis is that it is open to further development, further truths, and while they honor all people 'of a book'; in essence they feel, as Inayat Khan puts it:

> There is one Holy Book, the sacred manuscript of nature, the only scripture which can enlighten the reader. . . . The Sufi has in all ages respected all sacred books—the Koran, the bible, the Torah—the same truth which he reads in the incorruptible manuscript of nature . . . the perfect and living model that teaches the inner law of life; all scriptures before nature's manuscript are as little pools of water before the ocean . . . to the eye of the seer every leaf of the tree is a page of the holy book that contains divine revelation, and he is inspired every moment of his life by constantly reading and understanding the holy script of nature . . . When man writes he inscribes characters upon rock, leaf, paper, wood or steel; when God writes, the characters He writes are living creatures.
>
> (Khan, *The Sufi Message*, I:47)

"The best of the Sufis, the poets and mystics, to whom the critics and scholars look for direction, go beyond any ordinary restrictions which demand that a 'Sufi' shall be a Muslim, a student of the Koran, must wear the patched robe or conform to a dress code, do certain dances and must belong to some order, because orthodoxy and Sufism do not travel the same road unless accidentally and then only for a short time.

"We begin to move from what it is not to more clearly what it is. Ghazzali, one of the Sufis who came closest to conforming to Islam claimed that Sufism is the inner teaching of all religions (Shah, *The Sufis*, 152) while Ibn El Arabi shocked the devout with this poem:

> My heart is capable of every form:
> A cloister for the monk, a fane [a forum] for idols,

A pasture for gazelles, the votary's Ka'ba [temple],
The tables of the Torah, The Quran.
Love is the creed I hold: wherever turn
His camels, Love is still my creed and faith.

(Shah, *Thinkers of the East*, 145)

"What is his religion? Love! To take the Sufis seriously is to take love seriously. Remember? 'All crime is due to a lack of love. All ignorance is a lack of love'—the quote with which we began this section."

They not only were quiet but had grown placid. Not good.

"The main thing to take away, aside from love and the book of nature, is the lack of orthodoxy, the insistence on the search itself and the freedom to discover. Nicholson says, 'The Sufis are not a sect, they have no dogmatic system, the tariqas or paths by which they seek God are in number as the souls of men . . .'"

"Would you interpret that," said Sam who, for ten minutes had been trying to say something. "And do you mind slowing down?"

"Sure, okay: Sufis, in effect, seek out their own path to perfection. There is no single way. Even if you are under a Murshid, or teacher, it is your choice to put yourself under that person's discipline, and even under that person it is *your* understanding of the teaching. Outside of that there is an infinite number of paths, as many as there are people. You move in your own way at your own speed . . . at your *own* speed, Sam.

"From *Life as Laughter*, Rajneesh says: 'Everybody will find his or her way to God if that person is not hindered by priests and prevented by religions' (Mullen, 35)."

Hands were going up to stop me right there but I read on: "'Religion is rebellion . . . against death, politics, greed, society, culture and civilization.'"

"Is he saying that religions stand in the way?" Joanne was laughing, like a child let out of school.

"Hindered by priests?" said Mike. "I was brought up in the Catholic religion and they were very helpful to me. And I *know* I'm going to heaven when I die."

"I've never heard of anything so *wild!* Religion is rebellion against *what?*" said Holly, who often took the side of society against those barbarians storming the gates.

"One at a time . . . but first, I can't believe that you haven't heard this kind of thing said before. Keep in mind that we're talking about two kinds of religion: esoteric and exoteric. And I don't, for a second, mean that the Methodist church, the Baptist church, or the Catholic church are in rebellion. Far from it. All of those just-named are exoteric, in form, and ally themselves with the government and the powers-that-be, in war and out the other side. But when we're talking about 'religion' in the inner, the most serious sense, the esoteric sense, we're talking, for example, about what Jesus stood for and what he was killed for: love, understanding, healing, and fighting the good fight against politics and greed."

"I thought he died for our sins," Mike said, although it was something of a question.

"Think! Can anyone take away *our* 'sins'? Our having 'missed the mark'? When we're hungry, can anyone eat a meal for us? When we're sad, can someone be happy *for* us? The first man who climbed Mt. Whitney, the highest mountain—Everest, thank you—Sir Edmund Hillary, gave his achievement to the Queen of England. Marvelous. So, without stepping out of her palace she had climbed Mt. Whitney . . . uh, Everest. Nice, and very courtly, but it was his achievement no matter what he says.

"What happened to Christ is, really, lost in history, lost in a myriad of conflicting accounts. 'He says he's God,' they claimed and, in the way we have been speaking of consciousness, we should be able to understand that. So? Let him be. 'I am the way, I am the truth, Love is the way . . .' It is complicated and filled with traps and depends on varying and different versions.

But when one begins to see that there is nothing that is separate from God, that it is *all* God, then one may be excused for claiming that he or she is God, because everything is God.

"Then others pick it up. 'That fellow calls himself God.'

"'So? Let it be.'

"'No, more and more people are coming to believe him.'

"'Then kill him.'

"'Yes! We can't have that sort of thing.'

"Then, in all their mercy, they give him one more chance to renounce. Who was the Italian astronomer-scientist who did the experiments from the Leaning Tower of Pisa? Yes, Galileo, and the Catholic church told him to take back the results of his findings or they would kill him. And so he did some additional calculations and decided he'd misspoken himself. I'm joking, and this is a very brief rendition, but he did recant, briefly, and lived to tell about it.

"Did any of you read about the basketball player who refused to stand for the playing of the national anthem? Incidentally, he is within his legal rights not to stand. But he was also receiving death threats and, when the management of the team realized that the fans would probably start boycotting the games, they suspended him and were ready to cancel his contract, etc. I think his manager explained to the player, and the management, and he's back. He still feels the same way, that the flag is a symbol of oppression, especially for blacks, but as long as he goes through the motions the people have calmed down again and will allow him to win games for them. Exoterically he played the game. Esoterically, his views are the same as they were before. And people are satisfied with the exoteric, the show . . . of respect, obedience, etc.

"Jesus tried to explain, in effect, that we are all sons of God, that we are all the Truth, in the same way Walt Whitman claims nothing for himself that he doesn't claim for every man and woman. No good. Jesus wouldn't renounce and so he was killed, in that peculiar way, hung up on a cross.

"But that was way back then before they knew how to kill people efficiently. In 1996 it just takes a little injection. No fuss no muss."

The board of trustees table was a seething mass of hands waving, moans and groans, heads flopping down on the table, up again to talk to others who were talking back at the same time.

I let them talk. Danny, I was surprised to discover, was totally for it. He agreed wholeheartedly, so did Carole and Sam, and Joanne, with some reservations. Carlito was laughing and nodding and seemed pleased. Jodie, who gained the floor for a minute, told everyone, "When the Catholic church wanted to control my sex life that was *it*—" but it was with a kind of angry regret. If they could have bent a little, she seemed to say, she would have been their devoted child.

Bess shouted for one and all, "Can we please have a break? I really need a cigarette."

"Good," I told them and we stopped.

I motioned for her to come over before she could leave. She did and I told her, "I *had* to let you out. I'm afraid to cross you. Your father might kill me."

"Now that's not fair," she said.

"I'm just joking."

She pointed a warning finger at me, but she was smiling.

* * *

When they came back I warned them again, "Whether you agree with a lot of this or not, you should know that one of the prominent Sufi mystics, Abu Bakr, in addition to agreeing that all religions are really one and the same, said, 'As to the term Sufi, it may not be applied, strictly speaking, to anyone who has not reached the End of the journey.'

"Of course, he is more orthodox than many others and states that without Sufism, the Islamic religion would be like a circumference without a centre, and that the first Sufi is the Prophet himself. So, he is dating the beginning of Sufism with Mohammed's life."

"Well, I'm confused," said Bess.

"Too much nicotine," I told her.

"On second thought, I'm not confused; I have some questions. We are being told that Sufism always existed, that all religions are really one and the same. And, now, that it begins with the life of Mohammed and that it is the very center of the Islamic religion. Which is it?"

"Very good question—"

"I want to talk about Catholicism and heaven," Mike demanded.

"Okay, we will, Mike—"

Carole was already answering Bess. "That's because no one single person speaks for the Sufis—"

"Good . . . Carole, good answer and good question. No one person does speak for the whole mass of people who follow the Sufi way or claim to. Not even other Sufis speak for the whole movement. But there is something else here. They don't argue, the Sufis who claim that it always existed, they don't claim that it was always called 'Sufism.' The Alchemists, esoteric Buddhism, Taoism, forms of Zen, Vedanta—under whatever name, the same search has always gone on, ignoring orthodox religion or the religion of the state, and still choosing the best from it, taking that, the inner core, of whatever religion or religions were in practice. Whether it was called 'alchemy' or 'esoteric Christianity' or whatever.

"I guess Rumi comes closest to expressing the attitude or philosophy or body of knowledge of Sufism, but I don't believe that even he meant to *fix* it at some point or other. Like the English language, it is still growing and needs new expressions in the language of the times. But, in the first place, you must have the inclination to know something different than is being taught in the world. People might call it an appeal to the commercial when I mention Peggy Lee's song, 'Is that all there is?' But I consider it a profound question. It embodies that wish to know something more than is being taught in the world.

"Inayat Khan, without insisting on prerequisites, says:

> . . . there is the feeling, especially after reading or hearing something about Sufism, that one is already really a Sufi, that one is at one with the circle of Sufis. One may now feel drawn to the spirit of the Teacher from whose hand initiation may be taken. . . . Initiation, or in Sufi terms *Bayat*, first of all has to do with the relationship between the pupil and the Murshid. The Murshid is understood to be the counsellor on the spiritual path. He does not give anything to or teach the pupil, the mureed, for he cannot give what the latter [the pupil] already has; he cannot teach what his soul has always known. What he does in the life of the mureed is to show him how he can clear his path toward the light within by his own self.
>
> (Khan, *The Sufi Message*, I:47)

"One more point, Mike, and then we'll talk about heaven, hell, God, and the Catholic church." Mike was a little defensive and, because of my answer, I added, "And those too are important points. Nothing that we've been brought up with can be taken lightly. Before we do that just keep in mind that when one person uses the term 'Sufi' it does not necessarily mean the same thing as when another person uses it. When one person uses it, it is a term for the highest achievement possible, only to be used for Jesus—yes, Jesus—or Mohammed, or Buddha. On the other hand, just a few weeks ago, a rather wealthy woman at a social gathering asked me what I was doing this summer and when I told her, she told me, 'Oh, how interesting. I was with some Sufis just a few months ago in Italy.' She mentioned the duke of so and so and the count so and so. 'We also went to Turkey,' she said, 'to Konya. You've been to Konya, haven't you?'

"'No,' I answered.

"'You *haven't*? You're teaching a course about Sufism and you haven't been to Konya?'

"Since I still had not gone to Konya, all I could answer was another no. I then made, in her eyes, the fatal mistake of asking her why it was so important.

"'But that's where it all started! That's where Rumi was born and is buried.'

"She was truly shocked. So, since I still haven't been to Konya perhaps we should cancel this group, and all go home."

"Call us when you get back from Konya," said Danny.

"Yes, I will. Her remarks reminded me of courses in Shakespeare, in which the Globe theater and London during Elizabethan times easily took preference over what Shakespeare was talking about. Alright, Mike, let's hear it?"

"Well," he squirmed in his chair, "I just think that the idea of going about it any old way, just choose your path, and do whatever you want, is a little wacky."

"So do I, Mike."

"But—"

"He's not saying that," said Sam.

"Close to it," said Holly.

"Look, I never said, do whatever you want and call it Sufism! And think of yourself as being on the path to enlightenment! And that you've got to go to Konya as a first step. Just because the quote is: 'The tariqas or paths by which they seek God are in number as the souls of men . . .'"

"Then I don't get it."

"I know that a lot of this is strange and new and so when I talk about our consciousness and never dying, and freedom, it is strange to your ears, but partly, when you say 'This *can't* be true,' I have to take a chance and without demeaning your point of view, tell you that, the main reason why it *can't* be true is that you've never heard it before. 'Nobody ever told me that before so it can't be true.'

"Got it? Things are true only if we hear them over and over again. Now, in terms of what we can understand more easily, that is called the Big Lie Technique, used by Hitler during World War II—"

"I don't know anything about that," said Mike. "I just know I'm going to heaven and, according to certain things you say, you make fun of it."

"Well, I'm sorry it seems that way but when I say that I don't believe in a heaven outside of us, what I'm really saying is that we are already in heaven, we're there but don't know it, and that makes all the difference. In the same way, if we see the rope in the road and take it for a snake, it might as well be a snake because of our belief. But we're wrong. It's a rope.

"The Buddhists say an interesting thing: basically, the sense of Buddhism is not trying to find something one doesn't have, like heaven, but simply to recover what one does have without knowing it.

"Alcoholics say 'heaven is when I stopped drinking.' Anyhow, I take it that heaven is where God is, right? Mike? Wouldn't that be your idea?"

"What? I'm getting lost—"

"When you say you're going to heaven . . . that would be to be with God, right?"

"Yes . . . of course."

"Well, Vedanta students believe that the only thing that stands in our way is our ignorance. That, really, we are already there."

"You see," said Mike, "but that's exactly the kind of thing I don't understand. Some of this makes sense, but . . ."

"That's all I'm asking for. That and to stay open, and listen, and pick up what makes sense to you. But don't *stick* on things, just because you've carried them around with you for years and years."

"But this I know! I just know it."

"About heaven?"

"Yes."

"Abu Bakr, Sufi, said, in refuting the charge of pantheism, that 'the Sufi . . . does not for one minute imagine that God is in the world; but he knows that the world is mysteriously plunged in God' (Abu Bakr, 11). And if the world is 'plunged in God,' then you are already there."

"You can talk like that all day and it's a mystery to me."

"But Mike, that's fine. It *is* a mystery. Let it be. To me these things are like jewels. They dazzle me. I play with them. Have fun. Lighten up. Let your mind play with these things. I'm only trying to make sense out of it all, for myself and for you. But in making sense, or trying to, I have to ask you and myself, what do you think of heaven? This place? And when I ask you and myself questions about heaven I'm not insulting you. I am only asking you to question what you believe in and that won't hurt your belief. I am not insulting you when I ask you to tell me something about it. Where is this Heaven? Is it in space? Is everyone weightless? Is it 'up there'? Because 'up there' is 'down there' in twelve hours. Is it on a different planet? Can you name the planet or the place in space? Can you tell me what the other inhabitants do when they're there? Can you give me a typical day? When a person dies we know that the body stays here. Does something leave the body? I think we can all agree that it does. But up there in heaven does your body eventually get there, too? And become reconstituted? At what age? Or do you have a body in Heaven? Is it the same as your earthly body? Can you have your favorite dish at any time of the day or night? Can you have sex in heaven? Is there ice cream?

"There's nothing flip about these questions. They are good solid questions. Mark Twain asked the same questions about heaven. He surmised that people would be singing hymns with the angels all day. He pointed out that people have a hard enough time sitting through an ordinary church sermon. Think about all day and night sermons and hymn-singing, for eternity.

Now, if that is *not* what happens, then try and conjure up a picture of what really does happen. What would you *like* heaven to be like? And is it going to be your choice what it will be like? Or will it be out of your hands? I mean, are you going to have a say in what happens up there, or out there? And if what is going to happen in heaven is totally out of your hands then are you sure you would like to go there?

"Look, I don't know the answers to these questions, and I am not saying that it doesn't exist, but the fact that no one can answer these questions adequately is the reason why this Sanskrit scholar and teacher of Vedanta, Swami Dayananda, says 'heaven is unverifiable' and if it is, since it is . . . let's at least examine it and talk about what the concept of heaven is all about."

"Well, I feel like you're making fun of my beliefs, even right now."

"Why do you say that? I think these are extremely important questions; and if you're certain you're going there it seems to me that someone, the ones who keep promising you that you are going there, must know something about it. If you can say you absolutely believe you're going there but no one has been able to answer even the most rudimentary questions about it— they have not been able to tell you one single detail of what happens in heaven—and if you still believe that that is where you're going when you die, then maybe you'd like to buy the Brooklyn Bridge—"

"Now, Taylor, I think Mike is right."

"Yes, about the Brooklyn Bridge—" said Holly.

Mike was quiet and allowed himself to be defended. My ears were burning.

"You're right. I was carried away. But, I guess, sometimes, I feel pushed . . . about getting you to see . . . a different view. And Mike, you say that you were not convinced by someone else about heaven but think hard, think back. As a little kid you were happy and not worried and you certainly didn't come upon the concept of heaven by yourself. Someone gave you the word 'heaven' and when you asked what it was all about someone had to have told you about it. Am I right?"

"I just know that I have this conviction."

"Okay, fine. And believe me when I truly say, someone can also have the absolute conviction that the piece of rope in the road is, really, a snake. They can be so convinced that they can even see the 'snake' move. And we *have* to use these stories, these little examples, and apply them to our innermost convictions. Which sometimes—I said sometimes—are only things we have believed for so long that they are like a skin graft, and just that hard to peel off of our body of beliefs.

"However, it is not part of the Sufi teachings to proselytize or to attack someone's convictions, only sometimes I have to wonder about your reactions. If I tell you that the Twenty-One Club has a new Mexican beer you go, 'Wow! Great! Let's check it out tonight!' But when I tell you that the bible was translated from Hebrew to Greek by the Essenes who made up the story of Eve and Adam's rib, and the serpent and the Garden of Eden, when, really, Adam and Eve, according to Moses, were created at the exact same time as 'Mankind . . . man *and* woman,' I get almost no reaction."

"Maybe that's because," said Jodie, "most of us, women, already know that men and women are equal and are just waiting for men to catch up."

"Good, Jodie, but you've missed the point. Whether you were ever taken in by this myth or not, you are still subject to the effects of 2,000 years of propaganda, give or take a few hundred years, which has affected all of us, that women are lower beings, that they are evil, because, after all, they took the first bite of the apple and charmed or seduced Adam into eating the apple also, and so women are the cause of the downfall of man. And that, still, like an evil wind, blows through the Western world.

"And you are affected by it because of every man you come into contact with who isn't as advanced as you are. And I might as well say, by every woman who has, in turn, been influenced by the same myths. And that may disgust you, or irritate you, or make you explain your view to them, but it still affects you. Directly and indirectly.

"That's enough. Next time we will take the story 'Why the Clay Birds Flew Away,' a story about Jesus as a young boy. Do that one, and think about what has been said today. Mike and anyone else of you who have questions, stick around and we'll talk some more. Okay? To the rest of you, bye bye, and see you tomorrow."

WHY THE CLAY BIRDS FLEW AWAY

One day Jesus, the son of Mary, while a child, was fashioning small birds out of clay. Some other youngsters who could not do so ran to the elders and told them, with many complaints. The elders said: "This work cannot be allowed on the Sabbath," for it was a Saturday.

Accordingly, they went to the pool where the Son of Mary was sitting and asked him where his birds were. For answer he pointed to the birds which had been fashioned and they flew away.

"Making birds which fly is impossible, therefore it cannot be a breaking of the Sabbath," said one elder.

"I would learn this art," said another.

"This is no art, it is but deception," said a third.

So the Sabbath was not broken, the art could not be taught. As for deception, the elders as well as the children had deceived themselves, because they did not know what the object of the fashioning of the birds was.

The reason for doing no work on Saturday had been forgotten. The knowledge of what is a deception and what is not was imperfect to those elders. The beginning of art and the end of action was unknown to them: thus it was also with the lengthening of the plank of wood.

It is further related that one day Jesus, the son of Mary, was in the workshop of Joseph the Carpenter. When a plank of wood was found to be too short, Jesus pulled it, and it was found to have become in some way lengthened.

When this story was told to the people, some said: "This is a miracle, therefore this child will be a saint."

Others said: "We do not believe it, do it again for us."

A third party said: "This cannot be true, therefore exclude it from the books."

The three parties with their different feelings, yet got the same answer because none knew the purpose and the real significance lying within the statement: "He stretched a plank."

* * *

Sufi authors make frequent reference to Jesus as a Master of the Way. There is, in addition, an enormous body of oral tradition about him current in the Middle East, which awaits a collector. This tale is found, in slightly different forms, in more than one dervish collection. Sufis say that "Son of a Carpenter" and other vocational names given to Gospel characters are initiatory terms, not necessarily describing the individual's work.

(Shah, *Tales of the Dervishes*, 56-7)

13

God's Tired; Don't Bother Him/Her

I wondered as I drove to the meeting. Wondered and asked myself about how much to share with them. Was God tired from making all those mountains? Were the Himalayas much harder than the rest? Tired from digging out oceans? And that is why we should rest on the seventh day? Because God rested then? Who kept track of it? Who was there? Did someone blow a whistle? Okay, time's up! You've either botched it or done it, but time's up! now rest.

Does God get tired? Does he get Almighty Tired? Do His Muscles Ache?

Adam and Eve were kicked out of the Garden of Eden. Why? Because they disobeyed God, who told them they could do anything they wanted but could not eat of the fruit of the tree of knowledge? Did God *want* them to eat of that tree? If he really didn't want them to eat of it, why put it there at all? And didn't he *know* they would eat of it? Doesn't he—or she—have foreknowledge?

And Eve was created from Adam's rib? Why didn't God create them at the same time? Didn't he know that Adam would need a mate? According to the bible, he created *them* mankind, man and woman and called *them* Adam. After that comes the rib story. So, then, was the rib story tacked on later? To make women depend on men?

Was Eve really an afterthought? Does God have after-thoughts? Does God make mistakes? Does God need a rest after working for six days? Does he take vacations? Where does he go?

Mr. Carr, the neighborhood father to me and my friends, was irritated with one of us. We were about ten years old and Walter had accidentally broken one of Mr.Carr's tools. "Walter," he told my friend, "You're as useless as a man's tits." All that day and most of the night I thought about it. What were my "tits" there for if they had no function? Did God make a mistake?

I pulled into the parking area and everyone was already there. They seemed enthusiastic and ready. I did tell them about Walter, and they enjoyed it immensely.

"Okay, Sara, what do you think? About 'Why the Clay Birds Flew Away'? Did you have a feeling I was going to call on you?"

"Yes, I did."

"Well, I didn't want to disappoint you."

"How about one day, just one day, calling on me when I raise my hand?"

"Sara, just tell me one thing about this story."

"You mean apart from not understanding it? . . . Okay, to me it doesn't seem to be a story about Jesus but about some little brats and their do-good parents."

"Excellent. See, you understand it but don't trust yourself. Jesus has very little to do with the story. Outside of making the birds fly away. And there's even something peculiar about that; what is it?"

No answers.

"Read that section where the birds fly away, Sara."

"Well, he just makes the birds, points at them and they fly away."

"Yes, but *when?* There's a sequence to it . . ."

"I see it," said Carole. "He first makes the clay birds and when the elders come back, because of the children complaining, they ask him where the birds are . . ."

By this time there was a full chorus of discoverers.

". . . they didn't fly till he pointed at them."

"Right. And he didn't point till the elders asked where the birds were. So, was there any miracle to it, until the elders came back in answer to the children's complaints?"

"No. He was just making clay birds. Is that work?"

"Good question. It seems more like play. So, then, what did the elders come back for?"

"I think," Sara said, "they just came back to stop him."

"Do you all agree?"

"Yes . . . they're like small-town cops who stop people because they have nothing better to do," said Carlito.

Sam was tickled about the remark because Carlito was a special favorite of the local police and had been stopped, as he said, "three days running."

"In Gurdjieff terms, the devil is man's terrible power of misunderstanding everything . . . the power of wrongly connecting everything. The elders in the story 'Why the Clay Birds Flew Away' don't see miracles; they see that whatever it was happened on the Sabbath. In *The Way of the Sufi* we are told, "To be a Sufi is to detach from fixed ideas and from preconceptions . . ." (Shah, *The Way of the Sufi*, preface) All of the people in the story, except for Jesus, are trapped by preconceptions and fixed ideas. You *can't* do that. Or you *shouldn't* do that! Or I won't let you do that. Or since I can't do it you should not be allowed to do it. Or you *didn't* do that! Or I don't believe you did that . . . do it again.

"Not one of them stops to wonder about why he did it, or how, or about the appropriateness of what is being done. Jesus is supposed to have healed a person who had been bedridden for thirty-eight years. He told the man to rise up and carry his bed and walk. The man did it. The authorities could only 'see' that it had been done on the Sabbath. The man explained that Jesus had healed him, and there was never a thought as to what was done or why, just that it was done on the wrong day. You get in an accident and it's not who is right; it's who doesn't have his papers. Either driver's license or insurance. If you don't have those you're wrong.

"The man he cured pointed out Jesus to the authorities and that was the beginning of the end. The children in the story are envious and so they tell on him. The elders arrive and dismiss the deed in various ways.

"But the story is not about miracles. The accent is on the reaction to whatever it is he's doing. The accent is on how they, the elders, and even the children, concentrate on everything *but* the miracle. People seem always to be looking in the wrong direction. They look at what*ever* happened as to whether it was at the right time, the right day, or if it broke a law. These are things they can understand.

"As for miracles in themselves, I'm afraid that for most of us we wouldn't *see* a miracle if it happened in front of us because we don't believe that certain things *can* happen. That only things approved of by Science can happen. Thus we have the numerous cases, presented in Charles Hoy Fort's *The Book of the Damned*, of thousands of people having witnessed a rain of frogs, a rain of mud, and many other unexplainable things that have happened, and because there is no scientific explanation for these things they are dismissed, as if they never happened. As a matter of fact, we can't even *see* things that take place . . . if we are convinced that they *can't* take place, or that they really *shouldn't* take place. It can't rain mud! It *can't* rain frogs. And down come the frogs. And down comes the mud. But . . . but . . . it *can't* be! And in 'Why the Clay Birds Flew Away,' the elders see it happening and don't believe it because they *can't* believe it, and so they haggle about the law being broken, or that what they've just seen didn't happen at all. Oh, on the wrong day, eh? Well, then, he's breaking the law. They never face what it was that was done. Some of them want him to do it again. Some of them would like to learn this trick. But Jesus can do certain things because he *is* . . . and what one *is* cannot be taught. What the Sufi hermit, who walks on water, *is* cannot be taught.

"There's an interesting note about Jesus making clay birds in the Koran. As the note mentions, Jesus doesn't 'figure largely,' but he figures:

> The miracles of Jesus do not figure largely in the Quran; v.3:43-46 . . . The last hemistich refers to 3:43. 'I will create for you out of clay as though it was the form of a bird, and I will blow thereon and it shall become a bird by God's permission.'
>
> (Keddie, 66-7)

"How many of you knew that Jesus is mentioned in the Koran?"

Oddly enough, Bess knew. Her father, who had been in the Middle East for a six-month stretch, had always been struck by the fact that Jesus and certain miracles attributed to him were in the Koran.

"You see, they recognize Jesus; healing the sick, stones into bread and so forth, but we don't recognize Muhammad.

"At the end of the story, the plank stretching takes place in the workshop of Joseph the Carpenter. The note states that vocational terms don't necessarily describe the individual's work. Maybe 'stretching a plank' is to do something that needs doing. The 'real but not the obvious thing to do.' Birds are also a symbol for thoughts. Hermes is represented as Sufi Truth, and is often represented as Simurgh, the king of birds. To breathe life into thoughts is to give *action* to them . . . to turn thoughts into action . . . clay birds into living birds—"

"Well, I don't mean to be disrespectful, but you're beginning to sound like the elders in the story." It was Carlito, and somehow he delivered that remark with respect and friendliness.

Carole gave him a big thumbs up. And Joanne added: "You know, *maybe* . . . he pointed at the birds and they *flew!* Just as the story says. I don't mind the miracle. In a way, it's not the miracles that get me, about religion; it's that someone should be worshipped . . . *because of a miracle*—does that make sense?"

All I could do was gaze in wonder.

Joanne was followed by Sam: "So, I don't *care* whether Jesus rose from the dead. We won't know, for sure, but maybe he did. At least, I have come to the point where I can believe . . . like you said, all sorts of things can happen. And life is more than we have imagined. I feel like my borders are . . . expanding."

"Do you guys realize how different this is from the way you were during those first days?" And you know, I was beginning to feel it myself. All of the words, all of the symbolism. Let the story be. Let it do for you what it can. Read it and let it work on you.

"As for the second part of the story, and stretching the plank. Again, we don't have to decide if it is a miracle, and what is the meaning of it. The reaction of the elders was the same as usual. One said it's a miracle, so he will be a saint, another said, do it again I don't believe it, and a third party said, it can't be true so strike it from the books."

"Well, what *is* the meaning of 'stretching the plank'?" asked Holly.

"I think it is in the realm of what is appropriate. The plank was too short, he pulled it, and it was found to have become lengthened, in some way."

"But, I mean, how do you explain it?" insisted Holly.

"I don't know, and, before you ask the question, I don't know about the birds being pointed at and flying off. It's a story, a teaching tale, and so keep your mind on that. So, we're back to Sara's statement, that it's not really so much about Jesus but rather a story about the elders and what they see and what they can't see. And what they make of it. The emphasis is not on the miracles, but on what is appropriate, on what needs doing. But I do say that people with powers don't talk about them, and they don't do them for the amusement of others or on social occasions, as if you'd ask a magician to 'do that trick again.' There's nothing casual about it.

"Listen, we could continue on with the topic of religion for the remainder of the meetings, but there are other things we have to do. There are stories that pertain to it and much other material besides that, but I am going to try and kill two birds with one stone . . . before they fly away. The woman question and miracles. What is a miracle? Something we believe can't, logically, take place. And yet it does. Depending upon our mind-set: we can't see it (believe it); it didn't happen; it shouldn't happen. Try not to either be dazzled or put off by the mention of miracles. If people claim they can fly, really fly, I'm not impressed until they prove to me they can fly from here to the West Coast, first class, and can get there in ten minutes. And even then, wouldn't it be an even greater miracle not to *need* to fly from here to the West Coast? To have everything you need right with you? To be complete in yourself? To stop needing the spectacular? I know that sounds old-fashioned but . . . As for real accomplishments, how about waking up happy in the mornings, and staying that way? How about having your pet corn stepped on and not losing your temper?

"Anyhow, this is about Rabi'a, the great female Sufi saint:

> From early on the Sufis counted women among those importantly contributing to their tradition and included such women as Rabi'a al-'Adawiyya (d.801) among the ranks of the most elect of spiritual leaders. Moreover, Sufi tales and legends incorporate elements that suggest a rejection of the values of the dominant society with regard to women.
>
> The narratives about Rabi'a al-'Adawiyya, for instance, most of which are clearly legendary, exemplify distinctly counter-cultural elements with respect to ideas about gender. The notion underlying all male-female interaction in the dominant society, that biology and sexuality govern relations between the sexes, for example, is clearly repudiated by one short

Sufi narrative. In it, the highly esteemed Sufi leader Hasan al-Basri (d.728) declares, 'I passed one whole night and day with Rabi'a speaking of the Way and the Truth, and it never passed through my mind that I was a man nor did it occur to her that she was a woman, and at the end when I looked at her I saw myself as bankrupt [i.e. as spiritually worth nothing] and Rabi'a as truly sincere [that is, rich in spiritual virtue].' The tale also reverses the dominant society's valuation of male over female, by representing not merely any man but one of the most revered male Sufi leaders describing himself as 'bankrupt' compared with a woman of truly superior merits. . . . In another tale, again featuring Hasan al-Basri, he approaches Rabi'a, who is sitting on a bank with a number of contemplators. Throwing his carpet on the water, Hasan sits on it and calls to Rabi'a to come and converse with him. Rabi'a, understanding that he wants to impress people with his spiritual powers, throws her carpet into the air, flies up to it, and sitting there says, 'Oh, Hasan, come up here where people will see us better.' Hasan is silent because it is beyond his power to fly. 'Oh, Hasan,' Rabi'a then says, 'that which you did a fish can do . . . and that which I did a fly can do. The real work [for the saints of God] lies beyond both of these.'

(Keddie, 66-7)

"What I am trying to call attention to—just as she is—is that the miracles are a minor issue. Don't decide for or against these ideas on the basis of miracles."

"I know we've talked about this before, but I'm not clear about the Sufis and 'right' and 'wrong,'" said Holly.

"In a way, that's an easy question but the problem is how to understand it:

In regard to the Sufi's attitude toward right and wrong—that these are man-made—one may ask how then it can matter what a person does. The answer is, it matters to those to whom it matters, and it does not matter to those to whom it does not matter. The first says that Sufis leave all religions and cleave to the truth. The other makes of it a religion and insists on ritual, set practices, an initiation fee, a 'recognized school.'"

(Khan, *The Sufi Message*, I:57-8)

"I don't quite get it. It's like not being praiseworthy or blameworthy? Is that it?" asked Holly.

"I think it's that we have got to stop seeing things in terms of right and wrong and good and bad. That they really are man-made. It should come as a relief but instead it comes as a shock because we are afraid of freedom."

"What??"

"Yes. Fearful of freedom. Whatever the issue is: right and wrong are man-made. Regardless of whether it is in books. Even if it's in leather-bound books. We're trying not to follow someone else; your own truth-search is what you are on. So, it is not 'right' and 'wrong' but 'hitting the mark' or 'missing the mark.' Not 'right' and 'wrong,' not 'good and 'bad,' and doing your best to hit the mark without guilt about missing it because 'guilt' goes with 'good' and 'bad' and we're leaving that.

"Look, let's take a break. Think about that but it's time. Besides, Bess is dying for a cigarette."

"I didn't say that! I didn't say anything. I'm fine."

"Well, *I* need a break," I told her.

"So do I," said Danny.

"I'm stunned," said Carole.

When I turned to her she just shook her head. "It's so simple," she said. "I agree, but I have to live with this awhile."

"I also agree," I told her. "It is a big change, and we're brainwashed and have been, for so long. Years and years of it."

* * *

When they came back in, Mike told us something that had been bothering him for a while. "I know what you're saying . . . and I can really see it . . . but, well, I think that people really ought to believe in *some*thing."

"I think they should be let alone . . . to discover."

"Well, aren't they? Don't you think they are?" he asked. "After all, we have freedom of religion; you can freely decide and practice your belief in this country. That's what our forefathers fought for."

"Okay, as a country Americans claim, and are very proud of the claim, that we allow freedom of religion. But if it isn't some form of Christianity, exoteric Christianity, the practice is looked on by a majority of Americans with a little suspicion. Even Judaism falls into this category. The others— Buddhism, Mohammedanism, and others—are more openly suspect. The very orthodox Christians want prayer-in-schools. They want Jesus Christ and God, and they mean the Christian Jesus and God. The others, those who claim religions other than Christianity, and still others who are concerned about our freedoms, worry about this infringement on their freedom to practice what they want. Are you with me so far? I mean, should people be allowed to practice what they want?"

Most of them nodded, some said yes, some abstained.

"Bess? Mike?"

"Sure," said Bess.

Mike said, "Yeah. I don't care what they do."

"Suppose, under their freedom, they choose to worship nothing at all? I mean, is that okay, too?"

"How do you worship nothing?"

"Suppose some say, because they have been either disillusioned or fed up with the whole thing, that they don't believe in anything? And don't want *any* religion in their lives?"

"That's okay, too," said Sam.

"And suppose those people forbid their children going to any church?"

"Well, that's interference in the children's lives . . . I think that's wrong."

"So? Who should interfere? Rather than the parents? The federal government?"

"No. I don't know."

"Suppose they want to worship snakes?"

"That would be dangerous to others around them," said Mike.

"Hey, freedom is dangerous. Okay? Are we going to allow it or not?"

"You're free as long as it doesn't endanger others," said Joanne.

"Okay, and that's just about where we are, legally. But as long as legal involves majority rule, or the loudest claque of voters, then our vaunted liberties are in danger.

"A few hundred years ago, although there are still practicing alchemists today, the alchemists were thought to be quasi-chemists, quacks or nuts who were trying to change iron or base metal into gold. And the language of their experiments was in terms of sulphur, mercury, iron, fire, and the melting points of various metals, and involved processes of how to go from one step to another. With just a little investigating it could be discovered that they were an ancient teaching, sometimes called The Work or The Great Work, in which the real purpose was revealed: they were trying to change the base metal of themselves into gold. And The Great Work is really 'work on oneself.' They worked in secret and since it had nothing to do with the 'state religion' they would have been classified as heretics or revolutionaries if their work had been discovered. In Inquisition times they would have been killed.

"So, for reasons of safety and so as not to be interfered with, the alchemists preferred to let the masses of people think that they were about the impossible task of changing iron or lead into gold. And wrote in code for the initiated. Anyone who didn't understand what they were really about thought they were crazy. 'They're all nuts, let 'em go.'"

"Well," said Danny, "they still haven't got prayer in schools, so that probably won't happen."

"Right. But, you know, it has been said, the measure of a society is its treatment of its minorities, and we in America don't do too well by ours. Either minority races or minority religions. Okay, let's break for ten minutes. What did you say?"

"I said 'minority races or women.'"

"Amen."

"Aye women!"

* * *

THE MAN WHO WALKED ON WATER

A conventionally-minded dervish, from an austerely pious school, was walking one day along a river bank. He was absorbed in concentration upon moralistic and scholastic problems, for this was the form which Sufi teaching had taken in the community to which he belonged. He equated emotional religion with the search for ultimate Truth.

Suddenly his thoughts were interrupted by a loud shout: someone was repeating the dervish call. "There is no point in that," he said to himself, "because the man is mispronouncing the syllables. Instead of intoning YA HU, he is saying U YA HU."

Then he realized he had a duty, as a more careful student, to correct this unfortunate person, who might have had no opportunity of being rightly guided, and was therefore probably only doing his best to attune himself with the idea behind the sounds.

So he hired a boat and made his way to the island in midstream from which the sound appeared to come.

Sitting in a reed hut he found a man, dressed in a dervish robe, moving in time to his own repetition of the initiatory phrase. "My friend," said the first dervish, "you are mispronouncing the phrase. It is incumbent upon me to tell you this, because there is merit for him who gives and him who takes advice. This is the way in which you speak it." And he told him.

"Thank you," said the other dervish humbly.

The first dervish entered his boat again, full of satisfaction at having done a good deed. After all, it was said that a man who could repeat the sacred formula correctly could even walk upon the waves: something that he had never seen, but always hoped—for some reason—to be able to achieve.

Now he could hear nothing from the reed hut but he was sure that his lesson had been well taken.

Then he heard a faltering U YA as the second dervish started to repeat the phrase in his old way . . .

While the first dervish was thinking about this, reflecting upon the perversity of humanity and its persistence in error, he suddenly saw a strange sight. From the island the other dervish was coming toward him, walking on the surface of the water . . .

Amazed, he stopped rowing. The second dervish walked up to him and said: "Brother, I am sorry to trouble you, but I have to come out to ask you again the standard method of making the repetition you were telling me, because I find it difficult to remember it."

(Shah, *The Tales of the Dervishes*, 84-5)

14

One False Step

"This is like a joke," said Holly. "The one who thinks he knows and the other who . . . who really does."

"I think the key is at the beginning," said Carole.

"Point it out."

"Well, if you take the description of the first dervish, you know that he is, sort of, being set up."

"Yes," said Dan, "the use of the words 'conventional' and 'pious'—well, you just know he's in for a fall."

"Yes, good. You people don't need me. And so, what else? In the first paragraph? What is he concentrating on?"

"On 'moralistic and scholastic problems.'"

"Yes, instead of what?"

Silence.

"Isn't this about *you?* About how you can overcome your own life attitudes and problems?"

"Yes . . . so—"

"So, instead, he's thinking about other people's problems. Maybe the problems of the world. You know, there's so much here. There's a Sufi quote about scholars: 'Beware! One false step and you might become a scholar.' This is not the direction of the Sufi. As you . . . pointed out to me the other day when I was going on about the Clay Birds: 'This is symbolic of this and that indicates . . .' Keep your feet on the ground . . . and you might be able to walk on water. I'm joking. So, as we see here, there are Sufi communities and there are Sufi communities.

Some are legitimate and others are 'pious' and 'conventional.' Anyone could begin a 'school' and call it a Sufi community or a Sufi order. Who's to stop it? That doesn't mean it's legitimate.

"How often do you see an old store, all boarded up, and in the window is a sign that says: OPEN! The sign is meaningless. Very often, so are words. 'How are you?' 'Fine!' Absolutely meaningless."

"How would you know the difference?" asked Bess. "I mean between a *real* group and the other kind?"

I was glad that Bess had asked about it. Perhaps I had piqued something in Bess, finally.

"Well, this story gives us some clues. If the point of concentration is on the form and on prestige and on right thinking, instead of a search for what is true, then you should know that it is conventional and more concerned with piety and appearances than real; if the concentration is on *you* and your own inner development and not on what only *appears* to be true, then the chances are that you're on the right track."

A number of the group members had asked how I first became interested in the ideas. Now seemed a good time to mention it. "My first contact with these ideas came about through Bayard Rustin, a black activist who, after a talk we had, told me I should get hold of some of the books of Gurdjieff and Ouspensky. I was going to Mexico to write and wanted a book that would challenge me. Not long after that time, just before I was to leave, I was at a party and saw Ouspensky's book *In Search of the Miraculous* on the hostess's shelf. I asked her to tell me about the book and she refused. She told me to read it myself. I told her that maybe she could save me some time by telling me about it, to find out whether I should bother. I'll never forget her answer: 'Read it or don't read it,' she said, 'but I'm not going to tell you about it.'

"Shortly after that experience—actually I had said, 'To hell with the book and to hell with her'—I picked up a copy in a bookstore. Since it dealt with both Ouspensky and Gurdjieff, I bought it. Went down to Mexico and practically ate the book. I have never been so engrossed in a book before.

"When I came back from Mexico, after reading the book twice, I had a chance to join two Gurdjieff groups. One of them insisted on group members wearing a tie and jacket to meetings and referring to Gurdjieff, who had by that time been dead for some thirteen years, as 'Mr. Gurdjieff.' To me these were signs. Do you see that, Bess? And the rest of you?"

"Yes," said Sara. "People insist on these formalities."

"Good. Does it mean I have more respect or love for God if I refer to him as 'Mr. God'? Or 'Mr. Jesus'? Or 'Mr. Rumi'? The emphasis, I felt, was on form, not on substance.

"The other group demanded only an interview. I met the leader of the group, Willem Nyland, and told him what I had read and that I felt I was more a Gurdjieff person than an Ouspensky person. Gurdjieff was the fire, I felt, the real thing, and Ouspensky was the secretary.

"I was accepted into an elementary group and stayed with him for nine years. I don't believe either 'Sufi' or 'Sufism' was mentioned. But Gurdjieff had gone through Sufi training with various teachers and was sent on from one to another.

"Everything I read, mostly after my immersion in the Gurdjieff work, which is also referred to as 'work on oneself,' made me realize that I had been part of a Sufi group. Exercises, tasks, everything about it was the same.

"Anyhow, let me continue with the story under discussion, because we could take any of these broad avenues and talk about them for days, but we have only three or four discussion days left and we still have a lot to cover.

"One question is, why does the Sufi from the pious and conventional school think that he knows the proper way to say the dervish call? I mean, by what authority is he convinced that *his* way is the correct way? Does he have an advanced degree from Harvard?"

"Maybe that's his problem," said Carole.

"Right. And has he himself walked on water or has he seen anyone else walking on water from having practiced the 'correct' way of saying the dervish call? Sara?"

"I *knew* it. No. Otherwise he wouldn't have been so amazed when the other one, the illiterate one, comes out walking on water."

"Well, then, what do you make of it? Anybody?"

Sara answered for us: "There's something in the way that the forest Sufi says the words that . . ."

"Is it just in pronunciation? What if the 'learned' one began to say it the way the other did? Would he then be able to walk on water?"

"No!" said Sam, with conviction.

"Why not?"

"Because . . ." The wind seemed to go out of his sails. "I don't know."

"I think you've got it. Just follow your thought."

"Well, it's not *just* the words. And, I think, because the other Sufi, the pious one, well, there's something wrong with his motivation. He wants to . . . walk on water."

"Or maybe there's something 'right' about the forest Sufi's motivation. Or, as the story says, 'with the idea behind the words.' So? Should that be your motivation? To do miracles?"

"No," said Carole, "your motivation should be to discover the truth, to understand, about life and love."

"Do you see it? You're not running around correcting the world's ills. You're working on yourself. Trying to perfect yourself. And the forest Sufi has been rewarded not for his pronunciation but, perhaps, for the sincerity of his prayers, and his life."

"I don't see that the pious Sufi did anything wrong," said Dan. "He was just trying to help."

"Good point. He didn't. He might have acted a little superior but—"

"He didn't *do* anything wrong," said Carlito, "he *was* wrong."

"Good, Carlito, but *how* wrong? Wrong to think it's just

pronunciation?"

"I don't get this at all," said Bess.

"How about what goes into an utterance? The *breath*, the *tone*, the wish behind the tone. The . . . quality, even of the sincerity . . . real prayer. But the story is also a comment on the pious and conventional.

> But if the following of Islam is understood to mean the obligatory adherence to a certain rite [and] means conforming to certain restrictions, how can the Sufi be placed in that category . . . [since] the Sufi does not follow any special book? . . . To a Sufi, revelation is the inherent property of every soul. There is an unceasing flow of the divine stream, which has neither beginning nor end.
>
> (Khan, *The Sufi Message*, I:56-7)

"One last run-through about heaven. Almost every serious religion or system of thought has included the central idea that we must know ourselves: 'To know thyself is to know God.' This is not limited to any particular belief but it occurs so often in all realms, and appears so regularly in all sorts of books that it cannot be ignored. Add to that the long quote I just read: 'I am all that exists,' and the view that God is all there is; that there is nothing outside of God, and you begin making some huge connections.

"John Milton, in *Paradise Lost*, said that 'the mind can make a hell of heaven or a heaven of hell,' which puts it directly in our laps. And Leo Tolstoy, certainly one of the greatest writers who ever lived, wrote a book called *The Kingdom of Heaven is Within You*. These are Western writers, telling us *we* are responsible. It's in our own hands; but, instead, it's 'Hey, I'd rather just worship in the church. They tell me that if I continue to come regularly, believe in Jesus, that I'll go to this place they call heaven. I also have to live a good life. But if I don't, God will forgive me, if I sincerely repent (be sorry for my sins). Even on my deathbed.'"

Mike waved me away with his hand. "That's not it at all . . ."

"But what if it's true? What if the kingdom of God is really within me? And not 'out there' or 'up there'? And what if I overcome my ignorance—difficult as that may be—and find that heaven is really within me?

"I've told you that Jesus appears in the Koran (Quran) and is recognized as a 'completed man' or a 'perfected man,' and most of you know his last words. Mike, do you know them?"

"No, I'm not sure."

"Forgive them. They know not what they do," said Joanne. "Or something close to that."

"Good. That is our translation of it, anyhow. Well, here is an account of the Sufi martyr Hallaj, known popularly as Mansur:

> He was executed in 922 for saying such things as "I am the truth," and refusing to recant, thus uttering the ultimate blasphemy. He was alleged to be an alchemist. . . . For the Sufis, some of the greatest of whom were his friends and contemporaries, he is one of their greatest masters. . . . He taught that Sufism was the internal truth of all true religion, and because he emphasized the importance of Jesus as a Sufi teacher, he was accused by fanatics of being a secret Christian. . . . His assertion that the Mecca pilgrimage could be performed anywhere, by making suitable dedications and preparations, was considered to be impossibly heretical. . . . On Tuesday, March 26, 922, Hallaj walked to the place of his execution. . . . He was tortured and dismembered, but showed no fear. This was his last public prayer, while he could still speak:
> 'O, Lord, make me grateful for the *baraka* which I have been given in being allowed to know what others

do not know. Divine mysteries which are unlawful to others have become thus lawful to me. Forgive and have mercy upon these Thy servants assembled here for the purpose of killing me; for, had Thou revealed to them what Thou hast revealed to me, they would not act thus.'"

(Shah, *The Sufis*, 425)

"Practically the identical sentiment," said Joanne.

"What's *baraka*?" Sam asked.

"In this case it means 'powers' or 'gifts'. . . . Yes, the speech was a little longer but the same feeling, the same sense. So, here are the two men, both martyrs to the truth, holding almost identical views. Notice that Hallaj (or Mansur) also calls Jesus a Sufi teacher. I am not going to get into that but it could probably be supported, in a few hundred pages. He studied with the Essenes, it is believed. And now we have to move on, even though there are hundreds of areas still to be covered.

"Next time we will begin with You and the World."

"Have we finished with Religion?"

"No, but we haven't *finished* with any other section, either, so let's not break with tradition. And before we finish—I mean, *now*—I want to hear about your three days, your reports on how the experiment went; did you remember to pause at your particular times? Or to pause before picking up your fork, or spoon? Or before reaching for that first bite of food at each meal?"

Again, despite their efforts, they were amazed that, except for a few successes, they had missed their "times" again and again. The pause before eating seemed even more difficult.

"One time," said Sara, "I was ready beforehand, at just before 5:00—my time was 5:00—and I couldn't get away—"

"So, what happened?"

"I was talking. Talking. I didn't do anything about it. Next time I looked at my watch it was 5:20."

"You couldn't get away?"

"Well, it didn't—"

"Couldn't you have excused yourself and gone to the bath-room? Couldn't you have planned ahead and told your friends you would be right back, and go out for a walk?"

Dan caught himself eating, realizing that he had not paused. He failed so completely that he gave up even trying after the second day.

Sam had done quite well the first day, waking up at 6:00 and taking that time to pause and come to himself, but the next day an old roommate came to visit and he had two late nights, and didn't wake up till 8:00 or 9:00 the next two days.

"How do you fail at something like this?" I asked them.

"By not doing it?" said Bess.

"Not quite," I said.

"By not realizing . . . that, in a certain way, we are asleep," said Jodie.

"Jodie," I told her, "that is it, exactly. That was the purpose of the exercise. Even to succeed at the task or exercise should still remind you of all of the thousands, *thousands* of mechani-cal actions we go through each day. Putting on our clothes, putting on your make-up, combing hair, dressing, socks and shoes, brushing teeth, opening and closing doors, walking, reading and studying, jotting down notes, paying for things, counting change, going to the bathroom, eating meals, getting into cars, all of the thousands of things at work that you just *do* without even a thought. This is what is meant when we are told that we go through our lives in sleep. But telling you is no good. You must see it for yourselves. *They* are not asleep . . . *you* are.

"Before the next discussion, we are going to go out on an old road for our exercise. So wear your walking shoes."

You and the World

15

Problems, Choices, Donkeys, and Facts

"Do you all know that road they call the Maple Road? The back road to Jaffrey?"

They nodded.

"Well, get in your cars. We're going out there for about half an hour to work on something. Actually, two cars ought to do it."

Maple Road is not its name, neither is The Back Road to Jaffrey, but it goes by both. It is behind the college, a one-lane road that meanders for about a mile and a half through the woods to join a tarred road near a big maple farm and then, after another mile or so, becomes a paved road to Thorndike Pond and Jaffrey, another small town in southern New Hampshire.

We parked and I collected the group. The entrance to the road is truly like entering a deep forest and the road itself is more like a trail than a road. Pine trees abound and the hardwood trees, maples and oaks, meet overhead, giving the gravel road a sun-dappled effect. On this day the wind was blowing in little gusts. The group was quiet and waiting.

"Okay, here's the plan: I'm going to drive ahead and park about half a mile from here. I want you to walk to the car but I want you to walk with certain things in mind. 1. Whatever awareness or consciousness means to you, we're going to try for it. 2. Do not walk with anyone else. 3. I want you to find your very own pace and don't think of anyone else or where they are.

Maybe you've never walked at your own pace before in your life but now is the time to try and find your own *slow* pace. 4. Now we're getting down to it. For this little walk, I'm asking you to saunter. The word 'saunter' comes from the French *sans terre*, which means 'without a land' or 'without a country.' So, you are trying to walk as though you have no land or, even, no home. You belong to no country. You have no destination. You have no destination because you are already home; you are *here* and this, wherever you are, is home. So, you are home. You carry your home with you. Remember; 'no place' is your home. There is no *where* to go. So, when you can really get into the feeling of no place, no magnet pulling you somewhere—when you are free of aims to get anywhere—that is when you begin, that is sauntering.

"I'll be down the road a ways, but that is my worry. Yours is to forget about time, distances, everything. Yours is to try, with all of your heart, to be there for every step. If you begin losing it, then stop. Collect yourself and start again."

How would they take it? How ready were they? I drove for half a mile, then parked in a little clearing beside the road, got out and sat on a log and waited.

About fifteen minutes later, Sam came into view. He was quiet, sober. A slow smile on his face. Why so quick?

"I wanted to get ahead so as to be really by myself."

"Ahead?"

He blushed. Then began telling: "It changed everything. I saw leaves shimmering. Sort of shivering. I noticed lots more; texture of the earth, rocks, and earth. The sun on my face. I never notice that . . . unless I go to the beach. And trees . . . the trees were almost speaking to me."

"Almost?"

"Yes, maybe *trying* to speak, to get through to me."

"The problem isn't with the trees."

"I know . . ."

In ones, some close on others, some more distant and

wrapped in a cover, auras separating them from each other, up they came, slowly, quietly but, it seemed, contented.

Their reactions, beginning slowly, soon were a waterfall; although I had told them to write down their impressions, it might come later but for now a waterfall:

> Different colors . . . even in the road itself . . . colors, the colors, hundreds of greens and browns, dark brown to tan . . . Earth without trees, that's a road, like the road has been carved out of the earth, like a cut, a wound . . . I was coming into touch . . . into touch with . . . I can't express it . . . My neck was loosening up. I was noticing little tiny flowers I've never seen before . . . That truck passed by. I was thinking, he must think we're all crazy. Then, what does it matter? What he thinks? I realized how much I worry about what other people think of me . . .

"Don't laugh at that. That's a real discovery."

> I discovered I look down a lot, and then let it go, I *let* it go and just looked down, my footsteps, my shadow, where do 'I' begin? . . . I saw water reflecting sky. Blue water looking up at the sky . . . I thought of water like eyes, looking out from the earth. I sat on that big tunnel of pipe that goes under the road and connects the water on both sides. The water was so still. I looked at the water for a long time. I love that swampy area. I just wanted it to *be* there, for always . . . I was thinking my shadow, too. That's *me?* No, I've got to move back to get to me . . . At first hard to slow down. I sat down. Wind like waves on the beach. Wind waves, like the sea; waves of wind . . . All the sounds, crisper sounds, walking sounds and pebbles under my feet. Perfect temperature. I never notice the little things when driving . . .

Pine trees bending in the wind. I was slowing down. Everything so peaceful. Trees making a canopy overhead. I'm relaxed now and refreshed. I was tired when I began . . . Everything was beautiful. Thinking about the wind, breezes, the shape of a breeze. The wind taking shapes and forms. There's a poem about it. Seeing only what it does, *not it*. Like consciousness, that you're always talking about. The wind, we see the results of it, not *it*. Then thinking about my life, how I never really think about my life. And time never stopping. The wind like time. The wind . . . is time!

We ended it there. Six of us piled in the car, the others walked. Another fifteen minutes and we were back at the cabin.

* * *

"We're beginning the last segment of our meetings. And once again I realize that there is no way to divide the various aspects of life. Any division is arbitrary. There is no way that any aspect of life can be separated from religion—unless we're talking about Sunday School and prayer meetings. There is no way that it doesn't involve teaching and learning. However, I will try and focus more on you, to make the focus *you* rather than a topic like Teaching or Religion. My hope is that once we have learned something about the difficulties of learning and teaching and the Sufis' attitude toward life and religion that we can home in on You and Our World.

"Wilhelm Reich wrote a wonderful booklet and the most wonderful part is the title: *The Problem With the World, Little Man, Is You*. There are only two problems with the book: (1) it's out of print, and (2) the title says it all. Swami Dayananda, whom I've quoted a number of times, wrote a similar pamphlet: *You Are the Problem and You Are the Solution*. A while back you might not have understood either title—"

"I hope you're not going to bring in 'rape' again," said Carole.

"And I hope you're not planning to get drunk in a bikers' bar."

"The thing is, that *shouldn't* have anything to do with it."

"But it does. It has almost everything to do with being raped or not."

"I'm going to write you a note about this little topic," said Carole.

"Good—"

"I'll give it to you before our next meeting."

"Okay. Meantime I will talk about problems in a more general way and you can draw whatever conclusions you can from that."

"On the heaven question and problems—"

"I thought we were finished with religion," said Jodie.

"You guys are so feisty today. What did you have for lunch? Don't answer that. . . . Anyhow, Jodie, we're not finished with any of it; we're just shifting gears. So, Swami Dayananda, Sanskrit scholar and teacher of Vedanta, who is here in this country about six or seven months out of the year, gives this funny little talk about the subject, and it goes like this:

> Heaven-promises are like commercial promises. One teacher says: 'Give me all your money, property, etc. and I'll solve your problems.'
>
> Another teacher says: 'I am only a signpost. I point the way. You must get there yourself. You do the walking.'
>
> The third says: 'I am an existentialist; there *is* no solution. There is none. And no heaven either.'
>
> The religious types say: 'There is no solution *here*. The solution is in heaven. After death there is the solution. But meantime you must do this and this and this. Then, when you die, you'll see. All problems solved, in Heaven.'

What do *I* say? I say *there is no problem!* Only our ignorance of the knowledge that free from smallness is fullness. That fullness is nothing other than what I am. . . . You are the whole! I am the whole! Many literatures talk about it. William Blake. The Sufis. None has provided the methodology to get there.

(Swami Dayananda, 1995 talk)

"Osho sounds very similar:

We have to accept ourselves and love ourselves and there is no problem: I have to repeat it: There is no problem. I have never come across a real problem—not up to now. And I must have listened to thousands of people and their thousands of problems. I have not come across a real problem yet. And I don't think that it is ever going to happen, because the real problem exists not. 'Problem' is a created thing. Situations are there, problems are not there. Problems are your interpretations of situations. The same situation may not be a problem to somebody and may be a problem to somebody else.

So it depends on you whether you create a problem or you don't create a problem, but problems are not there. Problems are not in existence; they are in the psychology of man . . .

But people don't like it: if you say their problem is not a problem, they don't like it. They feel very bad. If you listen to their problems they feel very good. And if you say, 'Yes, this is a great problem,' they are very happy. That's why psychoanalysis has become one of the most important things of this century. The psychoanalyst helps nobody—maybe he helps himself, but he helps nobody else. He cannot. But still people go and pay. They enjoy—he accepts their problems.

Whatsoever absurd problem you bring to the psychoanalyst, he listens to it very sincerely and seriously, as if it is there. He takes it for granted that you are suffering greatly, and he starts working on it. . . . And it takes years!

. . . When you bring a mad person to a Zen monastery, they simply put him in a corner, in a small hut, far away from the monastery. They give him food and tell him, 'Just be there, quiet.' Nobody goes to talk to him; food is supplied, his comforts are looked after, but nobody bothers about him. And what psychoanalysis does in three years they do in three weeks. Within three weeks the person simply comes out and he says, 'Yes, the problem is finished.'

(Osho, *The Tantra Experience*, 46)

"Okay, Carole?"

"What?"

"Do you see what he's saying? About problems? We went over this in one of the early discussions but we've covered a lot of ground since then. Remember? We talked about having a flat and whether it was a problem?"

"I know what you're saying. I know what he's saying. Yes, I remember the earlier discussion. I'm stuck on this point. Not that I agree entirely with you."

"Let one problem slip by and they'll all slip by . . . I'm joking. Let me ask Carlito again. What about it, Carlito? You're driving along the highway and you get a flat. Is that a problem?"

"Of *course* it is," said Carlito. But even he knew enough by now to realize there was more, and when the laughter died down he waited. "I hear you. But I kind of agree with Carole."

"But I thought this was cleared up a good while ago. Is it a fact or is it a problem?"

"It's both."

"Is it really . . . both?"

"Well, you do have to get it fixed!"

"Watch!" I stood up and with one sweep of my hand I knocked everything off of the table in front of me onto the floor: books, pens, a glass of water, papers, a sandwich half-eaten. The desk was clear. Nothing left. There was a moment of pure awareness everywhere. No doubt of it. I had their attention.

"Is that a problem? *No!* It's just stuff on the floor. I can pick it up. I can leave it there forever. I can ask someone else to pick it up and they'd probably refuse, since I did it willfully. But it is *not* a problem. Maybe the sandwich is ruined. Maybe I've damaged the book. Maybe water is all over it. But these are not problems. Either I pick it up or not. Tonight, I want you to practice that. Hit yourself. Bang into something. And, *click,* as fast as that, catch yourself before you make it a problem."

"Is that a task you're giving us?" said Sam.

"Yes."

"But it's ruined," said Jodie, "because we *plan* it and it is not an accident. It's not spontaneous."

"Good point. But it's practice. And if you can practice not allowing it to become a problem then you can transfer the practice to things that *do* happen to you, accidentally, as we say.

"As for the flat . . . you *could* just walk away from it. But, okay, say you decide to fix it. And you have no spare?"

"That's another fact," said Sara, who came out with surprising contributions from time to time.

"How about if you have to meet your girlfriend's parents and this is going to make you late?"

"Another fact," said Sam, laughing at Carlito.

"Okay, okay, I get it," said Carlito, "but none of these facts are funny."

"Another *fact*," said Holly, joining in.

"I'll read it again," I told them.

So it depends on *you* whether you create a problem or you don't create a problem, but problems are not there. Problems are not in existence; they are in the psychology of man . . .

Something had dawned on Holly's face; it was a nice thing to see. I asked her to speak up.

"Well, it's not a problem until I make it one."

"And how would you do that?"

"I don't know. Start kicking the car, or crying, or cursing."

"Do you guys see it? I know this is not as simple as reading some quote from a book and having the light dawn because it depends not on just words but on your actions, on putting those words to use, the next time you see a problem coming up. Well, the cursing and the kicking come after you have decided . . . *decided* . . . that this is a *real problem*. And the difference and the difficulty in teaching is right here: You hear something—'there are no problems'—and even though you heard it and can repeat it, the crazy thing is that it's not *yours*. You can make it yours only when you act from the standpoint of that knowledge. That is the meaning of the phrase *changing knowledge to understanding*. To taste is to know . . . to experience is to know. As long as you just deal with the situation there *is* no problem. Do all of you get that? And I'm not saying I don't get angry, or that I don't create problems out of just plain situations. But the thing is, if you're on a path to get over that, and simply deal with situations and facts instead of moaning and crying and cursing about it, then begin, just begin to realize, by watching yourself, how you create problems out of facts and situations. When you become fully convinced that you are doing this to yourself things will begin to change."

"You know," Carlito said, as calmly and as seriously as I'd ever seen him, "I don't know if I *want* to be that cool."

There was a kind of silent agreement among some and others were trying it on for size.

"I know exactly what you're saying, Carlito. The thing is don't get so *hot* about it that you do something stupid, like selling your car for five bucks, which a friend of mine almost did. Example: I used to get furious when someone got in line in front of me. One day I saw the donkey in myself. Someone, without excuse, got in front of me in a line. It was at a post office in Mexico. I told the man to get in line behind me. He asked me if I knew who he was. Wrong question. I told him I didn't care if he was the president of Mexico; get in line. Does this seem silly? I was ready to kill or be killed over this issue. In that moment, I saw some things in myself. I was ready to fight to the death over this simple injustice. The next time it happened was in a grocery store in the states. I forced myself to go to the end of the line, without saying a word to the person, and start all over again working my way up. This is what is meant by a choice. *We* can choose. Donkeys simply react."

"What happened?" asked Sam. ". . . in Mexico?"

"I killed him! . . . I had to, you see?"

"*What?*"

"No . . . I elbowed him out of the way and put my letters ahead of his. But, you see? I could have killed him, or he could have shot me. Stranger things have happened.

"Listen, all of these things you have to take home with you and think about and then get out on the road and work on. There's no room in here for feeling stupid. We're all stupid. Admitting it is the first step to becoming less stupid. Remember the 70,000 veils? The Koran says, 70,000 veils of ignorance separate us from Allah. We're far and away from it.

"I assigned 'When the Waters Were Changed,' so let's take that next. . . . Look, we're planting seeds now. Okay? These are seeds. And, Carlito, it's not a matter of being cool, it's just a matter of realizing that you're in charge; you can get hot or cool but just realize that it's *you* running the show. You can run it any way you want. Still, you are the problem. I'd say that's a truth. You have a choice. As my favorite Swami says, 'Don't walk behind donkeys. They kick. That's what donkeys do. They have no choice. But you do.'

"Let's break for five or ten minutes. And come back for the story."

* * *

WHEN THE WATERS WERE CHANGED

Once upon a time, Khidr, the Teacher of Moses, called upon mankind with a warning. At a certain date, he said, all the water in the world which had not been specially hoarded would disappear. It would then be renewed, with different water, which would drive men mad.

Only one man listened to the meaning of this advice. He collected water and went to a secure place where he stored it and waited for the water to change its character.

On the appointed date the streams stopped running, the wells went dry, and the man who had listened, seeing this happening, went to his retreat and drank his preserved water.

When he saw, from his security, the waterfalls again beginning to flow, this man descended among the other sons of men. He found that they were thinking and talking in an entirely different way from before; yet they had no memory of what had happened, nor of having been warned. When he tried to talk to them, he realized that they thought that he was mad, and they showed hostility or compassion, not understanding.

At first he drank none of the new water, but went back to his concealment, to draw on his supplies, every day. Finally, however, he took the decision to drink the new water because he could not bear the loneliness of living, behaving, and thinking in a different way from everyone else. He drank the new water and became like the rest. Then he forgot all about his own store of special water, and his fellows began to look upon him as a madman who had miraculously been restored to sanity.

(Shah, *Tales of the Dervishes*, 21)

"Well, what do you think? Sam?"

"I think . . . it's one of the saddest stories I've ever read."

Others were surprised or hadn't thought of it like that.

"Why sad?"

"I don't know . . . in a way, it's hopeless. And even if I were in his shoes . . . I mean, knowing that I was sane and that everybody else was nuts . . . I don't know . . . just . . . just sad. I think I . . . would probably do what he did. I mean I'd be torn."

"Sam, I think that's a brave answer."

Some were amused at the idea of Sam being "brave."

"Not funny," I told them. "He suffered over it. And what good are these stories if you don't take them to heart? If you don't *live* them? Let me begin from a different tack. You all probably know the Lord's Prayer, right? 'Give us this day our daily bread—'"

"You told us," said Mike, "that bread means understanding."

"Right. Exactly that—"

"You say this comes from Nicoll? And where did he get it? From the sparrows?" Holly offered it with an indeterminate smile on her face.

"This in itself is an important question, Holly; but it is also elementary. I could tell you this comes from the Rishis, the earliest wise men—men and women—but at some point you really must face it. Go into yourselves and ask *there*, does this make sense or not? And if it does then drop the search for some ultimate authority. This *is* the Sufi search. It's for meaning, not for authority. You know the bumper sticker: 'Question Authority'? It should be 'Disregard Authority' or even '*There is no Authority*.' That doesn't mean disobey the law. It can be troublesome, time-consuming and costly not to obey the law. It just means there's nothing holy about the law or the people in power. Meantime—yeah, he got it from the sparrows."

Holly sat there. I asked if she understood me.

"I'm seeing something about myself, and it's . . . it's a lot to deal with."

"Okay, then deal and deal and deal with it. So, we are being starved of meaning and we need our daily bit of understanding for the development of our lives. And, in keeping with our group motto, there is always a necessity for plain common sense. Take cooking. Common sense demands that you taste something before you serve it to others. Is it done yet? No mystery; taste it.

"So 'bread' is really understanding. Give us this day our daily bit of understanding, from each story. In the story under discussion right now, all I can say is I'm glad if it makes you think. If it puts you in the shoes of the man who has to decide; do I remain up here on the hill with the truth, and my loneliness? Or do I go down into town and join the lunatics? I think I've mentioned to you that more than a few people have called earth 'the lunatic planet'—George Bernard Shaw and Gurdjieff, to name two—and all you have to do is read just one day's newspaper seriously to know they're right. I tried it one day recently and discovered that on the same day we got the news that there was no money for research into a possible cure or vaccination for the outbreak of the dreaded Ebolla disease—not even a hundred dollars—right next to that article was an article about two defense contractors in Washington battling over a sixty-billion-dollar contract for thirty attack submarines. Two billion dollars a sub. This was in 1995, with no enemy in sight. The articles appeared together. The submarine article to the right. But let's not take up time with any further discussion of it; the news is enough.

"Anyhow, Nicoll speaks of water and it pertains directly to this story:

> What then does water mean psychologically? . . . A hundred examples might be quoted. Let us take one from the Gospels. Christ spoke to the Woman of Samaria . . . and told her that he could give her 'living water.' Christ says to her when she has come to draw

water at the well: 'Everyone that drinketh of this water [from the well] shall thirst again: but whosoever drinketh of the water that I shall give him shall never thirst; but the water that I shall give him shall become in him a well of water springing up into eternal life' (John 4:13-14).

. . . Again in the Old Testament, in the book of Jeremiah, it is said: 'For my people have committed two evils; they have forsaken me the fountain of living waters, and hewed them out cisterns, broken cisterns, that can hold no water' (Jeremiah 2:13).

. . . In the ancient language *water* means Truth. But it means a special kind of Truth, a special form of knowledge called 'living truth.' It is living Truth because it makes a man *alive in himself*, and not dead, once the knowledge of it is assented to and applied in practice. In esoteric teaching—that is, teaching about inner evolution—a man is called *dead* who knows nothing about it. . . . For no one can change, no one can become different, no one can evolve and reach this higher possible level and so be re-born, unless he knows, hears and follows a teaching about it."

(Nicoll, *The New Man*, 8)

"Is *this* the teaching?" said Jodie.

"No, this is a discussion group."

And when they subsided, ". . . about the teaching."

"Would you say," said Jodie, "that when fundamentalists talk about being re-born it is the same thing?"

"What do you think?"

"I don't know."

"Yes, you *do*."

Almost everyone was jeering at her, pushing her, yelling across the table at her.

"Well, I wanted to hear it from him."

"Let's go on with a discussion of the story. Mike?"

"I think it's a very simple story. He either goes with the herd or he doesn't."

"Do you think it was, maybe, a harrowing experience?"

"No, I really don't think so . . . because . . . because he forgets what he once knew and—"

"Yes," Carole said, "and became just as crazy as everyone else."

Sara told us, "I think Sam is right. I think it's very sad. Because what he really wants is to bring them to *him*. I mean he wants the social contact with sane people, not to become insane along with them."

"Yes, Sara, and once he loses it he doesn't even remember what he had or what he has lost, as Mike said. Let me read something about Charles Hoy Fort. I've referred to his book before—*The Book of the Damned*. His enemy was dogmatic science. And Oliver Wendell Holmes, one of the most famous of our Supreme Court justices, was a great fan of his because Fort attacked things that were taken for granted. Holmes said, 'We have been cocksure of so many things that were not so' (Fort, 10).

"A very prominent critic, in a review of *The Book of the Damned*, said: 'He was one sane man in a mad mad world—and for that reason very lonely'(Fort, 11). His book has been called one of the ten greatest books ever written, if not the greatest. Is Fort the sane man, looking down on a mad mad world? Is he the man in the story? Because if he is that makes *us* part of the madmen.

"Look, in a way, I do think this is a simple story. A great story but more a story to think about than to discuss. I want to bring up some other things and remind you of some things we began to talk about during the first days of this . . . discussion group."

"Please," said Holly, "let me bring up just one thing here. How do we know that the *entire* population drank the water and became mad? All except for one person?"

"Holly, I know I've told you, all of you, before now but these things are so important. We *know* it because in the story we are *told* that that is what happened when they drank the other water. That is *story*. It is *true* within the story, and within the bounds of story see how much you can learn. Even if you don't believe it's possible, imagine, for the moment, that it is true, 'as if' it's true. Again, these are teaching tales."

She nodded, but was troubled. I nodded for her to go on.

"Well, it's not realistic. *No* one else listens?"

"Look. You get what you get from it. Understand that. Let the story *in* and take what you can from it. Reject it and you get nothing. Take! Be selfish! *Be* unrealistic, use your imagination so that from the 'unreal' you gain something that can be applied to your very real life. I think all of us, in thinking about this story, want at least one other person to be sane, just one other, for companionship. Otherwise it's just too bleak. But there's a great deal more to the story. It's not simply being 'sane.' It is being enlightened. And since we haven't tasted that bliss we think it's no different than the difference between being sane or insane. Like the difference between being sick or not being sick, which we call being 'well.' But there is at least one other category to consider: 'Sick,' 'not sick,' and blissfully healthy.

"Hi, man! How're ya feeling? Fine, he says. His mouth hardly opens up wide enough to let the word out. Fine? Is that *fine?* In the same way, the state of at-one-ment (atonement) is in a different league.

"To continue with the Koran and the separation by 70,000 thousand veils:

> . . . the passage through the veils has brought with it forgetfulness (nisyan): and for this reason man is called *insan* (long 'A'). He is now, as it were, in prison in his body, separated by these thick curtains from Allah.
> (Nicholson, *The Mystics of Islam*, 15)

"Perhaps orthodox Muslims would want to have me killed for saying this, but it seems to me that the 70,000 veils is a metaphor for the separation between ourselves as we are and Allah, or God. And a lot more picturesque than saying 'It's a long way to get to God.'

"So, way back then at the beginning of our group sessions, we talked about 'I' and what is really 'I' and our bodies. And I want to go back to that. I obtained a tentative agreement, I believe, among most of you that we are not our bodies but that we are our consciousness, the thing which sparks us, which uses our muscles, our eyes, our ears, and our brains through which we function. And without that consciousness we die. In fact, that *is* life itself. Our legs, without consciousness, are useless. And, as Blake said, we see *through* our eyes, not merely with our eyes. Because, when a person dies the eyes are still there but there is no 'sight,' etc.

"Now, if the life in us is the same as the life in everything else which moves and emotes and plays and sings, then we must, truly, identify not with our skins and our physical shells but with the *real*, the thing that moves all of us, the life *in* all of us. You might even say 'all of life.' Okay?

"Now, I know this is a big piece to bite off but . . . if that spark, that fire, that *life* thing, that consciousness, is the same in me as it is in you, and everyone else, then it brings up thousands of questions: about killing, racism, love, and hatred.

"Think about what was just said.

"Now, how do we account for the differences from one 'shell' to another? I'm taking this from the standpoint of 'as if' you have swallowed all of this and agree. If so, then, how do we account for the differences from one person to another? And I think I told you that wind through a reed pipe makes a different sound than wind through a saxophone, a clarinet, a trombone, a tuba. The wind is the same only playing through different instruments; the same wind sounds different when it comes out. And so maybe that is our condition. We are instruments and life plays us, or plays through us. But essentially, we are one consciousness.

"It seems to me that if the life in each of us is 'I' and if that 'life' is the same as the 'life' in everyone else then the 'I' of me is the same as the 'I' of you, the real 'I,' which moves me and is behind my emoting and playing and singing; then, if that is true, we ought to be identifying not with our skins but with something else, and, incidentally, we ought to be able to get along. We should, but why can't we? Is it because we identify with the 'shell' rather than the consciousness?

"How to account for the differences from one 'shell' to another? We're only different instruments played on by life itself; so how and why the differences in the instruments called people?

"Where was one 'instrument' born? Under what influences? What were the parents like? What were the first impressions? The climate of the house and neighborhood in the first years? The fears? Who were its teachers? What were the books it read? What were the stories it was told? Who were its friends? What were the early experiences? Traumas? Punishments? Rewards?

"All of these elements fashion each of us. Here is a little story, about instruments named John Wetzel and Mary Jane Simmons. These instruments were fashioned by their own ele-ments; is it any wonder that John Wetzel does not understand Mary Jane Simmons? And, yet, they are married.

"Two years after the ceremony, they both look up and ask: How in the world did this happen to us? Mary Jane, with totally different parents, who saw things out of different eyes than John, had different fears and views of education, punishment, sex, friends, alcohol, habits, health, diet, pleasure, religion . . . Mary Jane, whose parents pushed her out into the world to a school that appeared to guarantee all of the things they believed in so they could give over all of that to the school, thus allowing them to go about their jobs and lives and let the school do its job on Mary Jane . . . Mary Jane is a little puzzled.

"So Mary Jane and John are married. And what is the basis of their courtship and marriage? In a word, the very basis of their marriage is 'misconception.' Mr. and Msconception.

"And, when they discover how different they are, do they get a divorce? It's very common and very popular in their crowd to do just that but there is a complication. There is a little baby. Baby Betsy. And Betsy, by the time the smoke has settled—I use the word smoke because they have a fierce and passionate physical relationship—or by the time they can look at each other clearly, without jumping into bed or wanting to, Betsy is two years old. And that poses a problem. For, whatever love is, they 'love' Betsy. And they wouldn't dream of leaving Betsy. So John and Mary Jane can separate and pass little Betsy back and forth between them—John on the weekends and Mary Jane during the week—or they can investigate and find out if there isn't something, some basis out of which they can renew their love or revive it, perhaps some link that they have overlooked, to try and discover if there is something important that they may have missed, before they get a divorce.

"And the link is the 'life' or the 'consciousness' which they discovered that they have in common. But despite that, how can they both keep their minds on this common link when one of them says or does something so 'utterly stupid'?

"End of Story. Can this marriage be saved? Sometimes Mary Jane and John see it through, and sometimes they get a divorce. It happens thousands of times every day in the U.S.

"But to get back to the larger question, there was a wonderful cartoon in *The New Yorker* some years ago. Two people, a man and a woman, are sitting in bed. They are middle-aged. And one says to the other: 'I never did understand you, and it's too late to start now.' The cartoon is funny since it states a truth which most of us have realized, that you can actually live with someone for years and, one day, discover that you don't know the person at all. How can it happen? For all sorts of reasons. First, because, according to the sources which we are studying, everything we do is in a state of wakeful-sleep. We marry, procreate, go to school, divorce, and it is all in a state of wakeful-sleep. Second, there has been no real effort to *try* to know each other.

217

Third, we *think* we know one another and that will do and, besides, the invitations are already sent out. Fourth, we not only do not know our mates, we don't even know ourselves. And fifth, there is nothing in our 'education' to help prepare us, either to know ourselves or to know another person. Our education is concerned with the world outside of us. For the inner life, you're on your own.

"Let's break for ten minutes."

"Just a minute," said Jodie. "Are you really saying that when people know, in their heart of hearts, that they probably shouldn't get married that they actually would go on through with it just because plans have been made and the *invitations have been sent out?*"

"Let me get this perfectly straight," I told them. I waited for perhaps ten seconds in silence, looking out from one to another of their faces that had by now become very dear to me. ". . . Let me make it perfectly clear. Do I believe that people will go through with it? With the wedding? Despite feeling it is not going to work? That it is the wrong decision? That they will go through with it? . . . Because the invitations have been sent out, and presents are coming in? . . . *YES!*

"Now, let's take a break and when we come back we'll talk about 'The Dreams and the Loaf of Bread.'"

Carole handed me her note, and at least eight of the others, led by Carlito, plunged into the lake on this muggy day in August, with only three more sessions to go.

THE DREAMS AND THE LOAF
OF BREAD

Three travelers on a long and exhausting
journey had become companions, and shared
the same pleasures and sorrows, pooling all
their resources.

After many days they realized that all they
had between them was a piece of bread and a
mouthful of water in a flask. They fell to quarrel-
ing as to who should have all the food. Making
no progress on this score, they tried to divide
the bread and water. Still they could not arrive
at a conclusion.

As dusk was falling, one finally suggested
that they should sleep. When they awoke,
the person who had had the most remarkable
dream would decide what should be done.

The next morning the three rose as the sun
came up.

"This is my dream," said the first. "I was carried away to places such as cannot be described,
so wonderful and serene were they. I met a wise
man who said to me: 'You deserve the food, for
your past and future life are worthy and suitable
subjects for admiration.'"

"How strange," said the second man. "For
in my dream, I actually saw all my past and my

future. In my future I saw a man of all-knowl-edge, who said: 'You deserve the bread more than your friends, for you are more learned and patient. You must be well-nurtured, for you are destined to lead men.'"

The third traveler said: "In my dream I saw nothing, heard nothing, said nothing. I felt a compelling presence which forced me to get up, find the bread and water—and consume them then and there. And this is what I did."

(Shah, *Tales of the Dervishes*, 111)

16

Drunk Again, in a Bikers' Bar

"I want to read your note, Carole, if you don't mind, but first let's take up the story."

"*This* is my favorite story, I think," said Sara. "All the talking, the dreams . . . then the one just wakes up and takes it all."

"Quite selfish, I'd say," said Holly. "Is that fair?"

"Oh, come on," said Sam. "Do you think those guys, the other two 'dreamers,' were telling the truth?"

Mike's face was a study. "What do you think, Mike?"

"I don't know," he answered slowly. "It didn't occur to me that they might have been lying. But . . . I think maybe they were."

"I read a book on dreams," said Carole. "The two dreams in the story were too direct. Dreams, according to my own observation, *and* the book are very indirect—"

"So, are you saying that you distrust the two who described their dreams?"

"Yes—"

"They just wanted the bread and the water," said Dan, "and would lie to get it."

"Yes, now a little wrinkle. In Sufi terms what does water mean?"

"*Got* it!" said Jodie. "Water equals truth!"

"Okay," said Mike, "and bread is understanding."

"Okay," said Joanne, "but is the story saying that there was only a little truth and a little understanding . . . to go around? I mean, not enough for all three?"

"Yes, that's what the story says; but, I think, the amount of bread and water in the story is really only a device to set us up for the solution."

"I think there's something great about it," said Sam. "His *need* was greater."

"Go on. So?"

"Maybe his *need* for truth and understanding was so great that it woke him up."

"Yes? Sam, good. Woke him up from what?"

"From . . . *sleep!*" Carole burst out.

"Exactly. From sleep and dreams. And instead of scheming and plotting to get it he wakes up, out of sleep, and takes it. Can we eat and drink in our sleep? No. We have to wake up, we have to leave the sleeping state before we can make truth and understanding . . . ours. The other two travelers are almost incidental to the story."

There was more discussion but soon enough it dried up. A simple little story, simple and complex.

"Okay, Carole? May I read your note?"

She nodded.

> I agree that women should definitely have had a larger role in religion since its development. Maybe if they had, all the sexism that has gone on and still continues would not exist. Who helped to establish and lead people in the formation and teaching of different religions? MEN! And that is that.
>
> C.

I did not want to fight this battle again. Even from the time she had threatened to write the note till now so much water had passed under the bridge.

For years I have been uncomfortable (*comfortable*—that catch-all word) about the Women's Movement, and the Black Movement and, of course, the White-Racist Movements, and have felt that movements which exclude anyone are divisive and pit those in the "movement" against those excluded from it. And these groups distract us from the real battles which need to be fought against war and injustice. Recently, I have felt that the current movement on college campuses of having the male first ask permission—"Mary, may I touch your breast? The left one?"—involves a certain kind of insanity. Incidents are brought up before committees of students who don't know either one of the participants. Behavior and conversations are discussed concerning incidents that are weeks old by the time they're considered.

I read Carole's note out loud and told them: "You might not recognize it but that note is a series of sexist remarks. Women have tremendous power, just as students have over the college curriculum. The problem is that students don't realize how much power they have. They pay for the school. They pay teachers' and administrators' salaries. They pay for the buildings, the staff, the upkeep. And they have little or no say in their education. I think women are the same. They have a reservoir of unused power; untapped except with their husbands or intimate partners. Whatever has happened has happened with their passive or active agreement. They *have* the power . . . but often they don't use it."

Hands were waving and interruptions were being voiced.

"Look, I'll agree to everything but that women are better than men. Are we talking about equality or superiority? Equality? Yes. Superiority of one over the other? *No!*

"I want to read something that has been hanging over this discussion for a long time. The Sufis say we don't know ourselves. Then it follows that we don't know what a 'man' is and we don't know what a 'woman' is. Because of the obvious differences, we treat the question as if the question can be resolved at a glance.

As a student in a graduate class at Harvard, some years ago, I was a member of a seminar which was asked to identify which of two piles of a clinical test, the TAT, had been written by males, and which of the two piles had been written by females. Only four students out of twenty identified the piles correctly, and this was after one and a half months of intensively studying the differences between men and women. Since this result was below chance . . . we may conclude that there *is* finally a consistency here . . . the teachings themselves are simply erroneous.

(Weisstein, 212)

"Is this shocking? One more item from the same source:

In 1952, Eysenck reported the results of what is called an 'outcome of therapy' study of neurotics which show that, of the patients who received psychoanalysis, the improvement rate was 44 percent; of the patients who received psychotherapy, the improvement rate was 64 percent; and the patients who received no treatment at all, the improvement rate was 72 percent. These findings have never been refuted; subsequent studies have confirmed the negative results of the Eysenck study.

(Weisstein, 212)

"Of course, it can be argued that tremendous, oh just *tremendous*, strides have been made since those cave-man days way back in 1970. At any rate, that is what was being practiced back then by the experts in the field and those results, if old, are disturbing enough for us to request some updating to refute those results and restore our confidence in 'establishment' psychology. A book written recently—*We've Had a Hundred Years of Psychotherapy: And the World's Getting Worse* by Hillman and Ventura, 1993—does nothing but further undermine our confidence in establishment medicine since the seventies.

224

"I can't answer questions about this, but it seems to me that we are self-correcting organisms if we're only given the chance. I believe that gender and sex questions are questions that women have been just a little upset about. Not that their opinions count for a great deal in scientific circles, but still . . ."

"Are you avoiding this subject? The subject of sex and gender?" Carole asked.

"No, but it would take us through August and into September to properly deal with it. And we have only two more discussion meetings. I'll only say that, as with other subjects, the Sufis have no set criteria. All of love, any and all aspects of it, are legitimate and are, hopefully, part of one's movement toward realization of our human brotherhood, and, of course, sisterhood.

"What is it to be a man? What is it to be a woman? Women are peace-loving? Men are war-like? In a book called *Men in War*, first published in 1918 by Andreas Latzko, the author tells us that the very worst thing of all was not the war itself, which is horrible enough, but that women send their men off. And that if they, the women, had objected, or fought against it, or told the men they'd never look at them again if they went off and became murderers, no general could have made them go.

"Keeping that in mind, along with the story of Mary Jane and John Wetzel, we have to decide what Jesus was talking about when he said 'I am the truth I am the way. And love one another as I have loved you . . .' I think we have wrongly interpreted his words as 'We *should* love one another,' something like a command or an earnest wish or a 'nice' thing to strive for. Of course it's impossible but, as my mother would have said, 'We should *try* to love one another, it's the civilized thing to do.'

"Instead, Jesus was telling us that love is the way. The *way*. That we *do* love one another and only our ignorance prevents us from seeing it. Seventy thousand veils of ignorance, says the Koran. Jesus is saying that love is the way to the Kingdom of

Heaven. We *do* love one another or we *should* love one another? Those two are so close, and so far away. What is the best analogy to show this? What is an obvious truth? Two and two equals four. An obvious truth. Instead we are imposing 'should.' As in: 'It would really be nice if two and two should equal four.' As if we had to get to heaven before two and two can equal four."

"Wooooooeee, but what in the world are you talking about?" said Sam, seconded by Danny. And this time he did have supporters.

"I'm saying," one second away from giving up the attempt, "that we *do* love one another. That's all. That's Jesus' message. He's not telling us to be civilized and *try* to love one another. As if he were a parent instructing a child on how to behave. Okay?"

"So, are you saying that everyone else has missed the message?"

"No, I'm just saying it's quite a leap for our conventional world of war and religious sects and countries and patriotism. Hazrat Inayat Khan got it. Sufis. Gnostics. Esoteric Christians. Many others . . . yes, even the sparrows got it—"

"I was *just* going to mention them," said Jodie.

"So," said Joanne, "you're saying that love is—"

"—the truth. Because we are our consciousness. And because we are our consciousness, really, that we *do* love one another, we are bound together in consciousness and in that way we are God."

"The . . . truth? Yes . . ." she turned away, and the look was of a child walking off the playground with all of the marbles.

"'No,' people say, 'the truth is that I *hate* that dirty so-and-so.' Jonathan Swift once wrote a political satire about war between the Big-enders and the Little-enders. The Big-enders believed that one should crack the egg at the big end. And the Little-enders believed it should be cracked at the little end. And they were furious at each other for differing with 'the truth.' Is that ridiculous? But is it life-like? Do they say, 'Hey, you want to crack it at the big end? Go ahead.' No, they want to kill each other for differing.

"'Hey, you see that guy over there? He thinks he's God.'

"'Really? So what? I don't care.'

"No, it's not so simple. 'We have to kill him.'

"'Really? Why?'

"'Because a lot of other people are beginning to think so, too.'

"'Yeah, I guess you're right.'

"I recently met an Indian woman who collared me and insisted on telling me how great the English language was. Well, what's so great about it, I asked her?

"'*So what*,' she said. 'I love it. Somebody says something and Americans say, *So what!*'

"The Catholics preach that the wafer taken at communion is 'really' the body of Christ.

"*So what!*

"Protestants say it is only a symbol of the body of Christ.

"*So what!*

"The Catholics believe in the pope, the other Christians do not . . . *so what!?*

"Can't we allow these differences? Do these things matter? Thousands and thousands of people have been killed over these differences. Each one of the blind ones who had felt a part of the elephant found his adherents. These adherents formed a sect. Each sect was convinced that it had the entire truth about the elephant. Each sect hated the other sects that differed from them."

"So what!" said Carlito.

In my zeal he had twisted my brain and I looked to see which way he was taking it. I must have stared hard at him because he began explaining urgently.

"I mean, let 'em *be*. Let 'em think what they want," he said.

"Yes, Carlito, but for that we have to become tolerant. Truly tolerant. If you believe abortion is murder and your neighbor doesn't, it's not as simple as his saying, 'If you think it's murder then don't have an abortion. *I* don't think it's murder. I think it's murder the way you scream at your children, but, of course, I *could* be wrong.' No, that is not good enough. If it's murder, they reason, then 'murder' shouldn't take place at all, never mind your 'belief.' So they bomb a clinic and kill doctors. Very Christian.

"These things affect our lives, and these are not stories. But we can learn from stories. They are examples that can be applied. They are even farfetched examples, but ridiculous as some are and as far afield from the immediate problem, they can be applied. For that reason they are called teaching tales.

"One last item, and I want to take the next story. When the astronauts were sailing around out there in space did they notice that there were no demarcation lines between countries? Were their views changed? Did they wonder about their old views? Did they think about the destruction of the atmosphere on earth? Did they feel tender about it? Loving about it? Did they feel connected? Did they begin to feel patriotic about our planet rather than about a little part of it? Did they think about our *planet* instead of *their* country? Yes, they did . . . so, there's room for hope. Is the truer version the version from outer space or from here?

"The truth. How staggering a subject.

"German school children are given a certain view of how and why World War II began. Is our (the American) version of how it began the truth? Or the Italian version? Or none of the above? Is anything that comes later a 'revised' version and are those people who come up with new ideas on it the 'revisionists'? The very very truth is not and will not be known. And that is very difficult to swallow. But when we swallow it something else happens—if we can really swallow it—because suddenly everything becomes an adventure. It is all very simple and all very complicated.

"Even the truth of a scene in a cafe, 8:03-8:05 P.M., Wednesday night, July 17, 1995, Boston, Massachusetts. There are two of us, sitting opposite, at a table far from the door. Who is sitting at the next table from my line of sight? What about her line of sight? What do we appear like to people at the other tables? My view is entirely different from that of my dinner companion sitting opposite me. I'm watching people act and react, eating and exclaiming, that she doesn't even see. Conversely, she is watching scenes, very dramatic scenes, proposals of marriage, proposals of separation, that are not in my world-view of the cafe. And all of this going on simultaneously. Then there's the waitress. She sees our table and moves through the tables eyeing others, passing them, re-passing, wondering all of her thoughts as she swishes in and out between diners, kitchen, cashier, bar. She has to deal with the chef and any exceptions her patrons suggest, and he has a certain mood back there, facing the unprepared food and the orders piling up. He has a date with the waitress later. And he's married and doesn't want that to get around. Then there's the manager who wants to fire the waitress because he knows what's going on between his chef and her (she's already turned him down) and besides he has someone else in mind. So there's her job. Her fears of getting fired, and whether it will be a big night or slow. Then there's the cashier with a three-year-old at home who has an infected ear and a babysitter neither one of them trusts; customers in and out, and putting credit cards through the machine. The in and out of people. And their thoughts. And from the cooks? And the cooks' helpers? And the dishwasher dreaming as he picks up sudsy plates and passes a sponge over them? All of this and much more in two minutes? One minute? Instants! While the termites eat away, supporting themselves on the beams supporting the entire scene.

"It hurts to imagine the complexity of a fight between just two people, not to speak of a battle between two armies. So an objective, total view of *anything* is impossible.

"Someone asked, is Sufism a religion? No, Sufism *is* religion. But no churches, no degree at the end of the course, no priests, no censors, no sins. Only truth and its pursuit.

"Here's a little story, just a tidbit and then we'll take a break."

THE TRUTH OR DIE

Once an emperor decided that the trouble with his kingdom was that people would not tell the truth. He determined to change all of that. The very next day he'd have his hangman stand at the gates to the city and before anyone could enter that person would have to answer a question. If the person was lying then he or she would be hung. The next morning Mullah Nasrudin was first to volunteer an answer.

"Where are you going?" asked the hangman.

"I'm going to be hung," said Nasrudin.

"You're lying," said the hangman. "I don't believe you."

"Then, since it's a lie you have to hang me."

The hangman looked puzzled. "But that would make it the truth. I can't hang you for telling the truth."

"Yes," said Nasrudin, "your truth. But if you don't hang me it will be a lie."

The plan was abandoned.

(Willem Nyland, talks, 1965)

"Okay, on to the bloodiest story of all: 'The Cure of Human Blood.' We'll pick it up when we come back from break. See? I brought my swim suit."

* * *

THE CURE OF HUMAN BLOOD

Maulana Bahaudin Naqshband was asked: "How is it that ignoble men or infants, as in so many stories, can be spiritualized by a glance, or in some indirect way, merely by coming into contact with a great teacher?"

He gave the following story as a reply, saying that this method paralleled the indirect route of spiritualization.

In the days of the great empire of Byzantium, one of its emperors was sick with a dreadful disease, which no doctor could cure. He sent ambassadors to every country with full descriptions of the ailment. One arrived at the school of the great El-Ghazzali, who was a Sufi whom the emperor had only heard of as one of the great sages of the East. El-Ghazzali asked one of his disciples to make the journey to Constantinople.

When the man, El Arif, arrived, he was taken to the court and treated with all honour, the Emperor beseeching him to effect a cure. Sheikh El-Arif asked what remedies had been tried, and which further ones were contemplated. Then he made an examination of the patient.

Finally he asked for a full audience of all the Court to be called, while he made his declaration of how the cure might be effected.

When all the nobles of the empire had assembled the Sufi said: "Your Imperial Majesty had better use faith."

"The Emperor has faith," answered a cleric, "but it does not take therapeutic effect."

"In that case," said the Sufi, "I am compelled to say that there is only one remedy on earth which will save him. But I do not want to speak it, so dreadful a thing is it."

But he was pressed, promised riches, threatened and cajoled. So he said:

"A bath in the blood of several hundred children under seven years of age will cure the Emperor."

When the confusion and alarm occasioned by these words had subsided, the Counsellors of State decided that the remedy was worth trying. Some, it is true, said that nobody had any right to attempt such a barbarity at the behest of a foreigner of doubtful origins. The majority, however, considered that any risk was to be taken to preserve the life of an Emperor such as this, whom they all respected and almost worshipped.

They prevailed upon the monarch, in spite of his reluctance, saying: "Your Imperial Majesty has no right to refuse; for this would deprive his Empire of even more than the life of all his subjects, let alone a number of children."

Therefore the word was sent around that all children in Byzantium of the required age were to be sent to Constantinople within a certain period, in order to be sacrificed for the Emperor's health.

The mothers of these children in almost every case called down curses upon the head of their ruler, for being such a monster as to demand their flesh and blood for his own salvation. Some, however, prayed instead that the Emperor might be healed before the time set for the slaying of their children.

The Emperor himself, after a certain amount of time had elapsed, began to feel that he could not allow such a deed as the slaughter of young children, on any pretext whatever. The problem put him into such a state of mind that it tortured him night and day, until he gave out the edict: "I would rather die myself than see the innocent die."

No sooner had he said this than his sickness began to abate, and he was soon perfectly well again. Shallow thinkers at once concluded that he had been rewarded for his good action. Others, as shallow, attributed his improvement to the relief of the mothers of the children, acting upon Divine power.

When the Sufi El-Arif was asked as to the means by which the disease had abated, he said: "As he had no faith, he had to have something equivalent to it. This was his single-mindedness coupled with the constructive desires of the mothers who wanted a remission of the disease before a certain time."

And the scoffers among the Byzantines said: "What a special dispensation of Divinity it was that the Emperor was healed in response to the holy prayers of the clergy, before the bloodthirsty Saracen's formula was tried. For was it not obvious that he was only trying to destroy the flower of our youth, which would otherwise grow up, and would one day fight against his kind?"

When the matter was referred to El-Ghazzali, he said: "An effect can take place only through a manner devised to operate within the time allotted to its attainment."

Just as the Sufi leech had to adapt his method to the people with whom he found himself surrounded, so the dervish spiritualizer can activate the inner cognitions of the infant, or the ignoble, even, in the realm of the science of Truth, the employment of the methods known to him, given to him for this purpose. This latter was the explanation of Our Master Bahaudin.

(Shah, *Tales of the Dervishes*, 96)

"Okay Sara . . . no, I mean Mike—we haven't heard from you for a while. What is your comment about this story?"

"The human blood story? The Cure of Human Blood?"

"Yes, Mike . . ."

"The story we just read?"

"You know, when I was in grammar school and the teacher asked me something I didn't know—such as, for some reason, eight times seven, well I just couldn't seem to remember 'eight times seven' and so—if the teacher asked me what is eight times seven, I would ask her: 'Eight times seven?' And she'd say, yes, 'Eight . . . eight, the number eight, times seven, yes, that's it, eight times seven.' And I'd answer, 'Ohh, *eight . . . eight times seven!*' I guess I was hoping for an earthquake or some natural disaster to take me out of it. Anyhow, Mike, will you tell us about the story?"

"I really liked the story. It's a little bloody, but other than that . . ."

"Come on, Mike. We've got one and a half meetings left. Give us some inspired thought about this."

"Well, I can't say exactly what cured him but he's cured right after . . . right after he decides not to do it."

"Good. So, the doctor, I mean, the Sufi—just like the Sufi in 'The Horseman and the Snake'—comes up with this peculiar cure. The Horseman says, 'Here, try some of these rotten apples.' No, he actually crams them down the man's throat. And *this* one, this Sufi, says what you need is a bloodbath. Do you think that antibiotics would have cured the Emperor? How about it . . . Sara?"

"I really did know it that time! No. I think definitely not."

"Why not?"

"Because it's an internal thing. . . . I mean, really internal."

"Well, most medicines cure internal things, right? They go down the hatch and into the stomach and internal organs."

"I mean, this seems to me like a sort of soul sickness."

"Okay. And we need a different kind of medicine for that. It is not a physical thing, the cause. Maybe the symptoms are physical, but the real cause is not. Good. You guys are learning to trust yourselves. But it's like a major effort before you look and speak from what you see. But that's it. The Sufi sees it. The others are as sick as the Emperor is. Sick or jaded."

"So," said Sam, "the bath is a device . . . right?"

"*You* said it. Do you believe that?"

"Yes, I think so. I think the Sufi did not, maybe did not ever, maybe never meant for it to happen."

"Who agrees with Sam?"

Practically everyone raised a hand. Bess was one of the conspicuous loners.

"You know something? We have to get over trying to guess which way is the 'right' way to go! Just get over that. It doesn't matter about getting the 'right' answer to somebody's questions. It matters to really and truly listen to yourself. And that is ten times better than getting some kind of 'right' answer. Then you'll be right even if you're wrong. You learn to really listen to yourself and you're on the path no matter what anyone thinks. If you just get that I'd be happy as hell. Good, Sam.

"So, Bess, you don't think so; then stick by what you believe. What do *you* think?"

"I'm not sure. But I guess it *was* kind of a plot to get this Emperor to . . ."

"To what?"

"To maybe wake up to what he was about to do."

"Alright, so we're pretty much agreed. Yes, it's a device. An amazingly cruel notion. He has to knock this Emperor over the head; something really shocking. But now, I've got to know about his ministers."

"They're 'yes' men," said Joanne.

"Do you think any of them have children the 'required' age? From zero to seven years of age?"

"I doubt it," said Sara, who was suddenly wide awake.

"What about the scoffers? Three paragraphs up from the

end of the story, calling the Sufi a 'bloodthirsty Saracen'? And the ministers?"

"The ministers *agreed* to it!" Danny yelled. "The Sufi proposed the bloodbath, and he wasn't necessarily really proposing it, only as a device. But the ministers went for it and were actually rounding up the children. *Who's* bloodthirsty? And the Emperor goes along with it, too!"

"Good, Danny—"

"And the mothers, maybe even worse. They were actually about to send their children or *were* sending them!"

"Down, Danny," said Sam. "Down, boy!"

Never mind, I was pleased; Dan, when he came through, came in a burst of enthusiasm.

"So, the Sufi arrives and talks to everyone. What has been done, what is going to be done. After listening and sort of sniffing the air, he says the Emperor better use faith. Remember, he never accuses the Emperor of not having faith."

"No," said Holly, "and they immediately, the ministers, protest that he *has* faith. And I find that interesting. Maybe they say it because they have to say the right thing."

"They're like a bunch of U.S. senators," said Holly.

"Well, they say he has faith but it just doesn't seem to work."

"Look at the beginning of the story; the word 'indirect' is used twice in the first six lines. So the story is an illustration of the 'indirect' method of accomplishing something. I can't tell you enough about the importance of the beginnings. What other tipoff do we have at the beginning of the story?"

"Well, it says the word 'ignoble' and I think that refers to, well, the Emperor."

"Good. Why not? Can't Emperors be ignoble? Can't presidents be ignoble? This doesn't need an answer. My real question is, what exactly is the cure?"

"That he take a bath in the blood of—"

"That's the device to effect the cure. The medicine. But what is the cure? And how do we know that he is cured?"

"I'd say," Joanne began, "when he was tortured night and day because of his thoughts about it, about sacrificing the children for *his* benefit."

"No," said Sara, "when he said 'I would rather die myself than see the innocent die.' That's when the disease leaves him."

"Yes, the cure and the teaching are one. He learns—whether he ever understands or not—he learns and is cured. He *can't* be that selfish. As selfish and self-centered as he is, there are limits, even for an emperor. And some of the people of the town think he was rewarded for his 'good action.' What do you think about that?"

"*Not* to murder hundreds of children isn't a good action," said Carlito.

"*Hear hear!*" said Sam, but seriously complimenting Carlito.

"Yes, it is not a *good* action. The Emperor was sound asleep in his luxurious life, surrounded by his 'yes' men. His sickness is that he is totally out of touch with his subjects and only by this bizarre 'cure,' or plans for it, is he, at last, awakened. He needed a *severe* knock on the head, and El-Arif gave it to him. The mothers are fairly clear about it: 'Such a monster,' they say. They aren't even shocked. That should give us an idea of what kind of an emperor he is. And at the end of the story, El-Arif says, 'As he had no faith . . .' he had to do something else.

"The Emperor loses his jadedness, for the moment, and becomes a human being again, identifying with the innocent rather than with: 1. the disease, 2. the cure, 3. the state or empire, and 4. his importance. Okay. Interesting story. Any questions about it? About anything?"

"Excuse this jump, but what about Whitman? We've not covered much of it and it seems very important and we don't have much time left," said Sara. "I *love* Whitman."

"I know. These are tough choices. There are a lot of stories that we could cover, or we could talk and ask questions. Don't worry, we will definitely take up Whitman, but first there are a few more things I want to tell you.

"When I was just a little bit younger than you, my stepfather told me to get a job one summer after high school. That I shouldn't just be hanging around all day; I was too old for that. In fact, he wanted me to get a job entirely on my own. Without pull. Without the help of the family. My feeling was, 'What's wrong with hanging around?'

"I didn't want to work at all. So, I went downtown with the Want Ads, and sat in some coffee shop, had some coffee and a Danish and sat down and 'looked' for a job. I even went so far as to mark out some phone numbers, and put them down in my notebook. Along with a brief description of the job. Then I went about eliminating jobs. 'I can't do *that* one because . . . well, I'm really not a house-painter. I *could* do that but what fun would that be?'

"Then I wrote in my notebook about the different characters all around me. What they were drinking. How they were eating. How many spoons of sugar they took. How they bit into stuff. Very superior to that whole roomful of people. By that time it was 12:00 and time for lunch. Besides, those jobs I had marked out were all taken by now, probably. They were in the *morning* paper. So, then I got the afternoon papers—no such thing nowadays—and went through the same process.

"I came home that first night and told my stepfather about my day, how I'd looked all over but no job. I felt I was covered. Do you see? I had 'tried' to get a job. I sort of believed it myself. 'I don't want your *story*,' he told me that evening. 'I want you to get a job. So don't come back tomorrow night with a story. Come back with a job.'

"Oh, really! Now, how does he know I wasn't out there all day, looking? My mother was satisfied with my stories. Why wasn't he? He wanted to hear where it was, doing what, and how much per hour. No stories.

"Next day I went to an employment agency, filled out papers. Got a call. Was sent way out somewhere. One of the worst jobs I've ever had. But he taught me something I've since decided is invaluable: Just get it done, get it done, one way or another. As for my stepfather, I never got chance to thank him because he began drinking and became a full-fledged alcoholic. They were divorced. And he drank himself to death."

"Couldn't you have thanked him anyway?" said Sam. "Even though—"

"You know something? I didn't realize till later what he had done for me. Years later. He caught me by the scruff of the neck and said, 'Stop it! Cut out the blah blah. Get it done!' We don't thank people for these really important steps. To really teach someone something is a painful process. One more story of mine and we'll then get to *your* stories.

"I had a very good friend. A friend who was so valuable and so difficult that I couldn't take him. I couldn't afford the hours of talk that we went through every time we got together. I had a family and a teaching job. And we'd have tremendous arguments that might last six or even eight hours. One evening he was with five or six of us and he suddenly made the statement: 'We're all full of shit.'

"'What? What did you say? I mean, *what?*'

"'I said, we're all full of shit.'

"We're all full of shit? Not very nice, right? But can we be 'nice' and still learn anything? Still teach anything? This is the water up the nose, inevitable for learning to swim. Well, we hear something like that and immediately want to say 'Wait a second. Speak for yourself. You don't know me that well.'

"'*We're alllll full of shit!*' he said again, louder than before.

"It took me three days before I could admit he was right. And does it really matter that he hadn't made an objective study of the human race? With a sampling of 8,000 people from a cross-section of city, country, small-town groups? What does it take to tell the truth? It takes courage. Knowing something is true and speaking it are so different.

"Incidentally, does this offend anyone? I asked you at the beginning of this . . . discussion, not to waste time resenting the things I said. Just pick up what you can and let the rest go. Don't waste time building a case against me. Don't waste time with theories about how this example could have been expressed in more pleasant terms.

"'When somebody gets raped is it the rapee's fault? Did they ask for it?' I'm not going into cases. All sorts of things happen. I also said that our Being attracts our life. Put more simply, I'm saying: the way we are attracts the things that happen to us.

"I have a good friend who just got over a very traumatic relationship. If she got sick, Hal, the man she was with, would run off to Maine and go sailing for three days. She had no idea when or if he was coming back. In a day or so she'd be okay and she'd fix meals again. On one of those occasions, before he had come back—and before he knew whether she'd died—I went over and found a note on the table: 'Dear Hal: Your dinner is in the frig, blah blah blah, Love, Mary.'

"I asked her if he had called her. 'No, but he'll probably be back tonight.'

"'And you fixed dinner on the *chance*—?'

"'Yeah . . .'

"'And of course you took care of his dog, let him in and out, and his boat is still parked in the yard?'

"'Yes . . .'

"'Mary, why don't you put a sign on your back, *Please kick me?*'

"'What are you talking about?'

"'You *tell* him—if he ever pulls that again. Just runs off when you get sick, that he can take his dog and his boat and his clothes and get the hell out of here.'

"'Oh,' she said, 'I would *never* tell Hal to leave.'

"'Then I'm going to make the sign myself and put it around your neck.'

"Next case, this friend, who said we were all full of shit, was over one night and he and I got in a furious argument. My fiancee at the time, who was a little shy but very opinionated, sat there for the whole time, while we went at it. After about an hour he turned to her, suddenly, and accused her of sitting there criticizing both of us.

"She was amazed. 'I haven't said a word the whole time!'

"'I know,' he said. 'You're just sitting there, *stinking up the air.*'

"Could he prove it? Of course not. No words had passed her lips. She was furious. He was crazy! He was presumptuous as all hell. He was a bully! No wonder his wife was ready to leave him. There was now another furious argument. She was also angry at me for not defending her. It went on and on.

"One week later she admitted to me, 'You know,' she said, somewhat sheepishly, *one week later*, she said, 'Paul was right.'

"'About what?' I asked her.

"'He was right. I *was* just sitting there, stinking up the air that night. I was criticizing both of you.'

"I credit her for owning up to it. She has a conscience. But, my God, *one week later!?!* A furious defensive argument and one week later a person admits she was wrong?"

"Some people go their whole lives," said Carlito, "and *never* admit things they *know* are true!" Carlito spoke as if it came right from his immediate life.

"Good. True, Carlito. And think what that does to the people who are trying to tell the truth. Next time you hear something that you know is a lie, ask yourself why don't you speak up? You *know* it's a lie. And what prevents you from speaking up? 'Let it go,' we say. 'It takes too much energy. Besides, she or he will get angry. I might lose a friend . . . a boyfriend, a girlfriend, a job, a ride home. If I just keep my mouth shut we'll be in bed in an hour or so, we'll talk about other things and it'll all be fine.'

"Does the person want to get raped? Hell no. But you, also, have got to take responsibility for the things you get yourself into. Of course it's a male-oriented society. I know that. But so do you. And, of *course* the rapist has to take responsibility for the things he does. And *of course* rape is terrible and despicable but, again, I'm talking to the rapees and the possible rapees, not the rapists. And I'm saying you can't be stupid, given the world as it is, so don't get drunk . . . I can't repeat it."

"Yes," said Carole, "or you might choke on that chauvinist cliché."

"I'll content myself by telling Jodie: Don't go to the Middle East *alone*. Now, we have got to take up something that directly pertains to you. The thing of stories and people's stories.

"Chuck is now forty years old. When he was twenty-four he was walking the Appalachian Trail and, while camping, watched his companion, the love of his life, fall from a ledge. She died in his arms. With that story he went from one pair of arms to another and is still going. Well, why not? Poor Chuck, the girl dying like that . . . and, of course he is afraid to commit to anyone because what happens when you commit? The loved one falls off a cliff. Well, you can continue that for all of your life or not. Your choice. And why should he commit to one person? Like this he can have hundreds!

"What is Chuck's story? *My girlfriend fell and died in my arms.*

"What is Mary's story? *I am an only child. I wanted brothers and sisters. My parents never gave me any.*

"What is Amy's story? *My sister hit me when I was seven. I've never been the same since then.*

"What is Lou's story? *I was babysitting my little brother and he ran out and was hit and killed by an automobile. I can never forgive myself.*

"What is Ann's story? *I was not wanted. Not by my mother or my father. It makes me not want myself.*

"What is Joe's story? *We never had any money. So I never had a chance.*

"What is Hal's story? *My mother seduced me.*

"What is Joan's story? *My uncle raped me.*

"What is Peter's story? *When I was sixteen a girl broke my heart.*"

"Are you saying that these stories are not true?" said Dan,

"because my story, if you want to call it that, is somewhat similar to some of the things you just mentioned."

"Not at all. I'm saying:

> Your possibility of transformation is in your future. The past is dead and gone and finished. Bury it! It has no meaning any more. Don't go on carrying it; it is unnecessary luggage. Because of this luggage you cannot go very high.
>
> (Osho, *The Tantra Experience*, 42)

"And in one of the stories we took up, Nuri Bey ('The Coffer of Nuri Bey') is burying the past. He's very 'reflective,' the story tells us, and, after he thinks about it for a while, he realizes this coffer is the thing that is the cause of the trouble. The servant thinks one thing, his wife knows the truth, and he's left to decide. Either open it or not. Side with my most faithful servant against my wife, or side with my wife against the servant. Or, maybe there's another way. That's it! Bury it! Forever. Do you get the message?

"Your father abused you? Don't identify with it. Do you see how it is not you? That you *have* a body but you are not your body? We are born new each minute. Each second, if we will allow it. But you don't allow it. You keep dredging up your 'story' instead of breaking that image whenever it comes up. And so it becomes your excuse, your crutch. Instead of saying that's not *me*, that's my *story*—I am my consciousness and the rest is theatre—we choose the story. It's easier. Did your father abuse *you*? Did that girl you were so in love with 'break your heart'? Did she betray *you*? Or the part of you which you wrongly take to be yourself?

"Drop it! Bury it! Little by little, perhaps in years, but in a progression along the path we realize that only in dropping the past can we progress. But the two are hand in glove. To drop the past is to progress and rise like a balloon with less weight. To rise is to see the past more easily and become able to drop it. To drop it is to rise. To rise is to see to drop it and rise higher. Eventually, you will have to forgive the person. No matter what was done to 'you,' no matter what 'your' reaction was. And don't be confused about why you're doing this. You're not letting the other person 'go'—you're letting yourself go."

"I don't understand . . .," said Holly.

"I don't blame you, Holly; and the longer we identify with our stories the more difficult it is to let them go."

"What I mean is," she said, "if we are, really, our consciousness . . ."

"Yes?"

"And that consciousness is the same in all of us . . ."

"Go on."

"Then it's *our* consciousness which did the abusing."

"No . . . listen . . . consciousness is the spark, the igniting spark that activates the body-mind-sense complex, the whole machine known as Holly. Now, what that body-mind-sense complex does once it is activated, once it is ignited, is due to whatever training and hard knocks and hugs and embraces that it has experienced. *Unless* something in us wakes up to the fact of how unconscious our reactions are. Of how our mechanism is playing out something that had been set up maybe early in Holly's life, that 'instrument's' life.

"Dostoyevsky wrote so well about crime. The more we understand about something, he said, the more we forgive. And to understand *all* is to forgive all.

"*Sniper Kills Fifteen People From Tower*. Almost without a doubt the man was quiet, responsible, an Eagle Scout, very kind, and then one day . . . We know nothing about it, but when we have all of the pieces we wonder why it didn't happen a year before it did.

"I know a student here at school who had to babysit a young boy. When the child was two his parents threw him in a tub of boiling water. Somehow, he was saved. I mean, he didn't die. But his genitals are useless. He is now twelve and has developed a tremendous interest in guns. Would it surprise anyone if he got hold of some guns and started killing people?

"Another student told me she was writing poetry in grade school when she was supposed to be doing something else. The teacher caught her, made fun of her efforts in front of the whole class, and then ripped her poems into hundreds of little pieces and threw the pieces into the trash can.

"These things happen. I believe there is an expression to that effect. But the thing is to identify your story and review it. Try to change toward it. And, finally, let it go. Your stories are really so much about burying the past. I say, even if you were raped, that's not a problem; it's an event. The problem is in the way you have taken it. When Osho says there are no problems, he means it. You were raped? That is history. Children are raped of love all the time. They are raped the slow way, a kind of Chinese torture, drop by drop: the cutting word; sarcasm; letting them sit there in shitty diapers, crying. Smacking them. Little children who don't know anything."

"Look, Taylor, I know what you're trying to say and do and all that but you're simply not a woman. *He who experiences knows*—I believe it. It's also true that *she* who experiences knows. And you don't know a woman's fears of being overwhelmed, overpowered and so—"

"Yes, yes, yes, and Carole, you are right. I *can't* know. All I can do is try and reach you across a gender barrier. And I do know this, Carole. I know that you're a human being. And so am I. And, before that, I am my consciousness, and so are you. And I do know about being overpowered because I have been there. Not raped but overpowered. And I know this: first we're our consciousness, next we're humans, and after that we're male and female humans, then Catholics, then Americans, Europeans, and on and on. And I also know that if you convince yourself that rape is the worst thing in the world and then it happens to you that it will probably be 'the worst thing in the world that can happen to you.' And that rope in the road is 'really' a snake.

"I know also that before the market crash of 1929 there were investors who convinced themselves that if the market failed they would die. And, do you know something? When it failed they died. Their hearts simply stopped. Long time ago we talked about belief and the power of belief. You can convince yourself you're really a lion. Fine. Totally convinced that you're a lion. You are convinced. Everyone around you, of course, sees that you're still just Joe. In the same way you can convince yourself that something that has been done to you is the most awful thing in the world. Listen to this from Camille Paglia:

> . . . one of the German magazine reporters who came to talk to me—she's been living in New York for ten years . . . She [now] lives in Brooklyn, and she let this guy in whom she shouldn't have, and she got raped. She said that, because she's a feminist, of course she had to go for counseling. She said it was awful, that the minute she arrived there, the rape counselors were saying, 'You will never recover from this, what's happened to you is so terrible.' She said, what the hell it was a terrible experience, but she was going to pick herself up, that it wasn't that big a deal. The whole system now is designed to make you feel that you are maimed and mutilated forever if something like that happens. She said it made her feel worse. It's absolutely American— it is not European—and the whole system is filled with these clichés about sex.
>
> (Paglia, 62-3)

"You're right, I don't know a *woman's* fears but I know a man's fears and both are human fears and they change with how big and strong we are and what kind of neighborhood we happen to be in, and what are the odds against us. But if we can enter all areas of life armed with common sense—and because common sense is so rare it is often called 'esoteric knowledge'—and if you can convince yourself that rape is an event from which we can recover, that we can survive it; and it will ruin your life only if you convince yourself that it *will*, and understand that it is our fears and the fears of those people who counseled us that it is a 'tragedy' and 'you'll *never* get over this' that make it so, then you could be okay. And recover from it the same way men can recover when they get assaulted, or raped, yes, men raped, and thoroughly humiliated.

"The woman who interviewed Camille Paglia had also been raped and she had this to say: 'It was a horrible experience, but it certainly didn't destroy my whole life or my psyche, as much as contemporary wisdom insisted it would' (Paglia, 62-3).

"Do you see how much we are influenced by 'contemporary wisdom'? We listen to our selves and know that it is only a rope up there in the road. And if, instead, contemporary wisdom insists that it's a snake, and they catch one at a vulnerable time in one's life, after a rape or assault and, after all, these 'experts' are only 'trying to help' and *they* say it's a snake . . . well, one thinks, I must be mistaken, I thought it was only rope.

"And, folks, we are winding up this discussion, and there are only a hundred thousand things left to say still and so we will, for this last class, tomorrow, take up Walt Whitman, American Sufi and ecstatic poet/transcendentalist, a giant big enough to take on all monikers and have room for a hundred more for none fits him and he wouldn't mind that at all. Yes, American Sufi among a hundred other descriptives. And no doubt he is immortal like the rest of us if we can only identify the real in each of us, as he has done so beautifully.

"Two more items and we are finished, till tomorrow. Then tomorrow we're finished."

"Tomorrow is the last meeting?" Carlito was reverting to type, the one to ask the obvious question, but I knew he was more than that.

"Yep. I don't want to even speculate how this has gone. I hope we've planted some seeds. And that they will come to something . . . maybe sooner than later. And before tomorrow I'd like each one of you to find a quiet place, a place where you know you won't be interrupted—if you haven't read them before—for the entire time it will take you to read the two poems of Whitman: *Song of the Open Road* and *Song of Myself.*

"One last word and we'll call it a day. Swami Dayananda, summer '95, was talking about the difference between leaders and teachers. Leaders, he said, want us to follow, and in following they want us to believe. That is the main thing, they want us to believe. Teachers want us to understand. The same is also true of commercial 'leaders.' When they tell us to drink Pepsi they want us to believe that it's a magic potion; that if we drink Pepsi that we will be young, popular, with it, that we will have oodles of fun. They don't want us to understand that it is really only sugar water with a little flavor.

"Teachers, on the other hand, want to help us see the truth. They want us to understand. They're not looking for followers and they don't care if others follow. So, then, teachers want us to understand and think for ourselves. To see the truth and think for ourselves.

"'Have you driven a Ford?'

"'Yeah, nothing unusual about it.'

"'Yes, but have you driven a Ford *lately?*'

"Their hope is that we'll keep on coming back so often, to drive one 'lately,' that we'll eventually succumb and buy a Ford. Not a bad plan, but one that has nothing to do with the truth, with understanding.

"Okay, that's it; and please read those two long poems, alone and undisturbed. Even if you've already read them. See you tomorrow."

17

I Am All That Exists

Man is asleep, must he die before he wakes?
— Mohammed

"I want to begin this last meeting with a quote because it seems so fitting to remind you once again of what Sufism is all about, and that there is no set formula or well-beaten path:

Is Sufism Muslim? Is a Sufi a Mohammedan? In joining a Sufi community, is one associating with Muslims? Is a Sufi a follower of Islam? The word *Islam* means 'peace'; this is the Arabic word. The Hebrew word is *Salem* (Jer-u-salem). Peace and its attainment in all directions is the goal of the world.

But if the following of Islam is understood to mean the obligatory adherence to a certain rite; if being a Mohammedan means conforming to certain restrictions, how can the Sufi be placed in that category, seeing that the Sufi is beyond all limitations of this kind? So far from not accepting the Quran, the Sufi recognizes scriptures which others disregard. But the Sufi does not follow any special book. The shining ones, such as 'Attar, Shams-e Tabrez, Rumi, Sa'di, and Hafiz, have expressed their free thought with a complete liberty of language. To a Sufi, revelation is the inherent property of every soul. There is an unceasing flow of the divine stream which has neither beginning nor end . . .

(Khan, The Sufi Message, I:56)

"Do you see? Sufism has no argument with other holy books, other beliefs. But Sufis remain free to choose or reject, not for others but for themselves. He goes on:

> . . . mystics in Islam have been called Sufis; but Sufism, divine wisdom, is for all, and is not limited to a certain people. It has existed from the first day of creation, and will continue to spread and to exist until the end of the world.
>
> . . . Sufis leave belief and disbelief to the grade of evolution of every individual soul . . . and the Murshid's work is to kindle the fire of the heart, and to light the torch of the soul of his mureed, and to let the mureed believe and disbelieve as he chooses, while journeying through the path of evolution. But in the end all culminates in one belief, *Huma man am*, that is, 'I am all that exists' . . .

(Khan, The Sufi Message, I:57)

"What is he saying? That 'I', little 'I,' am all that exists? And on the path to that knowledge, that realization, that I can believe whatever I want? Just stay on the path? *As I see it?* Yes, I'm afraid that's what he said."

"Why-didn't-you-*sayyyyyyy* that?" Danny spoke in an exaggerated drawl, smiling broadly.

"Sam's *been* saying that!" Sara confessed for him.

"*Sam* . . . have you, really?" I asked him.

"Yes, I called home . . . I told them I was God."

The whole cabin rocked with laughter.

When we recovered, I asked Sam what their reaction was.

"They want to take me out of school! . . . They're ready to come get me. . . . Don't worry," he said to me, "it's just talk."

It took five minutes for everyone to calm down.

"That's wonderful. Well, I don't know if anyone can follow that act. Anyone or anything. Well, okay, that's true. That's the belief. And you're only separated from it by 70,000 veils of ignorance. Well, *now*, maybe only 65,000. But the reaction of Sam's parents is so interesting. They could have gone in any one of a hundred ways: That's fine, son. And how's the weather up there? Or, they could have laughed. They could have said college is the place to explore ideas, good; they could even have said, well, in a certain way, that could be true or Son, what's the name of that professor of yours? Does he have wings, or is he just ga-ga? Too bad they were closer to the last one, but, Sam, without any introduction, that's like waving a red flag in front of the papal bull . . . joke.

"Anyhow, Inayat Khan gives us another date for the beginning of Sufism, 'the first day of creation,' and the student, the mureed, is free to believe or disbelieve as he or she chooses, as the mureed journeys 'through the path of evolution.'

"How neatly he avoids Darwin's theory of evolution. He doesn't argue with it; he indicates, very subtly, that it is a one-person journey—individual evolution. Nicoll even says: 'The Gospels are about the inner development and evolution of a man.' (Nicoll, *The New Man*, 24) But the truly revolutionary conclusion, which frightens Sam's parents so much, is: *I am all that exists*.

"We will talk more about that today. So, we're back to consciousness and all that it implies. Here, at last, is the freedom everyone has been dying for, a way which tells you to search in your own way, there is no one to say 'Stop!' Only you.

"When I was a kid, I was very rebellious. The cliché used about me was 'He rebels against authority . . . he hates authority.' But of course! At every turn someone is telling us 'Stop! Don't! Do it this way! That's bad! You *can't*! This is good, not *that*.'

"The emphasis on education in this culture/civilization is on making children learn to read and do mathematics and chemistry. But young people have trouble with academic subjects not because they lack the intelligence but because they are still struggling with 'What's it all for?' All of the emphasis is on academic subjects, not on meaning—how we can realize our significance as people, not as cogs in some corporate structure. But they sense it; deep down they know that the real subject is themselves, when the demand is chemistry. Educators worry about 'Why Johnny can't read,' and Johnny's question is more basic. His question is simply: 'Why?'

"Sometimes subtly and sometimes with sledge-hammer blows, we're forced to acknowledge society's conclusion that the bottom line is success (money). And Johnny really knows that money isn't the bottom line.

"In the breakup of young families, the lack of life-meaning is obvious—in their inability to have a job, raise a family, and follow their own hearts' desires. The saddest part is that most of them don't even have a 'heart's desire' because that has not been a part of the curriculum, at school or in their own upbringing, because both of *their* parents were working too. The lack of cultural and personal values leads to depression—psychological, not economic—and loss of humor, which, in turn, leads to estrangement between the couple and depression in the children.

"The subjects of physics, chemistry, mathematics become far removed from students who feel worthless and are suffering a maze of more personal problems and so are not free to absorb academic subjects, which they know are not the most central in their lives. And people will not turn from those problems until they are properly put away, i.e., after they have been made to realize that they are whole, valid, sane, and significant. Only then can they turn to the second order of things: reading, writing, and arithmetic. Even those children who do well in school and funnel their energy toward subjects have difficulties later because they have no training in choosing mates, friends, lovers. And can't live with them once they're chosen.

"Don't kill because you'll get life in prison. No, 'life in prison' should be the last in a long list of reasons. That example is obvious; however, it is less obvious but definitely there in other examples: Get good grades so you'll get into college. Get good grades in college so you'll get a good job. Get a good job so you'll make money. Make money so you'll have two houses and four cars. Have two houses and four cars so you'll be happy. Too bad it doesn't follow.

"Our most important work is work on ourselves, and the work of bringing up healthy and free children who know themselves and are not bought off by a few dollars. Instead of building the important background of self and values into the program, the schools have to hire psychiatrists and social guidance counselors—who, in turn, aren't equipped to answer the big questions—to take up, on a part-time basis, things that should be central to an education."

I stopped myself when I began hearing a madman who had been teaching for too long. "Sorry about that; it's a backward way of letting you know it's a relief to be discussing something that is relevant to your lives instead of preparing you for the corporate world."

"Are we going to do Walt Whitman?"

"Surprise. Right now. And I do hope you got chance to read it straight through—"

"I love it!" said Sam.

This was echoed by a number of others. Maybe it was what we had done by way of background, but for once no one objected to "poetry."

"Good. You know, the similarities between Rumi, perhaps the best-known of all Sufi poets, and Whitman—their reverence for life, for all of life—is impossible to ignore. I am putting various bits and pieces of Sufi poems and prose side by side with pieces of Whitman's poems. See how they fit. If I took away certain words it would be very difficult to say which was which, Sufis or Whitman:

1. Everywhere I look, I see Thy winning face; everywhere I go, I arrive at Thy dwelling place.
(Khan, *The Sufi Message*, I:20)

2. And I know that the hand of God is the promise of my own,
And I know that the spirit of God is the brother of my own
(Whitman, 25)

3. I am the poet of the Body and I am the poet of the Soul,
the pleasures of heaven are with me and the pains of hell are with me . . .
(Whitman, 39)

4. For the man who has realized the inner life every act is his meditation; if he is walking in the street . . . if he is working as a carpenter, as a goldsmith . . . that is his meditation. It does not matter if he is looking at heaven or at the earth, he is looking at the object . . . he worships. East or west or north or south, upon all sides is his God . . .
(Khan, *The Sufi Message*, I:79)

5. The true mosque in a pure and holy heart
Is builded: there let all men worship God;
For there He dwells, not in a mosque of stone.
(Khurqani, in Nicholson, *The Mystics of Islam*, 87)

6. 'Look in your own heart,' says the Sufi, 'for the kingdom of God is within you.'
(Nicholson, *The Mystics of Islam*, 70)

7. There is one Brotherhood, the human brotherhood which unites the children of the earth indiscriminately in the Fatherhood of God.

(Khan, *The Sufi Message*, I:18)

8. And that all the men ever born are also my brothers, and the women my sisters and lovers,
And that a kelson of the creation is love,
And limitless are leaves stiff or drooping in the fields,
And brown ants in the little wells beneath them . . .

(Whitman, 26)

9. There is so much to be seen by one whose every glance, wherever it is cast, breaks through every object and discovers its depth and its secret.

(Khan, *The Sufi Message*, I:79)

10. You air that serves me with breath to speak
You objects that call from diffusion . . .
You light that wraps me and all things in delicate equable showers!
You paths . . .
You flagg'd walks of the cities . . .
You ferries! You planks! . . .
You rows of houses . . .
You porches and entrances . . .
You windows . . .
You doors . . .
You gray stones of interminable pavements . . .

(Whitman, 120)

11. The fifth necessity in the spiritual path is the loving of the everyday life.

(Khan, *The Sufi Message*, I:97)

12. My faith is the greatest of faiths and the least of faiths,

Enclosing worship ancient and modern and all between ancient and modern . . .

(Whitman, 64)

13. If there be any believer, infidel, or Christian hermit—'tis I.

(Rumi, in Arasteh, 139)

14. I am not the poet of goodness only, I do not decline to be the poet of wickedness also.

(Whitman, 40)

15. If there be any lover in the world, O Muslims—'tis I.

(Rumi, in Arasteh, 139)

16. Smile O voluptuous cool-breath'd earth!
Earth of the slumbering and liquid trees!
Earth of departed sunset—earth of the mountains misty-topt!
Earth of the vitreous pour of the full moon just tinged with blue!
. . . Earth of the limpid gray of clouds brighter and clearer for my sake!
. . . Smile, for your lover comes.

(Whitman, 39)

17. The wine-dregs, the cup-bearer, the minstrel, the harp, and the music,
The beloved, the candle, the drink and the joy of the drunken—'tis I.

(Rumi, in Arasteh, 139)

18. The black with his woolly head, the felon, the dis-
eas'd, the illiterate person, are not denied . . . They
pass, I also pass, none can be interdicted,
None but are accepted, none but shall be dear to me.
(Whitman, 119)

19. A peaceful and harmonious life with his fellow-
men cannot be led until the sense of justice has been
awakened in him by a selfless conscience.
(Khan, *The Sufi Message*, I:17)

20. Clear and sweet is my soul, and clear and sweet all
that is not my soul.
Lack one lacks both, and the unseen is proved by the seen.
Till that becomes unseen and receives proof in its turn.
(Whitman, 24)

21. This earth and heaven with all that they hold,
Angels, Peris, Genies and Mankind—'tis I.
(Rumi, in Arasteh, 139)

22. . . . . the horrors of fratricidal war, the fever of doubtful news, the fitful events;
These come to me days and nights and go from me
again,
But they are not the me myself. Apart from the pulling
and hauling stands what I am . . . both in and out of the
game and watching and wondering at it.
(Whitman, 25)

23. Sufis are in the world but not of it.
(Sufi saying)

"Enough! I hereby declare that Walt Whitman, whether he
ever heard the term before—transcendental, ecstatic, giant

earthwalker, bisexual, tri-sexual—is also a Sufi poet."

"Did you read one from Sufis and one from Walt Whitman?" asked Joanne.

"I couldn't tell," said Holly.

"No, sometimes there would be two from Rumi, then one, then one from Rumi or another Sufi and two from Whitman.

"Fernando Pessoa, Portuguese poet, died in 1935, like Whitman, wrote about himself. On mysticism:

> My mysticism is not wanting to know.
> It's living without thinking about it.
>
> I don't know what nature is: I sing it.
> I live on a hilltop
> In a solitary whitewashed cabin.
> And that's my definition.

(Pessoa, 20)

"Like the Sufis, Pessoa did not like classifications. Once he was called a materialist poet and said, 'I'm not even a poet: I see' (Pessoa, 20). What he did was to define a poet in three words: 'One who *sees*.' I gave you copies of Pessoa's poem on Whitman along with questions about both men.

"I would guess that, outside of Homer and Shakespeare, more poets have done homage to Walt Whitman than to any other poet. Pessoa calls his tribute 'Salutation to Walt Whitman,' but it's much more than a salute, more than a tribute.

> . . . From here in Portugal, with all past ages in my brain,
> I salute you, Walt, I salute you, my brother in the uni verse . . .
> [and] I am not unworthy of you, Walt, as you well know, . . . I am with you, as you well know, and understand you and love you,

And though I never met you, born the same year you
    died,
I know you loved me too, you knew me, and I am
    happy.
I know that you knew me, that you considered and
    explained me,
I know that this is what I am, whether on Brooklyn
    ferry ten years before I was born
Or strolling up Rua do Ouro thinking about every
    thing that is not Rua do Ouro,
And just as you felt everything, so I feel everything,
    and so here we are clasping hands,
Clasping hands, Walt, clasping hands, with the uni-
    verse doing a dance in our soul . . .

Look at me; you know that I . . . Am not your disciple,
    am not your friend, am not your singer,
You know that I am You, and you are happy about it.
                                    (Pessoa, 72-3)

"Well, it goes on. I asked you to explain that relationship
and I got some strange answers."

"But, Taylor, that's a strange relationship," said Holly.

"Maybe strange but, for any of this to make sense to you, all
of you have to drop your fixed notions; call it 'strange' or 'wonderful,' but get out of your habitual modes of thinking. Already
you have had to become different, if not 'strange,' to understand some of this because this is not the usual fare, this is not
what they teach you.

"I do want to tell you something . . . no, I *have* to tell you
some things before we finish up, and now is the time. Most of
you did very well, but what do you do with a question which
includes this thought: Pessoa says he *is* Whitman. Pessoa has
discovered that he is his consciousness. Whitman *knew* he was
his consciousness. And by knowing that he was his conscious-

ness he *is* man and woman; men and women, leaves and trees and the earth ball itself. And so, of course he is Pessoa and Pessoa is Whitman and *we* are Whitman and Pessoa and ourselves and each other because we are, truly, consciousness. Okay? That's what it's all about and thank God for Whitman and Pessoa and that truth.

"If we are our consciousness, the same wind through different instruments then we are *all* related! So, *if* we are all related in that way, and if you really begin to see that, then you would not be able to drop a bomb on other people. Even if . . . I started to say, even if they are not Red Sox fans, but I really mean, even if they aren't from '*your*' country. To refuse to bomb others, knowing we are our consciousness, is not the same thing as pacifism. Not at all. To bomb others would be an attempt to destroy the very stuff which is *you*. It would be like trying to kill yourself.

"Now what is the alternative to believing that? We're back to square one and whatever you might have identified with before hearing it—your brain, your body, etc. Whatever else you've gained from this series of discussions, I don't think you're satisfied with the way you looked at yourself before this—not having really examined what it is when you say 'Who am I?' Or 'What am I?'

"Walt Whitman in *Song of the Open Road* says:

Listen! I will be honest with you,
I do not offer the old smooth prizes, but offer rough new prizes . . .

"Not the B.A. degree, not the Ph.D., not honors, not money, not high office but something no one can take from you, and a new way of seeing yourselves—these are the rough new prizes. Freedom from approval by others, joy, love, conviction!

"Picture yourself shipwrecked. You swim to land, and there you are, alive but naked on a foreign shore. No credit cards, no identification, no money, no titles or degrees. Being 'ship-wrecked' in Sufi terms means that a person is reduced to his or her *real* possessions, the things which are truly one's own: languages, skills, abilities; things that not even God could take from you, as my old teacher used to say.

"Now, we are truly running out of time—for these meetings. To repeat, you can continue seeing yourself as a little wave or you can begin to realize you are ocean. It is your choice. It is a little like saying the glass is half full or half empty. It is your choice. You can see yourself as deprived or blessed. Again it is your choice. And it has nothing to do with whether you were abused as a child: 'I've been deprived. I was an abused child' or 'I am blessed, even though I was abused as a child.' *You* were not abused; your body, your mind may have been, but consciousness cannot be abused. Do you see? It is your choice. You can continue to feel that you're only a little wave in the vast ocean or realize—I say *realize*—that you are ocean.

"Instead, we say, 'Noooo, I am just a drop, I'm just a little wave in the ocean.' And if I ask you, what is a drop? 'Well, a drop is water.' Yes, and what is a wave? 'Well, a wave is water, too.' Yes, and what is the ocean? And again you have to answer, 'The ocean is water.' That's right. The wave is water and so is the ocean. You are water, the ocean is water—"

"Stop . . . excuse me," said Jodie. "I don't know how to say this but . . . a wave is . . . *hardly* the same as an *ocean*."

"No," I told her, "it's not the same but, then again, it *is*."

"I don't follow that. At all."

"Okay, let's back up. To say the glass is half full is true, right?" They nodded. "And to say that the glass is half empty . . . that is also true, isn't it?"

Nods and murmurs.

"So, they are both true. The one you choose to describe that situation is so indicative of an attitude that it has become a classic joke. They're both true. Which do you choose?

"Okay, now to you and the ocean. You are on a boat, out in the ocean. You lean over the side with a bucket and scoop up part of what is a wave. When the water settles down, where is the wave? It is just water. It is also ocean."

"Yes, only . . ." The question seemed to die on Holly's lips, but her words went on. "Well, I was going to say that a bucket of water is not the same as a wave. But, I guess, I see . . . what you're saying."

"Good. And even if we could collect an entire wave from one end to the other, maybe miles long, we would find that it is still only water. Do you see? Look, let's take a short break and . . . our last break, and then we'll end it. A break and then just another few minutes to tie things up."

Sam, Carole, Joanne, Carlito, and Sara came up to me while the rest streamed out the door.

Within seconds came the shouts from outside: "*Come on, Carlito,*" Jodie shouted from the lake. "Come on *in!*"

"—Yeah, come on in the *ocean!*"

Carlito shrugged, Sam grinned. Jodie and Carlito had grown quite close in the last week.

"We were talking, four or five of us," Sam said. "This is really the *last* discussion!?"

I was glad that they, too, were shocked that it was over.

Joanne, with some impatience and a look at Sam, said, "Well, we feel like this is just an introduction . . ."

"I mean, you've raised a few thousand questions and, well, often enough, no answers. And now—" said Carole.

"Yes, well, it *is* an introduction."

"We'd like to go on," said Carlito.

Everyone laughed at the expression on his face. Carlito, the direct one.

"You guys laugh, but it was Carlito who got up, ate the bread and drank the water, while the rest of you were explaining your dreams . . . in any case, you guys are off for home right now. Let's see what happens when you come back."

They okayed that and went out the door to stretch or swim or smoke and I stayed in the cabin, sitting at the table wondering about the class, about teaching, learning, about what it all means. Even wondering about why I had given them a break and didn't end it a few minutes ago. What was there left to say? Time was up. According to the orthodox, God had only six days to create the universe. I had had about one month to try and explain something.

I kept waiting for something to come to me. I thumbed through one of the books in front of me, returning to the thoughts that had begun today's discussion:

> As soon as thought is restricted, it ceases to be Sufism.
> . . . The murshid's work is to kindle the fire of the heart, and to light the torch of the soul of his mureed, and to let the mureed believe and disbelieve as he [or she] chooses, while journeying through the path of evolution. But in the end all culminate in one belief, *Huma man am*, that is, "I am all that exists," and all other beliefs are preparatory for this final conviction.
> (Khan, *The Sufi Message*, I: 57)

They joked about "being God." Are they ready for that?

* * *

Ready or not, they straggled in for the last bit of discussion—stretched, smoked, wet from the lake.

"Sooo . . ." I faced them for the last time. "A final few minutes, and a chance to tell you that I have enjoyed this.

"So, as I was saying, before the break; you're never going to realize your ocean-ness as long as you insist on your wave-ness. 'I hate rice!' Or '*I* take two spoons of sugar, please.'

"No. 'It' hates rice. '*I*' don't. 'It' is sitting there repeating, 'I can't talk to anyone in the mornings till I have three cups of coffee, and I'm only on number two,' while 'I' is dancing with Whitman and Pessoa, clasping hands with the universe doing a dance in our soul. And that is a rough new prize worth the taking. And it is as easy as that, as easy as choosing.

"If you remember nothing else, remember that you have choices. The glass is half full, or half empty. Both are true. Which do you choose?

"The leader of a little seminar I went to once said: 'Life is a feast. Why are we all starving to death?' Keep asking yourself. Why? And listen to your own answers."

I looked around at them. Perfect. As they are. With a ton of work to do, but perfect.

"Maybe that's the best way we could end this," I told them. "Learn to listen. To other people, and to yourselves. Keep asking if what you hear is true. Then listen to yourselves. Your real selves for the answers . . ."

To their stoic patience, I could only add, "Nothing spectacular about those words, I know. You could probably hear the same thing from your grandmothers. Listen . . . listen . . . listen to yourselves. All the answers are there."

It was over and done with. I could feel it. Let them go.

"Let's join hands for a minute. I want to read something to you."

I had Walt Whitman in front of me, with a mug on it to hold the book open. We joined hands around the table, Mike leaning across the table to join hands with Bess at one end.

"We're all travelers, in life, in understanding. Walt Whitman has put this in his unique way, and it applies whether the road is physical, or introspective and imaginary. So, this is for us:

Camerado, I give you my hand!
I give you my love more precise than money,
I give you myself before preaching or law;
Will you give me yourself? Will you come travel
    with me?

Shall we stick by each other as long as we live?"
(Whitman, *Everyman*, lines 220-224)

Then it was hugs and goodbyes; cars starting up, addresses exchanged and promises to call, shouts and laughter echoes.

I took one last look around, closed and locked the door and drove home.

The End

Works Cited

Abu Bakr, Siraj Ed-Din. *The Book of Certainty*. New York: Samuel Weiser, 1970.

Farber, Jerry. "The Student as Nigger." In *The Rhetoric of No* by Ray Fabrizio, Edith Karas, and Ruth Menmuir. New York: Holt Rinehart and Winston, Inc., 1974.

Farzan, Massud. *Tale of the Reed Pipe*. New York: E.P. Dutton, 1974.

Fort, Charles. *The Book of the Damned*. New York: Ace Publishing Corp., 1918.

Gatto, John T. *Dumbing Us Down: The Hidden Curriculum of Compulsory Schooling*. Philadelphia: New Society Publishers, 1992.

Gurdjieff, G.I. *All and Everything*, Bk. III. New York: E.P. Dutton, 1964.

Han-Shan. *Cold Mountain*. Trans. by Burton Watson. Boston: Shambhala, 1992.

Hearn, Matt. *Deschooling Our Lives*. Philadelphia: New Society Publishers, 1995.

Hemingway, Ernest. "Indian Camp." In *The Conscious Reader*, 5th Ed., ed. by Caroline Shrodes, Harry Finestone, and Michael Shugrue. New York: MacMillan Publishing Co., 1992.

Keddie, Nikki R., and Beth Baron. *Women in Middle Eastern History*. New Haven: Yale University Press, 1991.

Khan, Hazrat Inayat. *The Sufi Message*, Vol. I. London: Barrie and Jenkins, 1970.

Mullen, Bob. *Life as Laughter*. London: Routledge and Kegan Paul, 1983.

Nicholson, R.A. *The Mathnawi of Jalalu'ddin Rumi*, Bk. IV. London: Luzac and Co. Ltd., 1968.

Nicholson, R.A. *The Mystics of Islam*. London: Routledge and Kegan Paul, 1979.

Nicoll, Maurice. *The New Man*. London: Vincent Stuart, 1986.

Nicoll, Maurice. *Pyschological Commentaries on the teaching of Gurdjieff and Ouspensky*, Vol. I. Boulder: Shambhala, 1984.

Orage, A.R. *On Love*. New York: Samuel Weiser, 1970.

Osho. *The Tantra Experience*. Shaftesbury, Dorset: Element Books Limited, 1994.

Ouspensky, P.D. *In Search of the Miraculous*. New York: Harcourt, Brace and World, 1949.

Ouspensky, P.D. *The Psychology of Man's Possible Evolution*. New York: Vintage Books, 1974.

Paglia, Camille. *Sex, Art, and American Culture*. New York: Vintage Books, 1992.

Pessoa, Fernando. *Poems of Fernando Pessoa*. Trans. by Edwin Honig and Susan M.Brown. New York: Ecco Press, 1986.

Rajneesh, Bhagwan Shree. *The Book of Secrets*. New York: Harper and Row, 1972.

Shah, Idries. *The Sufis*. New York: Doubleday, 1964.

Shah, Idries. *Tales of the Dervishes*. London: Jonathan Cape, 1967.

Shah, Idries. *Thinkers of the East*. Baltimore: Penguin Books Inc., 1971.

Shah, Indries. *The Way of the Sufi*. New York: E.P. Dutton, 1970.

Weisstein, Naomi. "'Kinder, Kuche, Kirche' as Scientific Law: Psychology Constructs the Female." In *Sisterhood is Powerful*, ed. by Robin Morgan, pp. 205-20. New York: Vintage Books, 1970.

Whinfield, E.H., trans. *Teachings of Rumi*. New York: E.P. Dutton, 1957.

Whitman, Walt. *Leaves of Grass*. New York: Bantam, 1983.

Suggested Further Reading

Abu Bakr, Siraj Ed-Din. *The Book of Certainty*. New York: Samuel Weiser, 1970.

Bennett, J.G. *Talks on Beelzebub's Tales*. London: Coombe Springs Press, 1977.

D'Olivet, Fabret. *The Hebraic Tongue Restored*. York Beach, Maine: Samuel Weiser, Inc., 1981.

Fabrizio, Ray, Edith Karas, and Ruth Menmuir. *The Rhetoric of No*. New York: Holt Rinehart and Winston, Inc., 1974.

Farzan, Massud. *Tale of the Reed Pipe*. New York: E.P. Dutton: 1974.

Fort, Charles. *The Book of the Damned*. New York: Ace Publishing Corp., 1918 (out of print).

Gatto, John T. *Dumbing Us Down: The Hidden Curriculum of Compulsory Schooling*. Philadelphia: New Society Publishers, 1992.

Gurdjieff, G.I. *All and Everything*, Bk. III. New York: E.P. Dutton, 1964.

Hearn, Matt. *Deschooling Our Lives*. Philadelphia: New Society Publishers, 1995.

Herrigel, Eugen. *Zen in the Art of Archery*. New York: McGraw Hill.

Huxley, Aldous. *The Art of Seeing*. Seattle: Montana Books Publishers, Inc.

Jung, C.G.. *Alchemical Studies*, in *Collected Works*, Vol. 13. Princeton: Princeton University Press.

Keddie, Nikki R., and Beth Baron. *Women in Middle Eastern History*. New Haven: Yale University Press, 1991.

Khan, Hazrat Inayat. *Personality; the Art of Being and Becoming*. New York: Omega Publishing Co., 1982.

Khan, Hazrat Inayat. *The Sufi Message*, Vol. I. London: Barrie and Jenkins, 1960.

Lefort, Rafael. *The Teachers of Gurdjieff*. New York: Samuel Weiser, 1966.

Lewisohn, Leonard, ed. *Classical Persian Sufism: From Its Origins to Rumi*. London: Khaniqahi Nimatullah Publications.

Morgan, Robin. *Sisterhood is Powerful*. New York: Vintage Books, 1970.

Mullen, Bob. *Life as Laughter*. London: Routledge and Kegan Paul, 1983.

Nicholson, R.A. *The Mathnawi of Jalalu'ddin Rumi*, Bks. I-VI. London: Luzac and Co. Ltd., 1968.

Nicholson, R.A. *The Mystics of Islam*. London: Routledge and Kegan Paul, 1979.

Nicoll, Maurice. *The New Man*. London: Vincent Stuart, 1961.

Nicoll, Maurice. *Pyschological Commentaries on the teaching of Gurdjieff and Ouspensky*, Vol. I. Boulder: Shambhala, 1984.

Orage, A.R. *On Love*. New York: Samuel Weiser, 1970.

Osho. *The Tantra Experience*. Shaftesbury, Dorset: Element Books Limited, 1994.

Ouspensky, P.D. *In Search of the Miraculous*. New York: Harcourt, Brace and World, 1949.

Ouspensky, P.D. *The Psychology of Man's Possible Evolution*. New York: Vintage Books, 1974.

Pessoa, Fernando. *Poems of Fernando Pessoa*. Trans. by Edwin Honig and Susan M.Brown. New York: Ecco Press, 1986.

Rajneesh, Bhagwan Shree. *The Book of Secrets*. New York: Harper and Row, 1972.

Shah, Idries. *The Sufis*. New York: Doubleday, 1964.

Shah, Idries. *Tales of the Dervishes*. London: Jonathan Cape, 1967.

Shah, Idries. *The Way of the Sufi*. New York: E.P. Dutton, 1970.

Shah, Idries. *Wisdom of the Idiots*. London: The Octagon Press, 1970.

Welch, Louise. *Orage With Gurdjieff in America*. London: Routledge and Kegan Paul, 1982.

About the Author

Taylor Morris, educator and writer, has taken to heart the Sufi dictum "He who tastes knows." He has traveled extensively and has had, by his count, nearly 100 employments in diverse fields since his youth. His pursuits have included teaching English on all levels, and he was the founder of a bilingual school in Jaltipan, Mexico.

As a professor at Franklin Pierce College in Rindge, New Hampshire, Taylor has led a number of student long-distance Walks. The first, to Nova Scotia, is recounted in his book *The Walk of the Conscious Ants*. He has also led Walks up the coast of Mexico; across Spain; through the British Isles; and, five times, across Europe—from Spain through France, Italy, Austria, Hungary, Germany, and Corsica, to Yugoslavia.

Taylor resides in Peterborough, New Hampshire, with his wife Jan and teaches Introducing Sufism at Franklin Pierce College.

Those who are interested in further investigation
of Sufism in America are invited to contact:

The Sufi Order
P.O. Box 30065
Seattle, WA 98103